D0884747

OH THANK HEAVEN!

THE STORY OF THE SOUTHLAND CORPORATION

BY ALLEN LILES

ACKNOWLEDGEMENTS

The preparation of the Southland history was made possible through the assistance and cooperation of many people. Mrs. Jaunell Storey, secretary to Joe C. Thompson for 14 years, organized hundreds of historical documents and personally interviewed nearly 100 company employees or retirees. Without her guidance and insight, structuring of the history simply would not have been possible. The other members of the corporate public relations department—Jean Thompson, Jean Robertson and Melinda Mitchell—contributed greatly through countless hours of interviewing, cataloguing of facts and materials, manuscript typing and information gathering. My special thanks to Kermit Ruppenkamp and Kittie Norwood, who were indispensable in verifying dates, figures and the English language. Credit for the superb visual presentation of the history belongs to Dee Ann Steiger and Hans Streich of Southland's design department. Special thanks also should be expressed to: each individual who favored us with his valuable time and priceless recollections; Walton Grayson III, who saw the need for a comprehensive company history and encouraged us to go forward in preparing it; and Joe C. Thompson, Jr., whose 50th Anniversary Committee and personal interest provided the necessary support for the successful completion of the project.

ALLEN LILES
Dallas, Texas
December, 1976

PUBLISHED IN COMMEMORATION OF
THE 50TH ANNIVERSARY OF THE SOUTHLAND CORPORATION

JOE C. THOMPSON, JR. 1901–1961

29932

PROLOGUE

All day and night they come. Mostly working people moving to and from their labors. In the early morning there are many from the offices and factories, stopping for their first coffee, forgotten cigarettes or a fresh pastry. Before noon the traffic into the store increases. They flow in and out, taking their mid-day break with sandwiches, chips, soft drinks or milk. In mid-afternoon, after school, the kids begin to arrive. Slurpee cups are filled, ice cream novelties or candy chosen, an errand for Mom handled. Late afternoon and evening brings the tide of returning workers, stopping to fill needs that have accumulated during the day. Milk, bread, groceries, beer, cigarettes and thousands of other products or services are waiting, ready to be found, purchased and carried to home or destination. From late night to sunup the customers still come. Many seek the friendly lights because all other places are dark. In the quiet hours after midnight there are many who must fill regular and emergency needs. The glow reminds these night people that a neighbor is ready to serve, prepared to help. As the sun makes its appearance and another 24-hour cycle begins, the process will repeat itself. Several million people will enter the little stores before this day ends. Their lives will be touched, their needs will be served in a way that is far more a necessary part of their lives than they might ever realize.

It's 3:25 A.M. The neighborhood sleeps, with the exception of the house with a sick child. When the coughing does not improve, a car leaves the driveway and the search begins for a simple item, cough syrup. The driver tries to recall. *Some place* near must be open in the middle of the night. Of course some place is, and the driver remembers. He is relieved to see the glow quickly appear ahead. Within a few minutes the short drive home will end happily, or at least more hopeful than before. Perhaps for the first time a thought will occur to someone involved that just being there when needed could be the most important service of all.

A thousand miles of Interstate is numbing when it comes at you without a pause. Through a 30-mile construction maze, a two-inch thunderstorm and a stalled trailer in the express lane, the rig scarcely loses a fraction from the precious schedule. But when the friends ahead call for a break the trucker agrees. From the four-lane overpass a familiar sign looms a block off the next exit. The three huge rigs converge for brief moments of coffee and friendship. The men know the pot is always on here or 50 miles up the road under the same sign. Oh, you cannot find this special brew everywhere the trucks roll, but just about. That is what really counts, saving those precious seconds when the wheels outside must stop so the wheels inside can stay in gear.

She simply cannot accept what has happened to her. It might not be that irritating any other time, but she does not need the hassle today. At nine o'clock she has an appointment with her department manager. He requested the meeting and she suspects there will be good news. It has to be a raise, a promotion or maybe both. Not bad for a kid three years out of business school. That is why a dumb thing like snagging your pantyhose can really upset a person. There just is not any time for *that* today. Wait a second—she remembers seeing that pantyhose display yesterday. Sure, when she was picking up cigarettes after work. As she swings into the parking lot she spies the display inside the store. Yes, it is just what she needs. She will make her appointment now, with time and good looks to spare.

It was his first chance ever to win a game for the team all by himself. He had come to bat with the score tied and bases loaded in the bottom of the last inning, wanting to blast the baseball a thousand feet. However, that is simply impossible when you are in the third grade, so he decided to settle for any kind of solid hit. He tried not to think of Mom, Dad and the grandparents, who sat cringing in the stands behind him. His sister was there, also, silently relishing every painful second. Boy, how he craved a hit. It was not meant to be, though, knocking in the winning run with a slammer. Can you believe it? That dumb pitcher walked him on four straight bad balls! Anyway, his team still won the game and the happy coach rewarded him with two big Slurpees instead of one, like the other kids got. You know, those Slurpees never tasted better.

CHAPTER 1

In the mid-1920s two profound changes began their sweep across America. In retrospect, they proceeded gradually. However, for five decades their progress has only sometimes been affected by more dramatic happenings, such as wars and the Depression.

The first change involved the mass production of the automobile. When Henry Ford announced that he planned to build cars in such numbers and at such prices that ultimately everyone would own a car, most wrote it off as eccentric nonsense. But when the assembly lines in Detroit began churning out cars in amazing volume at relatively low cost, the heyday of the Flivver and Tin Lizzie began. Three hundred million cars later our devotion to the personal freedom created by the automobile remains largely intact, unshaken by pollution concerns and assorted other negatives. The automobile drastically changed a nation. Streets and roads were improved and expanded. Huge industries were born, millions of jobs created. People were free to move, live and play far away from their original environment. And the coming of the auto age produced a second major change.

As population, affluence and personal mobility increased, a gradual migration began into the suburban areas surrounding the large cities. With masses of people pouring into relatively distant areas, the need for goods and services for these newly-formed neighborhoods began to grow. Shopping centers blossomed, providing a miniature of the older, larger downtown section. And as the population continued to spread out over millions of square miles, an already valuable commodity took on even more importance. This precious commodity was "time," minutes and seconds. Everyone is allocated the same amount but there the similarity disappears. Some use it well; others scatter it foolishly. To most, though, time is important and the saving of time is desired.

The automobile reshaped our lifestyle and created the suburbs. The growth of these new areas established conservation of one's personal time as a needed service. These major changes created an aftershock of their own. One of the most unusual, which now affects millions of lives daily, occurred when the fortunes of three quite different individuals merged in 1927.

CLAUDE S. DAWLEY

Claude Dawley had touched history before. His family's next-door neighbors for a brief time in Denison, Texas, were the Eisenhowers, of German stock. As young "Ike" Eisenhower was becoming famous during World War II, Dawley's mother would recall when Dwight David was born and what he was like as a weeks-old baby.

Dawley's father was a pioneer in the ice business. In the late 1890s he built one of the first ice manufacturing plants in the Southwest in Denison, a North Texas city not far from the Oklahoma border. Since his family's home was located near the ice plant, young Claude was a frequent visitor there. His father enjoyed explaining to him the mystery of making ice. To a small and curious boy the whole process seemed incredible.

In those days the use of ice for the preservation of food was slow in gaining acceptance. The price was high, two to three cents a pound, and ice boxes were often poorly built. People would wrap ice in blankets and newspapers to make it last longer.

However, there was one field where ice was in demand: the cooling of beer in kegs or bottles. The pasteurization of beer was yet to come and shipments were still being made in railroad cars cooled with natural ice and then stored in vaults.

The Dawley ice plants were very profitable. The operation, called Southern Ice, expanded rapidly and by 1920 the company had some 40-odd plants located throughout the Southwest. By this time Claude had joined his father in the family business.

In 1926 Dawley began investigating the possible formation of his own company, primarily through the acquisition of existing ice plants. Several friends expressed an interest in joining with him and by early 1927 enough financial commitments had been gathered so that the effort of selecting properties could seriously begin.

After researching a number of possible opportunities Claude Dawley and his group settled on four separate companies which operated a total of eight ice manufacturing plants. These were Consumers Ice Co., which owned five plants and 16 retail ice stations in the Oak Cliff section of Dallas; City Ice Co. of San Antonio, which had one plant and five retail ice stations; McKinney Ice and Cold Storage Co., consisting of one plant in McKinney, Texas; and Crystal Ice Co., which owned one plant in Sherman, Texas.

Dawley obtained options, which were exercisable until June 1, 1927, on purchasing the four companies. Now only one formidable obstacle remained before the new company could be formed and operations commenced. Dawley and his associates needed to locate $1,387,500, the total purchase price of the combined properties.

At the suggestion of a friend Dawley traveled to Chicago to call on Martin Insull, head of the enormous Middle West Utilities Company and a brother of Samuel Insull, the billionaire utility tycoon, then regarded as one of the most powerful men in America.

In the 1920s ice was considered a utility, and Middle West owned many ice companies throughout the nation. Even though their investment in several Texas utilities was already into the millions, the Insulls were interested in most any proposition that might strengthen their holdings.

Sensing at once the potential of Dawley's proposal, Martin Insull offered to take any unsubscribed common stock at the same price other investors were paying. There were 12,500 shares available at $10 per share and Dawley, surprised but pleased, accepted the offer. Insull ordered Middle West's treasurer to draw Dawley a check for $125,000 immediately. He then pledged his assistance to Dawley in helping to arrange additional financing for the proposed new company. Since the Texan considered himself a "shoestring operator" compared to the Insulls, Dawley was flattered.

SOUTHLAND ICE COMPANY

CONSUMERS ICE CO.

Claude S. Dawley

Insull then telephoned two Chicago financial houses and told them that a man named Dawley would call upon them shortly with plans to organize an ice company in Texas and that he should be accommodated. Dawley's reception was indeed cordial. He later estimated that the price his proposed company received for its securities resulted in a saving of $20,000 in comparison with another arrangement made some weeks before.

So, as a result of the Chicago conferences, definite financing for Dawley's new company had materialized. The Hill and Joiner Company contracted to purchase proposed first mortgage six percent bonds and the Utility Investment Co. agreed to buy the preferred stock.

As June 1 and the expiration date of the options approached, final preparations became hectic. Appraisals were made by a nationally known company, audits were completed by recognized accountants and titles were approved. The legal papers required for incorporation were filed. Stock certificates for both the common and preferred stock were designed and printed. The deed of trust was prepared and bonds were printed.

During the completion of the final details Dawley approached the president of the North Texas National Bank in Dallas, in accordance with a promise that he had made the banker earlier regarding preliminary financing for the new company. Dawley explained he was now ready to go forward and that he wished to borrow $1.1 million on a personal note in order to purchase the ice properties under option. Dawley recalled that the bank president gulped audibly. A million dollar loan represented a rather large transaction in Dallas banking circles in 1927.

When the banker questioned him about plans for repayment of the loan, Dawley offered to pledge his financing with the two Chicago investment firms. The bank president informed Dawley that he would have to send one of his officers to Chicago for verification before any loan could be made. Two days later Dawley received a call. The bank had approved the loan. The Insull magic had worked again.

Dawley personally took title to all properties under option and began immediately to secure the charter and create the corporation. On June 28, 1927, the first meeting of several of the subscribers to the common stock took place. Present at the meeting were Arthur Hardgrave of Kansas City, representing Middle West Utilities, and W. W. Rodgers, J. W. Hassell, Joe C. Thompson, Jr. and Claude S. Dawley, all of Dallas. All of those in attendance were named directors of the new company. The board then proceeded to elect temporary officers. They were Claude S. Dawley, president; Arthur Hardgrave, vice president; W. W. Rodgers, secretary-treasurer.

The new directors also selected a name for the new corporation: THE SOUTHLAND ICE COMPANY.

Dawley was pleased. With the financial support of the Insull empire, the solidness of the combined ice companies and a strong demand for manufactured ice almost guaranteed, the future appeared bright indeed.

JOE C. THOMPSON, JR.

Joe C. Thompson, Jr. first began working for a salary when he was eight years old, sweeping the floor in a printing plant during his summer vacation from elementary school. Young Jodie Thompson worked every summer from that time on. He enjoyed hard work and approached even the most menial task with a ferocity and spirit that astonished his fellow workers and his employers.

The Thompson family lived at the corner of Edgefield and Tenth Street in Oak Cliff, a section of Dallas. Joe C., Sr. and Minnie Redding Thompson had moved to Oak Cliff from Waxahachie, Texas, in 1901, before Jodie had celebrated his first birthday. The Thompsons had little money, so thrift and hard work were absolute necessities. Jodie's father repeatedly stressed their value and his mother, a tiny but deep-spirited woman, also taught him the benefits of self-discipline.

In every family there usually is one more bestowed with promise and potential than the others. The Thompson family was no exception. His father, mother and older sister soon realized that Jodie had a rare mix of positive attitude, uncommon intelligence and powerful drive that promised great potential. From the moment that assessment was first confirmed the family dedicated itself to Jodie and his progress. With this complete endorsement from his family and his own considerable talents, Jodie confronted the future with confidence.

Mr. and Mrs. J. O. Jones lived next door to the Thompson family. Jones was vice president and general manager of Consumers Ice Co., a firm which operated several ice plants and retail ice docks in Oak Cliff. Since the Joneses had no children of their own it was quite natural that J. O. would be drawn to the likable young Jodie Thompson. As the boy loved to work and regarded no job as too difficult, J. O. decided to teach Jodie the ice business.

Consumers Ice operated horse-drawn wagons which delivered ice throughout the Oak Cliff area. The horses, and sometimes mules, required grooming and feeding. Their stables needed cleaning. The youngster gladly donned his overalls and went to work, laboring hard but learning as well.

When he became a teenager the work became even more physical. During summer vacations from Oak Cliff High School Jodie began loading ice into the wagons. Handling the heavy block ice tested his strength severely. J. O. had warned him of what to expect in the seven-day-week ice business and Jodie had prepared himself mentally. It helped that J. O. had promised him if he would stick to it, he would do well.

Jodie stuck through the stable cleaning, the horse grooming, the ice loading

and even the mixing and pouring of cement for the driveways to the plants. By the time he left for college in the fall of 1918 he was helping to keep the company's books as well as doing his share of physical chores. Most importantly, he was developing a deep, thorough knowledge of the ice business.

At The University of Texas in Austin Jodie's enterprise and spirit blossomed further. He was into a multitude of activities. He was student manager of the Longhorn basketball team and the Shorthorn freshman football team. In his senior year he was named class president. His willingness to work, friendliness and diligence were rewarded with honors and responsibilities. Jodie paid close attention to his academic chores, too. After all, the family had sacrificed so that he could have his education. Even his sister had quit school and was working to help finance his years at the University.

In August 1922, with bachelor of arts and bachelor of business administration degrees in his suitcase, Jodie headed back home to Dallas. He already had a job waiting for him. Not surprisingly, he had accepted J. O. Jones' offer to rejoin the Consumers Ice Co. on a fulltime basis.

Although J. O. loved Jodie like a son, there were some unavoidable conflicts. Jodie's mind, always quick and responsive where new ideas were concerned, had been sharpened further by four stimulating years at the University. J. O. was basically conservative in his traditional approach to the ice business. He also had learned it from the stables to the office and he was hesitant when confronted with a change in thinking or procedure.

In the summer of 1924 Jodie presented J. O. a new merchandising plan to increase Consumers' summer sales. Jodie's motives also included the possible financial boost the idea might bring to him personally. He was in love with Margaret Philp, daughter of the Dallas postmaster, and they wanted to marry. However, his salary of $150 per month offered a slim base on which to establish a household.

So Jodie came up with an idea. He proposed to J. O. that Consumers promote the sale of chilled watermelons through its retail ice docks. Although no one remembers for sure, J. O. probably scowled, scratched his head, voiced a few well-expressed doubts and then gave his approval.

During that summer of '24 Oak Cliff residents flocked to the Consumers ice docks to buy the first ice-cold watermelons ever sold in Texas. By the end of the summer Jodie was $2,300 richer. On September 30, 1924, he and Margaret Philp were married, with their financial security considerably bolstered by the results of a previously untried idea.

By 1926 Jodie had advanced to secretary-treasurer of the company. The Consumers Ice Co. now included five ice plants and 16 retail ice docks in Oak Cliff. Although a relatively small organization, its future looked fairly promising.

Sometime in early 1927 Jodie first became aware of an outsider's interest

Even as a small boy, Jodie Thompson helped next-door neighbor J. O. Jones. Later he worked in the stables of Jones' ice company.

Joe C. Thompson, Jr. and his new bride, the former Margaret "Peggy" Philp.

in acquiring the company. The prospective purchaser was Claude S. Dawley. It was rumored that the young Dawley was seeking to locate a group of several small ice companies for the purpose of consolidating them into one corporation with himself as president.

Jodie was admittedly intrigued with the possibilities. His horizons were beginning to expand beyond his successful relationship with Consumers. As for J. O., he was well-satisfied with the size of his present operations and cared little for further growth. He willingly gave Jodie his blessing to become involved with Dawley in any acquisition discussions.

As the talks progressed Jodie became excited with the opportunity of becoming personally involved with Dawley's group of investors. Impressed with Jodie's intelligence and knowledge of the ice business, Dawley offered him the chance to purchase stock in the proposed new venture. Jodie quickly accepted. Through his own savings and various loans, Jodie bought 2,500 shares of the new company at $10 per share. It was a major commitment for a young executive of modest means. It required belief in himself and his abilities. Fortunately for Jodie, these considerations were not in doubt.

On June 28, 1927, Jodie attended the first meeting of the subscribers to the common stock of the new firm. Dawley and his associates had been successful in their efforts to put together a solid group of ice plants and retail ice stations, of which Consumers Ice was the largest and most profitable operation.

Before the meeting ended directors were named and officers were elected. Twenty-six-year-old Joe C. Thompson, Jr., groomsman, stable cleaner, ice loader, bookkeeper and executive, became a full director of a brand new Dallas corporation—THE SOUTHLAND ICE COMPANY.

UNCLE JOHNNY GREEN

John Jefferson (Uncle Johnny) Green had been doing quite well in the summer of 1927, operating his small frame ice dock at Twelfth and Edgefield in Oak Cliff, a sleepy Dallas section of about 80,000 people.

The neighborhood folks seemed to appreciate the convenience of Uncle Johnny's little ice dock, which was one of 16 such retail stores scattered throughout Oak Cliff. The docks were owned by The Southland Ice Company, which had been formed only months before.

Uncle Johnny, always anxious to serve his customers better and thereby increase his own profits, was intrigued by various comments he had been receiving lately. He confided to his wife that he was getting lots of suggestions from his customers and they all had a similar theme.

It seemed almost all of the folks served by his dock appreciated that Uncle Johnny stayed open in the summer 16 hours every day, seven days a week, to dispense the block ice which was vital to householders for home refrigeration. Lately, however, his customers had hinted, or even asked outright, that he provide them other items besides ice.

Just the other day one fellow had allowed that it sure would be helpful if Uncle Johnny would stock a few loaves of bread along with the ice. A neighbor lady wanted a quart of milk for her children late one evening but had to settle for 20 cents worth of ice. Still another regular customer had needed a dozen eggs after church one Sunday, but the grocery stores were all closed.

Now, Uncle Johnny was a shrewd businessman. At 55, he had worked extensively in the theatre business besides his long experience in retailing. As a good salesman he recognized that an opportunity was being presented to him. He told his wife about an idea, one that really had sprung more from his customers than from himself. "I'm going to put in a stock of milk, eggs and bread," Uncle Johnny explained to her. "Customers keep saying they would buy things like that from the ice dock, especially on the weekends."

For the first few weeks he financed the "sideline" selling of bread, milk and eggs out of his own pocket. The venture was an immediate success. Uncle Johnny's regular cigar box, where he kept change and receipts, was overflowing with nickels, dimes, quarters and more than a few bills. His cotton change pouch, which he wore around his waist, seemed far heavier than usual as sales increased almost daily. To stock enough products to accommodate the extra business Uncle Johnny hired Troy Hammons, a friend and skilled carpenter, to put up three new shelves especially for food items. The extra shelves were needed as word of Uncle Johnny's new service spread throughout the immediate neighborhood.

Uncle Johnny was now convinced he had a winning idea. As summer waned and the demand for ice began to diminish, the sales of bread, eggs and milk continued strong. He decided the moment had arrived when he must share his idea and give it a true test. He knew that young Jodie Thompson, an executive with Southland Ice, literally worshipped an "idea." So he decided to confront Jodie with a proposal.

Although outranked, Uncle Johnny seldom addressed anyone less than half his age by "Mr." So he did not hesitate to lay out his offer rather directly to the younger company official. "Jodie, I have a little deal I want to make with you," he said. "I want to stay here this winter and put about 12 items in my station—milk, bread, eggs, cigarettes and a few canned goods. You furnish the items and I will pay the power bills and keep the accounts for the business. In the spring I will come in and settle up with you." Thompson agreed to Uncle Johnny's offer and then generally dismissed the arrangement from his mind as he had a new ice company to help operate.

The next spring, around May 1, Uncle Johnny appeared at The Southland Ice Company office in the Santa Fe Building, located in downtown Dallas. "Where's Jodie?" he asked. When told that Mr. Thompson was in his office checking ice sales reports, Uncle Johnny strolled back and handed young Thompson $1,000 in cash, the company's share of Uncle Johnny's profits.

At that moment the "convenience store" business was born.

*The Southland Ice Company plant at Page and Polk Streets
in the Oak Cliff section of Dallas in the early 1930s.*

The new Southland Ice Company moved off to an excellent start in the summer of 1927. Since its founding had coincided with the opening of the ice season in Texas, sales and profits mounted quickly. By the end of its first summer the firm was in a comfortable cash position.

On August 2, 1927, an important change occurred in top management. Joe C. Thompson, Jr. was named secretary-treasurer, replacing W. W. Rodgers, who had been elevated to vice president following the resignation of Arthur Hardgrave. The board set Thompson's annual salary at $2,700.

In September the young ice company expanded its operations. It purchased the Temple Ice and Refrigerating Company, which consisted of two plants having daily capacities of 100 tons and 45 tons, respectively. Soon after, Southland added the Perfection Ice Company in Fort Worth and the Ennis Ice Company in Ennis, Texas, each consisting of one ice plant. With these new acquisitions by early 1928 Southland numbered 12 ice plants, with approximately 20 retail ice docks in Dallas and San Antonio.

While Uncle Johnny Green was testing his idea of providing selected grocery items for the shoppers at his Oak Cliff ice dock, Claude Dawley was being exposed to this new merchandising concept from another direction.

In San Antonio Southland marketed its ice through a delivery company operated by Ernest Laubscher. Since Laubscher also operated Southland's retail ice stations, he and Dawley often toured these facilities when the company president visited San Antonio. On a routine inspection visit Dawley noticed a customer drive up and the station manager, in response to a request, hand the man a bottle of milk and a loaf of bread. The customer purchased no ice. When asked by Dawley about this transaction, Laubscher explained that he was experimenting with the idea of selling a limited number of grocery items at the stations. Laubscher's primary reason for the test was not so much a desire for increased sales and profits as it was a way to keep his summer ice crews working all year long. It was a long, costly and painful process to hire new crews every summer. Dawley agreed with Laubscher's concept as crew turnover was a thorny problem with any seasonal ice operation.

Laubscher related that the experiment was proving successful. He told Dawley that, indeed, many people would drive up and purchase grocery items without buying ice. Laubscher credited much of the appeal to the curb service provided by each station manager.

THE IDEA DEVELOPS

On Dawley's return to Dallas he discussed the new merchandising idea with J. O. Jones and Jodie Thompson. Predictably, J. O. was skeptical while Jodie was enthusiastic. Although the $1,000 profit had not yet been placed in Jodie's hands, the young man recalled Uncle Johnny Green's confidence when he had made the proposal to keep his own ice dock open during the usually dormant winter months. Jodie soon traveled to San Antonio to observe Laubscher's operations himself. Thereafter, Uncle Johnny's visit with the winter profits confirmed what Jodie now believed to be true. People did want the convenience of buying items other than ice, especially in the evenings and on Sundays. His eager brain began to whirl with the possibilities this discovery could offer his company.

Thompson could identify four possible benefits from this new merchandising concept:

1. It would increase revenue and profit from ice station operations.
2. It would ultimately provide year-round employment for ice station operators.
3. It would provide a much needed diversification of the ice business.
4. It would definitely offer the opportunity for the company to render a new service of great convenience to its customers.

Thompson immediately took a personal interest in the development of the idea. He had new shelves added in the other ice stations, or hot boxes as they were sometimes called. He also had actual new additions, in the form of lean-tos, built at many hot box locations. He encouraged all types of experiments with different kinds of convenience items.

Sales began to grow. Customers expressed delight with the new service and backed up this approval with their business. The early morning to late night hours, plus the Sunday service, soon became a topic of much discussion within retailing circles.

1 New products were added to the stock of the little retail ice stations, or "hot boxes."

2 An early ad for Tote'm Stores.

3 The world's first convenience store. B. C. Glenn, an early store manager, stands in front of Uncle Johnny Green's retail ice station at Twelfth and Edgefield in Oak Cliff.

Not all of the comment was good. One chain of local grocery stores notified Southland that it would refuse to buy any more ice from the company unless these clandestine grocery sales were stopped immediately. Another complaint sprang from a group protesting the Sunday operations as, first, a sacrilege to the holy day and, second, "dirty pool" to competitors who happened to be closed on that particular day.

The second complaint, regarding Sunday operations, faded away in time. But the threat of a boycott of future ice purchases by the grocery chain caused Claude Dawley to ask Thompson some difficult questions. Dawley wanted specific dollar figures on how the loss of the chain's business would affect company operations when compared to the potential sales gains from the new hot box grocery operations. Thompson worked diligently compiling and projecting the figures. When he finished totaling up the two sets of numbers, he related to Dawley that Southland would be much further ahead to stay with the new merchandising idea. Dawley agreed with the assessment and the grocery sales continued.

THE TOTEM POLES

Another innovation emerged which would help identify the new concept. One of the Southland employees had recently visited Alaska and had acquired an unusual souvenir, a real Indian totem pole. When he returned to Texas the

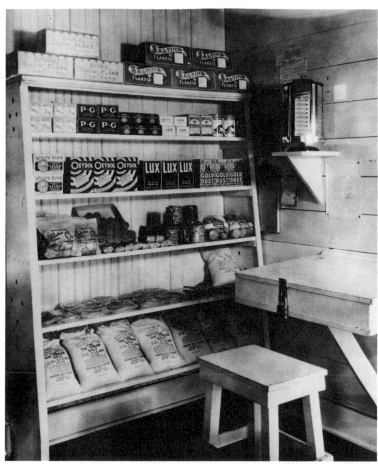

1

2

Southland Ice Company

Sole operators Totem Stations. 30 stations in Oak Cliff, one near you.

SERV-ICE
THE YEAR-ROUND

We have just received a car of fir Xmas trees from the State of Washington. Be sure to get one.

3

man erected the totem pole on his lawn at home and it became a curiosity which attracted many stares and comments. Soon the man (who remains nameless) suggested that the ice docks be called Tote'm Stores, capitalizing on the fact that people "toted" away their purchases. A real totem pole would be placed by each dock and used as a trademark and for identification purposes. The suggestion was approved. A surprised group of Indians in Alaska received a large order for a batch of totem poles from some crazy Texans and the "pole" sign, a forerunner of a type of retail identification which would later become standard throughout the world, was inaugurated beside the little ice stations in Oak Cliff and San Antonio.

Before too long facsimile totem poles began to spring up at ice docks other than Southland's. When the Navigation Ice Company opened stores in Houston, it asked permission to use the Tote'm theme and Southland officials agreed to the request. Soon totem poles were appearing throughout Texas, giving even more thrust to this new and novel service.

THE EARLY DAYS

Although the convenience store idea was gaining momentum, Southland still depended on the ice business for the major part of its sales and profits. Among the first Southland icemen was F. M. Dickerson. He recalled the early days of his career with the company: "In Dallas, Mr. Jones owned the Consumers ice plants and ice houses and Jodie Thompson ran them. The fellow I worked for, named Williams, was in the ice business down in Waxahachie, Texas. When he decided to start delivery routes in Dallas he brought my brother and me along with him. We bought all of our ice from Mr. Jones and Jodie. Later Mr. Williams decided he didn't care for the big city and he sold the routes to Mr. Jones. He then tried to convince my brother and me to go back to Waxahachie with him, but Mr. Thompson and Mr. Jones wanted us to stay in Dallas and run ice routes for them, which we did. The routes were called Oak Cliff Ice Delivery and they were operated as a separate company from Consumers. Oak Cliff Ice Delivery bought their ice from Consumers. When we decided to stay in Dallas, Jodie and Mr. Jones gave us a raise of 50 cents a day. We were then making $3 a day and we worked seven days a week. The first year we had 17 routes and by the second year we had increased them to 37. We worked 80-odd horses and mules. I drove horses and mules to deliver ice until 1931, when we got our first trucks. We did have some big horses which could pull wagons by themselves, but most of the wagons were pulled by two horses. We had a barn and feedlot and a man we called the 'barnman.' He fed the horses, groomed them and took care of the lot. That wasn't an easy job. At that time we couldn't cover much territory. My first route ran from Twelfth Street to Clarendon and Beckley to Polk. That spring I told Jodie I wanted to try to change my route by going Twelfth to Page and then Beckley over to Polk. He said, 'I don't know whether you can make a route on that.' Well, I ended up making the biggest route we had. I sold every house in the 400 and 500 blocks of Twelfth. We had about 120 independent routes in Oak Cliff, besides Lewis Ice Delivery. Lewis Ice bought from Southern Ice on Ninth Street, then Southland got their account and later on we bought Lewis Ice. Mr. Thompson continued to operate it as

The first Tote'm Stores (top photo) featured real totem poles ordered from Alaska. Later, the totem pole was painted on the sides of the stores.

1

2

3

4

5

1 Brothers F. M. Dickerson (in the straw hat) and Charlie Dickerson first went to work in 1923 for Oak Cliff Ice Delivery Company, which later became part of the Southland Ice Company. Charlie Dickerson is wearing the leather back pack used by ice deliverymen in early days.

2 Captain Worsham was the chief engineer at the Southland ice plant at Page and Polk in Oak Cliff. Early ice plants were powered by steam.

3 New uniforms for Southland ice deliverymen.

4 Motorized trucks at first supplemented, then replaced the horse and mule drawn ice wagons. The location is the Southland ice plant at Austin, Texas (formerly Dixie Ice Company).

5 Southland built and leased gasoline stations to oil companies in the late 1920s. Tote'm and Marathon Oil Co. shared a location at Llewellyn and Jefferson in Oak Cliff.

Lewis Ice because the man who had it, Mr. Ed Lewis, was such a fine gentleman and Mr. Thompson didn't want to change the name. Mr. Thompson used to ride with me when we started a new route. He would stay on the wagon all day. I remember once when we started on Cockrell Hill and we sold five blocks of ice the first day, and we thought that was really good. But I knew we could do better. An independent driver ran a route out there and the people didn't like him. Finally I built up my route to the point where we would sell 14 blocks a day. I remember some of the people had coupons from this independent driver. I went in and told Jodie I could do better if these people didn't have those coupons, that perhaps I could get them as customers. He told me to go ahead and pick up their coupons for the ice just like they were ours. He never did want to lose the chance to get a new customer."

THE ICE INDUSTRY

The history of the use of ice for refrigeration purposes dates back many centuries. As one of the oldest methods of refrigeration, ice had been cut and stored in China as early as 1000 B.C. In the United States in the 1920s some natural ice was still being cut and harvested from streams in many northern states for shipment and then storage in warmer climates until the summer months.

Between the 1890s and 1920s many fortunes were accumulated by owners of ice manufacturing plants throughout the United States. Ice was reasonably inexpensive to manufacture and was the only real source of refrigeration for foods and beverages. However, the invention of the mechanical refrigerator had an enormous impact on the manufactured ice business. Although never as satisfactory as the refrigeration produced by ice, the convenience of this new invention caused the disappearance of many ice boxes, ice manufacturing plants and ice-originated fortunes. The spread and acceptance of the mechanical refrigerator, introduced in 1926, promised significant changes in the ice business.

In the late 1920s the merchandising of ice was undergoing its own dramatic change. In a March 29, 1929, speech to the Southwestern Ice Manufacturers Association, Jodie Thompson told the group that recent surveys had discovered a trend away from home delivery of ice by wagon. Thompson said that 65 percent of the ice now sold by his company was bought by customers at Southland ice stations and hauled home on the running boards of private automobiles.

Thompson also discussed the modern training and education of ice salesmen, which included daily sales talks "just like those received by the expert salesmen employed by modern merchandising organizations." He added that Southland Ice was planning to put all of the service men at its various ice stations into company uniforms. He said that other extra "public relations" efforts would include the use of canvas sacks for the delivery of ice to customers' homes. The sacks would help prevent the product from dripping on the housewives' clean floors.

26

Thompson concluded his remarks by telling the group that the most important activity in increasing ice sales, and thus fighting the dreaded mechanical refrigerator, lay in home service work conducted by young women especially trained for this type of merchandising. These home service experts would visit residences throughout the cities where their company marketed ice and explain how better refrigeration results could be obtained through the use of standard ice boxes.

THE ERA OF ICE "WARS"

Ice "wars" were as troublesome to the manufacturing industry as the competition from the mechanical refrigerator. For example, a full-fledged "war" broke out in Dallas during the spring of 1929. Several independent Dallas ice peddlers from north of the Trinity River began hauling ice into Oak Cliff and selling it below the 50 cents per 100-pound price which had prevailed until then. J. B. Joseph, owner of the Republic Ice Company, and C. E. Kennemer, manager of City Ice Delivery, promptly lowered their price to 20 cents a hundred and stated their intention to stay at that price until the war was broken "even if it took all summer." These periodic "wars" would eventually end as did this 1929 battle, but not before sales and profits of all concerned were badly affected.

Other cities near Dallas also experienced their own ice "wars." The Central Texas ice market was affected by a 1928 skirmish which in turn led to another acquisition for the young Southland Ice Company. Ice operators in Waco, Austin and Taylor, Texas, were engaged in a price slashing vendetta which threatened ruin for the ice business in Central Texas. Dawley and Thompson were concerned because Southland's San Antonio operations might be affected.

After several months of uncertainty a solution was found. One of the companies involved offered to step out and sell its operations to Southland. So for $363,515.24, the company purchased the Dixie Ice Company with plants at Waco, Taylor and Austin and additional ice stations at Ennis, Wilmer and Midlothian. This would be the last of the major pre-1930 acquisitions for Southland, although two small ice plants located in Wilmer and Midlothian, respectively, would be added later in 1928.

While the ice business was doing well and the new grocery operations showed promise, Jodie Thompson was not hesitant to explore other possibilities for diversification. At several of the ice stations in Oak Cliff Thompson had noticed surplus, unused ground located adjacent to the Southland property. He soon entered negotiations with an oil company on the possibility of constructing gasoline stations and then leasing them on a 10-year basis. Thompson finally completed an agreement to build five stations at a cost of approximately $25,000, to be rented to the oil company for $8,220 annually. Both Thompson and Dawley felt this return would be satisfactory to Southland and would draw extra customer traffic to the nearby ice stations. This pattern of exploring previously untried and sometimes premature ideas was to continue and influence the company's fortunes throughout its history.

THE DEPRESSION BEGINS

Negative events occurring outside of Texas now began to crowd in on the new company. The stock market's Black Tuesday arrived on October 29, 1929, and the long downward spiral into national recession and depression began. Sales and profits for all businesses began to fall, first slowly and then more rapidly. Jobs were lost and standards of living declined daily.

As the Depression surrounded and engulfed the country in 1930, growth for The Southland Ice Company came to a halt. Financing for further expansion was impossible to obtain. New expenditures were practically out of the question. As Claude Dawley surveyed the stagnant condition of business in general and Southland's future prospects in particular, he made a decision.

On several occasions Martin Insull, the president of Middle West Utilities, had discussed the possibility of purchasing all of Southland's common stock. As Dawley and the other shareholders became more concerned about the fury of the Depression and the ability of their small company to withstand the economic decline, they decided to consider Insull's proposal seriously. After brief deliberation the decision was made to protect their own personal investments during this time of national uncertainty by selling out to Insull. The offer was generous. The shareholders received a price which doubled their original investments.

JODIE THOMPSON NAMED PRESIDENT

On March 31, 1931, only a few months after the Insull interests assumed ownership of Southland, Claude Dawley resigned as a director and president of the company. A new president was named by the board of directors: 30-year-old Joe C. Thompson, Jr., by this time a vice president of Southland Ice. Thompson suddenly found himself in charge of a company which was battling to survive and grow amidst an economic disaster. Although quite young by the usual business standards, he was obviously well prepared for his new responsibility.

There was no question that Thompson knew the ice business. The early experiences drawn from his friend and "partner," J. O. Jones, had given him the background on which to build and add his own personal business experience. But there was much depth to this innovative young entrepreneur who had just assumed the presidency of a promising million-dollar company.

There was one special facet of Jodie Thompson's character, although unrelated to business in the strict sense, that was a critical element in shaping his life and business destiny. In whatever community or environment Jodie found himself he was committed to being involved with its operation and improvement. He had confirmed it earlier during his years at The University of Texas, where he capped his accomplishments with the presidency of the 1922 senior class. His early civic activities following his graduation from college again demonstrated this belief in involvement.

It was not a guarded secret that Jodie Thompson believed one's dedication to community service was helpful to personal and business success. But far more importantly, he realized that the overall health of any community was directly dependent on the participation of its citizens in civic responsibilities.

THE OAK CLIFF COMMERCIAL ASSOCIATION

In 1927 the Oak Cliff-Dallas Commercial Association, a local chamber of commerce-type organization, elected Jodie Thompson as its new president. At 26, he was the youngest person ever to hold the office. He now assumed the responsibility for transforming a relatively unprogressive section of an otherwise booming city into a growth-oriented area. One of the Dallas newspapers, the *Times Herald,* editorialized on young Thompson's selection: "In the election of Joe C. Thompson to the presidency of their organization, the board of directors of the Oak Cliff-Dallas Commercial Association paid a noteworthy tribute to the younger generation of businessmen. The business ability and civic spirit he has manifested since taking his place in the commercial world have supported the argument of those who contend that the postwar young people are not all 'going to the dogs.' The new president has demonstrated that he has a correct perspective toward the past, present, and future and that he has not been thrown out of balance by the modern disruptive forces said to be causing the so-called 'revolt of youth.' The *Times Herald* predicts a year of unusual progress for the association under his administration."

One year later, as Thompson was being reelected president of the Oak Cliff group, the newspaper's prophecy could be viewed as an understatement. In just 12 months the association had shaken its accumulated lethargy. A new cycle of development was begun in Oak Cliff, stimulated by the dynamic young businessman/entrepreneur who saw only progress and opportunity ahead.

In late September 1928 a cornerstone was laid for the Oak Cliff Medical and Dental Building on Jefferson Avenue. More than 2,000 local citizens attended the dedication of the $750,000 structure which was hailed as only the beginning of a new day for Oak Cliff. Jodie Thompson, one of the speakers at the cornerstone ceremony, related that few Oak Cliff businessmen had believed the project feasible when it was first proposed. Now it was being widely predicted that Oak Cliff would soon have its first modern department store, a municipal market, additional banks and other commercial houses, perhaps even a new industry or two. The most important potential developments were the proposed bridges which would link Oak Cliff with the larger Dallas area north of the Trinity River. The Ulrickson bond issue, as it was called, later passed easily and the Dallas-Oak Cliff access became a much-needed reality. Naturally the Oak Cliff Commercial Association, headed by the young iceman, led the campaign to pass the bond issue.

Other accomplishments of the Commercial Association under the first year of Thompson's presidency included a successful bond issue to levee the Trinity

ATCH—MARCH 31, 1931

Here's Candidate Whose Secretary Thinks Him Greatest Fellow in World—Joe C. Thompson, 30

BY EDMOND M. BARR

If you see a crowd of men standing around a downtown corner you may, by breaking thru the group, find a smiling young fellow in the center. He is Joe C. Thompson, an up-and-coming business genius of 30, who heads several business enterprises and has a gluttonous appetite for hard work. He is a candidate at large for councilman on the Citizens' Charter association in the coming city election.

Thompson was drafted by his friends because they know he will make the same conscientous city official that he is business man. Thompson is the type of fellow who always has his hand out to greet you—and means it.

Secretary Likes Him.

A man is seldom a hero to his own valet and less often to his secretary. But his secretary thinks "Mr. Thompson is the biggest and greatest man in the country."

Thompson's worst habit is smoking cigarets. He likes to play golf but admits he isn't another Bobby Jones. While at Texas university he was manager of the basketball team. Friends say that long before Elinor Glynn thought of the word, Thompson had "it."

He is married and has two young sons who think there is no one in the world like their dad. His favorite hobby is to call home on the telephone and converse with the youngsters. Only privileged friends are permitted to listen in on the conversation.

Most Useful Citizen.

Thompson prizes highly the loving cup presented him last year by the Junior Chamber of Commerce for being the city's most useful citizen in 1930. He is the son-in-law of John W. Philp, former Dallas postmaster and now fourth assistant postmaster general.

His rise to business success has been meteor-like. His good nature, amiability and ability to make and hold friends, coupled with downright hard work, is responsible for his success at 30. He has never attempted politics before but is one of those fellows who is certain he can tackle and handle anything that comes his

JOE C. THOMPSON

WELL KNOWN YOUNG DALLAS BUSINESS MAN CANDIDATE AT LARGE FOR CITY COUNCIL ON CHARTER ASSOCIATION TICKET—

FORMERLY A BASKETBALL TEAM MANAGER

HELLO DADDY!

HE LIKES TO HAVE PHONE CONVERSATIONS WITH HIS TWO BOYS

Thos. F. Nash, president Dallas Junior Chamber of Commerce (left), and Joe C. Thompson, winner of 1928 Wilson Cup, holding the 1929 trophy.

Dallas Junior Chamber of Commerce Service Award for the Year 1929

River, providing official encouragement which led to the founding of a quality daily newspaper for the area, a pledge from the Dallas Chamber of Commerce and Dallas City Commission to support an aviation field west of the Trinity and re-organization of the Oak Cliff Post of the American Legion.

JODIE THOMPSON: CIVIC LEADER

Of course his achievements in Oak Cliff were beginning to draw interest throughout the entire city of Dallas. He was quickly being tabbed as a "comer" by the local establishment, always eager to identify young talent. His success at reawakening an entire area was being noted by various community service groups. In early 1929 he was selected by the Dallas Junior Chamber of Commerce as the winner of the George O. Wilson award. This honor, named for a former president of the U. S. Junior Chamber, was presented annually to the young man between 21 and 35 years of age who had rendered the most noteworthy service to Dallas and Dallas County during the preceding year. Thompson was cited specifically for his development of the Oak Cliff-Dallas Commercial Association and for creating harmonious relations between the civic and business bodies of Dallas and Oak Cliff. In his remarks delivered at the awards banquet held January 8, 1929, at the Dallas Country Club, Thompson predictably responded to the award by calling upon the members of the junior chamber to join with him in his association's efforts to build a "greater and finer civic structure." The Wilson award was a milestone in Thompson's life. His achievements and presence were now fully acknowledged by the leaders of the entire Dallas business community, including many who would later help determine the future of his struggling ice company.

Jodie Thompson's election as president of The Southland Ice Company on March 31, 1931, preceded by only one week another important personal honor. On April 7, at the age of 30, Thompson was selected by Dallas voters to serve as a city councilman. Dallas had decided to adopt the city council-city manager form of government and this particular election chose the city's first councilmen. A candidate of the newly-organized Citizens Charter Association, Thompson won the Place 8 (at large) position and joined the council as its youngest member. He now prepared to assume two new responsibilities at virtually the same time—president of Southland and servant to the people of Dallas. These two newly-won positions excited a hard-working fellow who prepared for challenges with barely concealed eagerness. If these had been the only two major tasks on Jodie Thompson's agenda in 1931, they probably would have been more than enough to keep him completely occupied. However, another surprise soon occurred in New York that would produce an impact felt throughout the world. The enormous Insull empire, regarded as all-powerful and financially untouchable, collapsed.

THE INSULL STORY

It was an ironic footnote to history that Middle West Utilities, instrumental in the birth of The Southland Ice Company, would become the primary cause for the fall of the House of Insull. Weaving the fabric of this colorful business

1 *From* The Dallas Dispatch, *March 31, 1931.*

2 *The Dallas Junior Chamber of Commerce recognized Thompson for "noteworthy service" to Dallas with its 1928 Wilson award.*

3 *The first meeting of the first City Council of Dallas, Wednesday, April 8, 1931. Front row, left to right, are E. R. Brown, V. H. Hexter, Mayor-elect T. L. Bradford, T. M. Cullum and W. H. Painter; back row, Mayor pro-tem C. E. Turner, H. C. Burroughs, A. B. Moore and Joe C. Thompson, Jr.*

history was Samuel Insull himself. To fully appreciate the origins of Southland it is necessary to know and understand, at least in some measure, the origins of Samuel Insull the man.

Armed with an Oxford education, an accountant's analytic view of his surroundings, a middle class background and an inexhaustible supply of energy, the tall, spindly 22-year-old Samuel Insull set out from London to New York in 1881 to assume duties as personal secretary to his lifelong hero, Thomas A. Edison. Insull had worked briefly with Edison's European investment representative in London and had become acquainted with the genius inventor.

Within a few months after arriving in America Insull held Edison's power of attorney, served as acting secretary to his many companies, signed his checks and even answered his mail. In 1883 Edison, having demonstrated successfully that his first central power station on Pearl Street in New York City worked, gave Insull his first major assignment. Edison formed the Thomas A. Edison Construction Department, put Insull in charge of it and told him to go out and sell the central station concept.

For the next 18 months Insull traveled the country over selling the Edison system. In 1886, with activity in Edison's enterprises accelerated suddenly by George Westinghouse's invention of the transformer making electrical transit systems practical for the first time, Edison consolidated his major manufacturing operations, relocated them in a large plant in Schenectady, New York, and put Insull in charge.

Edison had told Insull, "Run the whole show. Make it either a big success or big failure, but do it big, Sammy." Insull did. In two years he quadrupled sales and increased the annual return on the total investment to more than 30 percent. However, when Edison accepted an offer of $1.75 million in cash and stock from banker J. P. Morgan in return for an interest in the firm, Insull's happiness in New York began to dwindle. He regarded Morgan and his associates with suspicion and eventually began searching for a new opportunity in the emerging power industry.

He took a $24,000 salary cut to accept the position of president of the newly-formed Chicago Edison Company. The year was 1892 and it marked the beginning of the Insull era in Chicago. Through a series of shrewd business and political moves Insull owned the only electric-power utility in Illinois by 1898. Insull's success by then was best reflected by the growth figures for Chicago Edison and Commonwealth Electric, another utility he had acquired. Production quadrupled during Insull's first three years in Chicago. Within a few more years production totaled more than the combined output of New York Edison, Boston Edison and Brooklyn Edison. By 1907 the company was 60 times larger than when Insull took over.

As Insull's companies broke ahead of the pack, blazing trails that all others followed, Insull's stature grew apace. By the turn of the century few men in

The New York Times.

"All the News That's Fit to Print."

VOL. LXXIX....No. 26,307. **** NEW YORK, FRIDAY, OCTOBER 25, 1929. TWO CENTS

WORST STOCK CRASH STEMMED BY BANKS;
12,894,650-SHARE DAY SWAMPS MARKET;
LEADERS CONFER, FIND CONDITIONS SOUND

EDISON

Samuel Insull

the industry could be regarded as his equal; by 1910 all men in the business walked in his shadow; others in the industry and his own employees referred to him as "The Chief."

MIDDLE WEST UTILITIES FORMED

With Insull's so-called Lake County experiment of rural electrification becoming a prototype for such systems throughout the country, he formed Middle West Utilities in 1912 as a holding company to support such ventures on a regional basis. Insull placed his younger brother, Martin, in charge of Middle West. Under Martin's able direction the company grew steadily, if not spectacularly.

However, after World War I Middle West flowered and expanded to other areas of the country. In Central Texas, for example, the Insulls in six years bought, modernized and interconnected various plants, increasing their part-time service in 46 communities to full-time service in 87 previously unserved communities. In the process it cut rates by an average of 60 percent.

In the hero-worshipping postwar decade Samuel Insull had become the "Babe Ruth" of business. His total empire comprised nearly $3 billion worth of utility properties. Among them the various companies had about 600,000 stockholders and 500,000 bondholders. Together they served more than four million customers and produced an eighth of the electricity and gas consumed in the United States.

But in the process of climbing to the top Insull had succeeded in making a large number of enemies, both financial and political. Heading the former was a group known as "The Club," New York investment bankers who resented Insull's stubborn refusal to do business in the East. Under the wily direction of the mighty J. P. Morgan himself the New York bankers were able to take advantage of a series of errors by the usually infallible Insull.

To protect his holdings Insull had formed I.U.I.—Insull Utilities Investments, to which he turned over all of the empire's utility holdings. I.U.I.'s purpose was to purchase Insull stocks, but the wild stock market boom before 1929 grossly inflated the prices I.U.I. was forced to pay for the various holdings.

THE FALL OF INSULL

When the crash occurred in 1929 Insull was certain that the Depression would be neither longer nor more severe than he had endured in the past. He then made three fatal errors: he expanded far more than was prudent; he returned to debt financing and he bought the security holdings of Cyrus S. Eaton, who had been the premier raider of Insull stock. Before Insull could even sense the impending danger, I.U.I. found itself $48 million in debt, approximately $20 million of which had grudgingly been borrowed from the New York bankers.

The first axe fell, not on Insull's I.U.I. holding company but on Middle West Utilities. On April 7, 1932, Insull and financial advisor Charles Stuart were in New York to discuss means of financing Middle West's $10 million note issue coming due June 1. Neither Insull nor Stuart believed that Middle West was in serious trouble and, although it was in no condition to weather a financial hurricane, Insull was confident that a satisfactory agreement for financing could be reached.

The next afternoon a meeting was convened in the office of Owen D. Young, chairman of General Electric, who had agreed to serve as mediator. Besides Insull, Stuart and Young, a handful of Chicago and New York bankers—representing Insull's creditors—were present. The talks had barely begun when a group of Morgan bankers entered and asked Insull and Stuart to wait outside. In an hour Young appeared at the door, telling Insull that no one was going to put up any more money for Middle West and that receivership was inevitable. And so, for the want of a $10 million loan, a billion-and-a-half-dollar corporation went under, followed by I.U.I. and the Insull empire. On June 6, 1932, Insull resigned from the chairmanships and presidencies of over 60 companies, then quietly left for Greece to rest and rebuild his tension-shattered nervous system. Behind him lay the wrath of his ruined investors, an indignant public and grand jury indictments. He was later arrested in Istanbul and returned to the United States to stand trial. Although eventually acquitted of every charge, he was left a sad, broken man. For his 53 years of labor to make electric power universally cheap and abundant he had received his reward from a "grateful" people: he was allowed to finish his life outside of prison. In 1938 Insull died in Paris with less than $10,000 remaining of his billion-dollar fortune.

SOUTHLAND FACES UNCERTAINTY

The collapse of Middle West Utilities took its affiliate companies by surprise. For Southland it was an especially severe disappointment. The company, which was progressing nicely with its ice operations and Tote'm Stores, was in the midst of an expansion program.

This decision to expand had come at a time when the Depression was still gathering momentum for most businesses. While "For Rent" signs fought for elbow room in various commercial districts and "Going Out of Business" sales were more numerous than "Help Wanted" ads, The Southland Ice Company was building new Tote'm Stores.

Uncle Johnny Green had been assigned to move to Fort Worth, 30 miles to the west, and locate sites for new Tote'm Stores. He also was to supervise the planning and construction of the new Fort Worth stores. On March 21, 1931, a three column by 11 inch advertisement in the Fort Worth Star-Telegram announced that seven Tote'm Ice Stores were now open for business. The ad, which featured the totem pole logo, said, "Unique stores which feature ice and refrigerated products are conveniently located throughout the city . . . other Tote'm Ice Stores will be opened as quickly as we can complete them . . . one will be in your neighborhood . . . You never leave your car when trading at a Tote'm Ice Store . . . You drive in . . . give your order for ice, eggs, butter, milk, cheese, cold drinks, or a hundred other products and you are quickly served while you remain behind the steering wheel." Dock prices for the ice ranged from 10 cents for a 25-pound block to 35 cents for 100 pounds.

In addition to the seven stores opened in March, 18 more were then under construction. By the beginning of summer there were 25 new Tote'm Stores operating in Fort Worth. Sales and profits for Southland, bolstered by the new expansion, increased nicely despite the Depression.

The fall of Insull shattered this optimism. New York and Chicago were far removed from Dallas and the financial debacle shredding the Insull interests did take some time to comprehend. Finally the seriousness of the collapse was fully realized. A government decree placed all of the various Middle West Utilities affiliate companies under the jurisdiction of federal trustees. This arrangement was to continue indefinitely, until all legal and financial problems could be settled.

There was one positive development for Southland amidst the discouraging news. Jodie Thompson was designated to remain as its president while the company operated under federal jurisdiction. This at least seemed to assure some degree of continuity while the confusion existed.

The company proceeded about its business despite the obvious uncertainties. Ice sales continued, the Tote'm operations were not curtailed and the main office was even relocated. Late in 1931 Southland Ice moved its headquarters from the Santa Fe Building in downtown Dallas to 932½ West Jefferson in Oak Cliff.

SOUTHLAND ENTERS BANKRUPTCY

However, Southland's fate was still being determined elsewhere. As the once huge Middle West Utilities collection of companies disintegrated along with the Insull legend, there was dismay in the board rooms of affiliates throughout the country. For many there was simply no other choice but to seek relief through the protection of the courts.

On December 19, 1932, in the U. S. Federal Court in Lubbock, Texas, The Southland Ice Company declared itself bankrupt. Joe C. Thompson, Jr. was named receiver and was ordered to operate the company during the period of bankruptcy, until such time as a reorganization could be completed.

So, from its initial birth just five years before and through its early development into an aggressive ice merchandiser and grocery innovator, Southland now became a casualty of the Insull era. Its future never seemed more dubious and the question of whether the company would even continue to exist was yet to be answered.

CHAPTER
3

A s The Southland Ice Company sank into receivership and uncertainty, unforeseen events were occurring that were to affect its future in a positive way.

In 1933 the Eighteenth Amendment to the United States Constitution was repealed. Prohibition, which had been ratified in 1920, was dead. The prohibition era had created immeasurable wealth and power for organized crime. An alarmed citizenry had finally decided that only complete repeal would reverse this growth of criminal activity. In 1932 both the Republican and Democratic party platforms worked to have the question submitted to the people. Congress passed a resolution proposing repeal in February 1933. By December 5, 1933, 36 states had ratified or approved the Twenty-First Amendment to the Constitution and national prohibition was officially ended.

In turning the control of liquor and beer laws back to the individual states the lawmakers had correctly interpreted the nation's mood. By 1936 all but eight states again permitted the manufacture and sale of liquor and beer.

The resumed sale of beer became an important stimulus to the Tote'm Stores' business. Since most beer drinkers in the United States preferred their beer to be chilled, this became a natural merchandising combination for the little ice docks/grocery stores. Also, as beer is primarily a pick-up item, it fit nicely with the other merchandise carried in the stores.

Another positive development arising directly from the company's receivership status was its new ability to battle competition more strongly. Being in receivership, Southland was freed from the demands of bond interest and preferred stock dividends. The company was able to operate quite competitively in this atmosphere since there were virtually no demands on its funds other than the usual operating expenses.

THE MANAGEMENT TEAM BEGINS TO FORM

Perhaps the most important happening during this time of reorganization went virtually unnoticed because of more visible pressures. It involved the coming together of a group of talented and compatible people, many of whom would form the nucleus of the Southland management team for years to come.

Although its future still depended mostly on the business judgment and vision of Jodie Thompson, other strength was being transfused into the ailing company from a variety of individuals.

One example was W. W. (Bill) Overton, Jr., a young Dallas banker and close personal friend of Thompson who offered his assistance in straightening out the company's tangled financial matters.

Overton had long admired Thompson's ability. He had been especially impressed with the young ice executive's perceptiveness in anticipating the decline of ice manufacturing plants and the horse-drawn wagons caused by the new mechanical refrigerator. In order to get Southland's financial status clarified Thompson asked Overton to journey to Chicago and attempt to sort

1

ICE STORES

are announced for Fort Worth

Open Saturday, March 21st

Unique stores which feature Ice and Refrigerated Products are conveniently located throughout the city. Seven are now ready to serve you at the following locations:

COLLEGE AND BALTIMORE
MEADOWBROOK AND WARD
1962 HEMPHILL
NASHVILLE AND AVENUE D
COLLEGE AND BERRY
LITTLE AND AVENUE L
BROADWAY AND BOAZ

Other Tote'm Ice Stores will be opened as quickly as we can complete them — One will be in your neighborhood — You never leave your car when trading at a TOTE'M ICE STORE—You drive in — give your order for ICE, EGGS, BUTTER, MILK, CHEESE, COLD DRINKS OR A HUNDRED OTHER PRODUCTS and you are quickly served while you remain at the steering wheel.

Save a Part of Your Gasoline

Bill by Buying Your Ice Here

DOCK PRICES
25 Pounds 10c
50 Pounds 20c
100 Pounds 35c

OPEN UNTIL 9 P. M. . . . . 365 DAYS IN THE YEAR

Stores under construction which will be opened soon are—

1415 N. Main St.	3220 West 7th St.
25th and Refugio	Dashwood and Main
May and Magnolia	Clover Lane and Lafayette
21st and Market	1016 E. Hattie St.
Jefferson and New York	Kennedy and Chambers
Forest Park Blvd. and Pulaski	7th and Magnolia
Rosedale and Alston	Little and Avenue G
Central and Clinton	Sylvania and Chenault
Sylvania and Yucca	Essex and Vista

Watch for Their Opening Date.

SOUTHLAND ICE COMPANY

OPERATORS OF TOTE'M ICE STORES

2

out the Insull remains which pertained to Southland. Overton made the trip and contacted brokers and bankers who were handling disposition of various parts of the decimated empire. Overton was able to negotiate the purchase of the Southland bonds owned by Insull for seven cents on the dollar. It was a major step in putting the company's ownership back in the proper hands.

Other people crucial to Southland's chance of survival began to combine their talents in an effort to keep the organization alive. G. Allen Penniman, Sr., who joined the company in 1932, soon became a key member of the operations team. W. F. Leonard, Jr., an employee since 1928, became Southland's first traveling auditor, then corporate secretary, and later achieved national recognition as an employee safety expert. J. B. Langford was a 1931 addition to the office staff. Within 10 years he was secretary of the company, following Leonard in that position. J. R. (Jimmie) Temple, who would be a participant in Southland's entrance into the dairy business within a few years, also went on the payroll in 1931.

WORKING IN THE ICE OPERATIONS

Of course there were many other important new people, mostly in the ice operations, where the physical work was often very demanding. One such newcomer was Wiley Wesson, who began his Southland career in the Temple ice plant in 1929 when he was 23 years old. He retired in 1972 as a plant manager after 43 years and 45 days with the company. Wesson recalled: "In the early '30s we delivered up to 38,000 pounds of block ice every day to Temple businesses. That meant loading and unloading 19 tons of ice every 24 hours. We served no homes then—just businesses. Practically every building in town was an ice stop. We drove an ice truck with no doors, just a windshield and cab. That way we could move off the truck quicker. We started loading ice at 5:00 A.M. and finished our deliveries between 7:00 and 8:00 P.M. It was a seven-day week at $3 a day. I was proud that most of my customers really trusted me. They would let me personally get the money for the ice from their cash boxes. I never had a single complaint from any of them. We also used to ice down special railroad boxcars which carried poultry. I would stand on top of the boxcar and my helper would be on the ground right next to it. Using his ice tongs, he would literally throw a 100-pound block of ice up to me; I would catch it in the air with my hooks, swing it around and throw it between my legs onto the top of the car. Then one of us would get on each end and chip it up. It was mighty hard work but we really made good money out of that little Temple plant. I met Claude Dawley at a San Antonio ice convention one year and Jodie asked me to tell him how much profit I made from the Temple ice plant. I told Dawley we had made $65,500 from a 42-ton capacity plant the previous year. He couldn't believe it, but it was true."

During the company's receivership a committee had been formed for the purpose of preparing a plan of reorganization. After considerable deliberation the committee developed a workable plan and presented it to the federal courts. On December 10, 1934, the proposal was approved by the United States Court for the Northern District of Texas, thus ending Southland's receiv-

1 Tote'm Stores expanded 30 miles west to Fort Worth in the early 1930s. A 1931 ad in The Fort Worth Star Telegram.

2 A new Tote'm Store built in Fort Worth in the early '30s.

ership status. The company had survived.

Following the approval of the plan by the court a new corporation was created using the name THE SOUTHLAND ICE COMPANY and incorporated under the laws of the State of Delaware. The new charter carried very broad powers permitting many activities beyond the powers of the original Texas charter. It was created with the promising merchandising possibilities of the Tote'm Stores foremost in mind.

Southland shareholders elected a new board of directors for the revitalized company. They were Joe C. Thompson, Jr., J. J. Ballard, C. Goodfellow, W. W. Overton, Jr., T. E. Joiner and C. C. Adams. New officers were Joe C. Thompson, Jr., president; J. J. Ballard, vice president; T. E. Joiner, vice president; A. F. Hartfelder, secretary-treasurer; J. Scrivner, assistant secretary.

BALLARD AND ATWELL

Two more key people, also new to the Southland organization, added their talents to the reorganization process in 1934. One was J. J. Ballard of Fort Worth, who founded the Ballard Sales Company in that city in 1932. Ballard first became aware of Southland when he sold an ice plant to the Southwest Dairy Products Co. located in Dallas. Claude Dawley was an officer of Southwest Dairy at the time of the sale and he had introduced Ballard to Jodie Thompson. The Dallasite and Forth Worthian were each immediately impressed with the other's knowledge of the ice business and soon became associates. It was to be an important relationship that would eventually span two generations and nearly five decades.

In 1934 the new ice company also chose a new counsel and legal advisor. He was Webster Atwell, who was named to the company's board of directors. Atwell remembered the beginnings of his relationship with Southland: "Jodie Thompson, Bill Sailer, Bill Overton and I were all good friends. We saw each other a lot socially and through our Dallas civic work. We ran around together and naturally became somewhat interested in each other's business connections. When I first began doing some of Southland's legal work the company was owned by Insull, that fellow in Chicago. Jodie continued to work for him while the company was in receivership, even though his empire had collapsed like a house of cards. Believe me, Southland was really in bad shape during the time it spent in receivership. We were essentially bankrupt but somehow, mainly because of Jodie, we just kept going. He was great at operating on a tight budget with absolutely no frills. Thompson, Overton, Sailer and I bought bonds and received common stock of Southland Ice after it was reorganized. We owned the ice plants and about 30 Tote'm Stores at that time. We gradually began building more stores and things began to improve. However, it was truly a close call and we almost didn't make it."

PENNIMAN JOINS SOUTHLAND

The outlook for the Tote'm Stores operation began to improve soon after

termination of receivership. Naturally any expansion of the stores had been halted by Southland's financial problems. But with the future beginning to appear somewhat more positive, attention focused again on the little "convenience" stores. One key person assigned by Jodie Thompson to help oversee management of the stores was G. Allen Penniman, Sr. He reviewed the early store operations: "Prohibition went out in 1933. I did my best to persuade my boss, Jimmie Temple, to put beer in the Dallas stations but he strictly vetoed it, saying Oak Cliff was a 'dry' area and we would lose all our business. When I was sent to Fort Worth to run our Tote'm Stores there the first thing I did was to buy beer licenses. As a result the Fort Worth profits almost doubled what Dallas had ever done, and that is when the stations got into the beer business. It was and is a profitable item and definitely helped the development of our early stores. Of course we had lots of problems in the stores, some big and some small. One of the biggest problems we faced then involved the handling of returned milk bottles. Milk was always a big volume item in our stores and it always seemed we were running out of space to keep the bottles. In most cases we had a large cage placed outside the store for the returned bottles. In 1935 Ex-Cello came out with a paper milk carton which could be filled on a special milk bottling machine. We finally found a dairy in Fort Worth, which did not have much business, to package the milk for us. Everybody in the company was really excited about it, but we had a bitter disappointment. By noon the day we started merchandising the cartons every storeman we had called in to say he had milk leaking all over his coolers. Ex-Cell-O was very nice about it—they repaid us the milk we lost, reimbursed us for the cartons and the advertising expenses. However, they soon came out with a successful milk carton and our problem with the returned bottles became less troublesome. It seems amazing that those bottles could have been such an operations nightmare, but they were.

"In 1934 Uncle Johnny Green had accompanied me to Fort Worth, where we took over the operation of about 25 stores which the company had built very quickly. They were designed a little better than the ice docks for the merchandising of ice and food. We had one-half of the selling space for each. As far as administering the stores is concerned it might be well here, too, to give Uncle Johnny Green credit for the beginning of the quota and budget system. He kept a daily graph of sales by stores and each month he would call in the various managers and show them what the other managers were doing. This was the beginning of our chart meetings. He was pretty good at chastising people if they had fallen behind in their budget. The budget system also had another effect—in those days it was pretty easy for the manager to get his own money mixed up with the company's, and this just about eliminated that problem. No doubt about it, Uncle Johnny was one of the finest fellows who ever lived. He is responsible for a lot of ideas that are still good today. He was particularly conscious of the necessity of always being courteous. As a matter of fact, when he was running the station in Oak Cliff this particular man drove by the dock every day with a block of ice on the back of his car. One day when he turned the corner the ice fell off. Uncle Johnny very quickly ran to the vault, got a block of ice and put it on the man's car. From that day on the man was Uncle Johnny's customer."

THE MID-THIRTIES

In 1935, Southland's board of directors demonstrated its confidence in the convenience store aspect of the business. The directors approved an appropriation of $20,000 to improve the existing Tote'm Stores. Jodie Thompson, although he had never relinquished his dedication to the ice business, still believed the safest route for Southland was through diversification into related operations. W. W. Overton, Jr., the banker friend who was now a member of the board, continued to be impressed with Thompson's insight into the problems awaiting companies which chose to concentrate on manufacturing and retailing of ice. Overton recalled: "Thompson foresaw clearly the decline of ice plants and horse-drawn wagons. He anticipated the closing down of hundreds of plants and millions of tons of manufacturing capability. He planned to absorb this change by serving neighborhoods milk, cold drinks and groceries through small stores using their own chilling facilities. I don't know what influence he may have had elsewhere, but in Texas his insight and leadership saved the ice industry. Jodie had a keen mind and a belief that practically anything refrigerated would sell in a warm weather climate. He was right."

Southland managed to keep its share of the manufactured ice business in Dallas during the mid-'30s. A sales recap for the Dallas market for the period July 15, 1935—July 14, 1936 shows that the company produced nearly 31,000 tons of ice, or about 14 percent of the ice manufactured in the city. Southland was the market's top producing company, edging out the second largest company, which manufactured 29,500 tons.

HARD-WORKING EMPLOYEES

One factor that allowed Southland to come back strongly after its near collapse was the sheer hard work of the employees. J. B. Langford, who was a member of the office staff, was not untypical: "We called ourselves the seven-seven-seven-crowd. We worked in the office from 7 A.M. to 7 P.M. seven days a week. One Sunday morning I told Mr. Thompson that I was accustomed to going to church on Sunday and would like to go that particular morning. He said, 'Well, certainly, Bernard, by all means take off an hour and go to church.' I did, but I sure came right back in a hurry. Even when my wife and I were married, I remember asking the preacher to hurry with the service. That's right—I needed to get back to work. However, I must say that the company always seemed to make up for it. They had an ice convention in San Antonio shortly after we were married and Mr. Thompson insisted that I take my bride. I worked part of every weekend from 1931 until 1952, mainly because Mr. Thompson knew the store people had to work and he didn't want them to think the office staff was goofing off. If he ever came across you in the office when you were not busy, you suddenly found yourself with three different assignments. Believe me, we all stayed busy."

Carrie Goodman, also a bookkeeper in the office, was another Southland employee who remembered those demanding times: "I started with Southland on October 16, 1929. Our office was on Beckley then and we worked on

the daily reports which came in from the ice plants and Tote'm Stores. If we didn't finish the reports by the end of the day we took them home with us to finish. We just couldn't afford to get behind. They hired me for $75 a month and I even got up to $105 at one time, but after the Depression really got bad my salary was cut back to $95. There were some days that we didn't have $25 in sales to report, and we really had to work hard for everything we got. Mr. Thompson was so sweet and considerate to me. He was firm but he knew how to criticize in the right way. He was always in a hurry, running up and down the stairs. I only saw him get really mad one time. One Christmas Eve some of the men got to celebrating a little too strong and started shooting fireworks in the office. Well, one of the firecrackers landed on my coat and burned a hole in it. One of the ladies called Mr. Thompson and he came down to the office, really mad. He made every single one of the men go to church six weeks in a row and even cut the salaries of two of them for a month or so. One of them threatened to quit and Mr. Thompson told him, 'O.K., if you want me to tell your father, who is head of the Dallas Shrine Temple, that you quit because I docked you for being drunk, go ahead.' Well, the fellow didn't quit and just ended up working that much harder for Mr. Thompson. We all worked hard just to survive and keep the company going.''

4

In 1936 Jodie Thompson and his associates made a decision on further diversification for Southland. The Tote'm Stores had become the largest retailers of dairy products in the Dallas-Fort Worth area. Thompson now believed the timing was right for Southland to consider production of its own milk and milk products. Thus, in Texas' centennial year, Oak Farms Dairies was founded. The new dairy company was organized and opened in May 1936 at 1114 North Lancaster in the Oak Cliff section of Dallas. Thompson assigned Jimmie Temple, a five-year employee of Southland, to serve as general manager of the dairy operations. Temple remembered: "Jodie asked me to drive with him to Austin to look at our Southland Ice operations there. On the way down he broke the news to me that we were going into the milk business. He said that Jake Golman (Golman Bakery in Dallas) had done all right in the bread business and we should do okay with milk. Allen Penniman was running the Tote'm Stores and he was skeptical about putting our own milk into the stores. 'It ain't gonna sell,' he said. We did have trouble when we first opened. One of our competitors went down and got a statement from the retail credit people which said who our stockholders were and what our relationship was with the Tote'm Stores. They used this with other grocery chains to make them think they were helping their competition (Tote'm) by buying milk from Oak Farms. This particular competitor gave us lots of trouble with their dirty tricks. They would occasionally open up our milk cartons and put cigarette butts in them. They weren't the only ones. One of the other competitors was always hyping our milk with lemon juice. Naturally we never did anything like that and came out on top. Well, we would do little things like rearranging the milk on the shelves. We'd pull Oak Farms up to the front of a dairy case and push our competition back to the rear. Of course the next time their man was in the store he moved it right back. Anyway, getting back to Oak Farms, we lost money from May to December in 1936. In 1937 we made $10,000. After that we never really had an unprofitable year. We worked like hell, selling the restaurants, hotels and hospitals besides the grocery chains. We packaged our milk in glass and paper containers, including using glass bottles for cottage cheese. How did we decide on the name Oak Farms? There was a dairy with a *Farms* in its name somewhere up east, and we were located in *Oak* Cliff. We just put them together and came up with Oak Farms."

H. E. HARTFELDER JOINS SOUTHLAND

Another person who would be at the center of Oak Farms' and Southland's progress for more than four decades joined the new dairy soon after its organization. H. E. (Herb) Hartfelder began as an accountant with Oak Farms in 1936. When the dairy was having problems during its early months he was hired to help correct the situation. He remembered: "When Oak Farms was begun in May 1936 I was working for a greeting card concern in Kansas City. My brother, Arthur Hartfelder, was secretary-treasurer of The Southland Ice Company. He called me and said that Mr. Thompson had opened a dairy in May and had lost half of the capital in the first three months. They knew something was wrong, and they needed someone they could depend upon to come in and do the accounting. I quit my job making $175 a month for a 40-hour week to take the job at Oak Farms, which paid $135 a month, seven days a week, 12 hours a day. At that time Arthur Moore was president of the dairy, Jimmie Temple, vice president and general manager and Elsie Gage, office manager. We soon found out that one of the plant employees was engaged in some shenanigans that were costing the dairy a lot of money. I became office manager for Oak Farms in January 1937, but before I ever set foot in the office I spent a month

47

1

Dallas Men Open New Dairy

A. B. MOORE.

JIM TEMPLE.

Oak Farms, Dallas' newest dairy enterprise, began operation Friday as Oak Farms milk and dairy products appeared on the local market. A. B. Moore is president and Jim Temple is general manager of the new dairy, located at 1114 North Lancaster. Both men are well known in Dallas and Oak Cliff business circles. Offices and plant of the dairy, representing an investment of more than $60,000, are said by experts to be the most modern in the Southwest. "Every piece of our equipment is brand new and represents the last word in modern dairying science," Mr. Temple said. Mr. Moore explained that one large room of the new building, air-conditioned and beautifully decorated as a club lounge, has been set aside for the use of churches, civic and social organizations. Oak Farms milk and dairy products will be sold only by grocers and food markets, or served at restaurants and fountains. Most of the company distribution is in Oak Cliff.

2

3

4

1 May 1936. Oak Farms Dairies began operation.

2 Jimmie Temple designed the first logo for Oak Farms Dairies.

3 The original Oak Farms dairy plant.

4 Civic leaders and Oak Farms and Southland management commemorated the opening of the dairy's plant at Ennis, Texas. H. E. Hartfelder is pictured sixth from left.

5 The Oak Farms dairy fleet.

6 Oak Farms Dairies' first ad. Note that cottage cheese was sold in glass jars.

OAKIE DOKEY

Published by Oak Farms, Inc., 1114 North Lancaster, Dallas. Written, Edited and Blue-penciled by Oakie Dokey, himself. . . Read and enjoyed (we hope) by those whose interests lie parallel to ours.

VOL. 2   APRIL 1937   NO. 2

3

1 "Oakie Dokey" was Oak Farms' first employee publication.

2 Oak Farms customers came in droves to see Gary Cooper and Jean Arthur in "The Plainsman" at the Texas Theater in Oak Cliff in 1937. The double feature, which included "The Saga of Wild Bill Hickok," was sponsored by Oak Farms' Oakie Dokey. Six bottle tops from Oak Farms sweet milk gained admittance for more than 1600 "kids." Firemen and policemen were called in to help handle the crowd.

3 Oak Farms matchbook saluted the grocer.

Modern Air Conditioned & Old type Refrig.

Austin — 1935

Southland Ice Co. Refrigerator Store. — Dallas-Texas.

or two at the Southwest Dairy Products Company in Fort Worth during the fall of '36. While there I learned most of its accounting system. After we instituted many of these procedures at Oak Farms we started making money. You know, we have been fortunate that we could always take a loss situation and turn it around, insofar as our dairies are concerned. For one thing we have been tight, economical operators, and in the dairy business that's essential."

There were other interesting events occurring at Southland in 1936. On September 8 the board of directors approved giving John Jefferson (Uncle Johnny) Green a $100 a month pension for life upon his retirement. It was deserved recognition for the man who had conceived the idea of merchandising groceries and other related products at the company's ice docks nine years before.

A WELCOME STABILITY

Southland was, unquestionably, becoming a more solid operation in the middle-'30s but it still remained a relatively small and struggling company. It certainly was anything but a country club operation, as another key office employee could attest. Mrs. T. E. (Louise) Swift, the sister of Jodie Thompson, served as his secretary at the time: "Our office was at 932½ West Jefferson in Oak Cliff, in the smallest, most dilapidated building in the whole area. Our office was on the second floor and the Globe Cleaning and Pressing Co. plant was beneath us on the first floor. We had to have the windows up all summer because there was no such thing as air-conditioning. The warm moist air from the cleaners would come in through the windows and although we had ceiling fans, they just circulated the warm air. We were about as miserable as we could be. It is amazing how much discomfort you can endure if you believe it is for the good of the business. You see, ice was really still the thing in those days; the grocery part was doing well but not yet in its heyday. The company at the time was so small. It is unbelievable when you think back on it. Bernard Langford headed the accounting department, and they were all in one large room. We had four private offices. Arthur Hartfelder, Herb's oldest brother, was the general auditor; Mr. Scrivner was our plant engineer; Allen Penniman had charge of the stores and Jodie's office was a large room in the back. We walked up and down that old rickety staircase and it was an achievement if you could get up and down without an accident. It is absolutely incredible now to imagine the condition of that old building. All of us in the company worked very hard to help Jodie make the company successful. Jodie's favorite expression was, 'While you are resting, do this or that.' Of course there was not a moment of rest when he was in the office. You just sighed a sigh of relief when he left and you knew it wouldn't be long until he was back again. We worked until 1:00 P.M. on Saturday. He knew I always went to town on Saturday afternoon. When I would walk into the office he would say, 'You are just glowing—you have that Saturday glow. I can tell you just can hardly wait to get to town.' 'Town' was a big thing in 1936. Jodie hated Saturdays. He almost couldn't stand it, knowing the office would empty at 1:00 P.M. Jodie was such a believer in everything concerning Southland. I remember one time when he had brought me some vegetables that he had raised on his farm on

On one side of the Globe cleaning and laundry plant was the entrance to the second floor office of the Southland Ice Company; on the other was the company's refrigerator store (see picture, lower right). An employee noted on the picture at lower left the difference between the "modern" 1935 refrigerator and an older model.

53

1

2

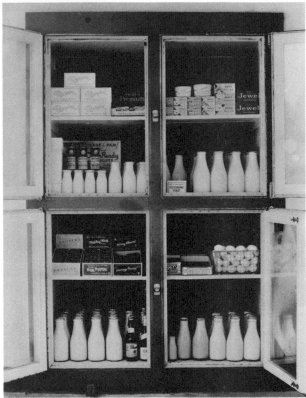

3

the Trinity River near Cayuga. I wasn't home but my husband Gene was there. Jodie went to the refrigerator to put the vegetables in and—how in the world it happened I don't know—I had a half-gallon of a competitor's milk—and also their cottage cheese—in the refrigerator. Jodie took them out, walked to the sink and poured them down the drain. Gene said, 'Your sister is really going to be mad.' Jodie replied, 'I hope she is. And you can tell her that every time I see a competitor's product in her refrigerator, it is going to meet the same fate.' Gene started to clean it up, but Jodie said, 'No, don't clean it—I want her to see what is going to happen. If our employees and their families don't use our products, we are in very bad shape.' He was so mad, which was not like him, but I got the message. It was Oak Farms products exclusively for me after that."

The late '30s were proving to be stabilizing years for The Southland Ice Company. In 1937 the board of directors added another new member. In November J. Y. (Johnny) Ballard of Fort Worth was appointed to fill the vacancy created by the death of his father, J. J. Ballard. Other actions taken by Southland's board in '37 included a directive to Jodie Thompson that he take a vacation sometime during the year. The board voted to give Thompson $1,000 to spend on the vacation as a token of its appreciation for his leadership of the company. In other decisions the board appropriated a sum for the remodeling of some Tote'm Stores, using the new accordion door fronts. It was also noted that the curb service provided for the Tote'm Stores' customers was continuing to prove very popular.

END OF A DECADE

By 1939 the company had 60 retail locations opened under the Tote'm name, mostly in the Dallas-Fort Worth area. The company had managed to prosper modestly during the difficult Depression years, mainly due to the conservative administration of Jodie Thompson and the exceptional hard work and dedication of the firm's extremely loyal employees. One major development was that Tote'm Stores' profits had now surpassed the earnings from the ice operations by a wide margin. The 60 convenience stores in operation by the end of the decade represented approximately triple the number operating soon after the company was founded in 1927. So, in a hectic 12-year period, the company had proceeded deliberately in building the financial and managerial foundation necessary for its future growth. Once again, though, events now developing thousands of miles away began to radically affect the course of world history and the fortunes of the small Dallas-based company. After a number of successful forays in Austria, Czechoslovakia and elsewhere, Adolf Hitler launched his blitzkrieg legions into neighboring Poland, bringing the nations of Europe into major conflict. In September 1939 World War II began.

1 The merchandise mix expanded, as seen in this Fort Worth store.

2 Refrigerated vaults held Oak Farms dairy products, eggs, beer, chocolate candy, yeast, shortening, bacon and oven-ready biscuits.

3 Tote'm Stores of the late '30s and early '40s. Doors widened, with accordian-style closures. Curb service was provided at all stores.

THE SOUTHLAND
ICE FAMILY
· 1939 — 1940 ·

Southland's management as the company entered the 1940s. At center is Joe C. Thompson,
Jr. Counterclockwise from upper left are H. F. McCormick, Jack Glover, Jim Scrivner,
W. F. Leonard, Jr., J. V. Cummings, E. H. Roberts, R. E. Inman, Sid Roper, G. Allen
Penniman, Sr., Elton Riggs, L. A. Orth, and R. H. Tresp. Inside center, left to right,
are W. A. Bohart, C. J. Nelson, and W. A. Moore.

CHAPTER

5

The war in Europe spread with dazzling and bewildering speed. The Lowlands, Belgium and France all toppled in a space of months. Mechanized warfare replaced old style troop movements. Airplanes, motorized tanks and trucks were the media of mobile warfare.

Orders for war materiel flowed into the United States and business increased at a rapid pace. In September 1940 Congress passed the Selective Service Act and immediately the construction of training camps began throughout the country, particularly in the Southwest. After December 1941, when Pearl Harbor finally brought the United States officially into World War II, these camps became home for hundreds of thousands of servicemen.

During the war years the ice business boomed all over Texas. Ice companies were especially busy in those areas where training camps were located, and Southland Ice enjoyed its share of this increased volume. Its Tote'm Stores flourished as a result of the general business revival. Again it was the beer business which showed one of the sharpest increases in sales during the war years. Jodie Thompson, with another demonstration of foresight, had somehow acquired a huge stock of empty bottles. As it was necessary for a customer to exchange bottles when buying beer regardless of the quantity bought, the Tote'm Stores were always able to have an ample supply of the necessary bottles on hand.

In many respects World War II presented as great a challenge to the ice industry as had the advent of the mechanical and electric refrigerators. For example, the manpower needs of the armed forces were rapidly draining away the type of men needed to operate the ice manufacturing plants. Ice companies were constantly scrambling to find enough capable people. In Southland's case, store and dairy operations also were affected by the manpower shortage. One positive factor for the ice industry was that, since its product was considered essential to the war effort and public health, repair parts for the plants were usually forthcoming.

CAMP HOOD IS BUILT

There are many recollections of the demands placed on The Southland Ice Company during the years when the country was at war. One of the largest training camps was the U. S. Army's Camp Hood, located near Killeen in Central Texas. The camp was served from Southland's Temple ice plant and represented an example of the importance of ice to the war effort.

E. H. (Pinky) Roberts, who first joined Southland in 1934, operated the Sherman ice plant until 1942. He was then assigned to oversee the Temple plant: "Our first contract with the Army called for 32,000 tons of ice for Camp Hood. We did not have a lot of help because most of the men had gone to war. Trucks were running all over Texas locating enough ice to fill the order. We even had ice shipped to us from as far away as Mobile and Chicago. It would usually arrive with about 60 percent of it melted, but we still needed that remaining 40 percent. Each soldier in training was supposed to be rationed so much ice per day and we had to deliver or it would foul up their system. I virtually never slept at home in those days. I would sleep in the ice plant on top of sacks of salt. We were running the ice plant night and day, and before I went to sleep I would mark the gauges with red paint so I could be alerted when one of the boilers malfunctioned. One night we blew a whole ammonia tank and nearly ran everyone out of

Temple. We started out by delivering ice at night to the construction people who were building Camp Hood. You know, they built that base from nothing to something in just 90 days. It was amazing what they did—but it was amazing what we did, too, getting that ice to them."

Wiley Wesson, who worked in the Temple plant then, added: "Yes, we delivered ice to Camp Hood when it first got started. Every 24 hours I carried them about a hundred 300-pound blocks of ice. It was a 60-mile round trip from Temple, so that meant two trips before lunch and two trips after lunch. I guess we loaded and unloaded 30,000 pounds of ice each day. When I got drafted and went into basic training it was like a vacation for me."

A CONSTANT NEED FOR ICE

Another Southland employee who played a direct role in servicing the new Camp Hood was Alfred Hudson. Alfred had begun his career with the company in 1932 at the Waco ice plant and managed Southland's Taylor, Texas, operation before he was transferred to Temple in 1943: "After I went to Temple I was put in charge of all refrigeration at Camp Hood. Many a time I wished that they had gone ahead and drafted me. All of the generals and colonels were breathing down our necks day and night. They wanted us to keep the ice coming 24 hours a day. With everyone's help we survived, and this is when Southland really began growing. Good help was hard to find. Once in Temple we had 15 or 20 young boys working for us. Many were goofing off—gambling. They would shoot dice all night long at the ice plant. I got tired of that. These boys were hard to catch in the act. One night I cut a hole in the roof and caught 'em. I fired every one of them, 15 in all. The next day I woke up with 15 trucks ready to haul ice to Camp Hood with no drivers. After hauling two truckloads of ice myself I came back and rehired seven of the men. We broke them of the dice shooting habit on company time. We really worked around the clock, 16 to 20 hours every day. At one time there were 90,000 soldiers at Camp Hood. It was quite a chore keeping all of those people supplied with ice. But, as I said, during the war was when Southland really started growing."

A man who would become one of Southland's top accounting managers began his career with Southland prior to World War II and was present as the company struggled with this busy period. Earl Monk recalled: "Up until the war Southland was really struggling. During the war we not only manufactured ice, we also brought it in from the North. They would cut the ice from millponds and lakes in Minnesota and the Great Lakes and ship it to Texas. People would line up for two or three blocks to buy ice in 12½- or 25-pound blocks because it was in such short supply. These blocks would sometimes have sticks, rocks, twigs and bolts imbedded in them, but it didn't matter as this type of ice was not for human consumption. It was shipped to us in boxcars, covered with sawdust. We trucked most of the ice to Camp Hood and sold ice to the Army and the families living at the post. Sometimes we would go down to Temple and help them count the money, and it would take us a week because they were so far behind in their counting. It was mostly nickels, dimes, quarters and 50-cent pieces."

W. F. Leonard, who later became an important contributor to Southland's performance in the safety and insurance area, added a postscript to the company's Camp Hood days: "When World War II started we had access to 35–40 ice plants. We got the Camp Hood ice contract, which was determined by sealed bid, on April 17, 1942. Mr. Thompson sent me to the Camp Hood finance office to await the outcome of the bids that day, and we got the job. From that day on the Camp Hood brass told us, 'Don't bother us with the details and problems; just keep our ice vaults full.' Sometimes, however, when we would accidentally short them a little on ice, we would hear from the colonels and even a general or two. But, all in all, we really kept Camp Hood iced down during World War II."

ICE AND THE WAR EFFORT

The war years severely tested the entire Texas ice industry. Southland's G. Allen Pénniman, Sr. discussed the overall demands on the industry during this wartime period in a 1943 speech to an Ice Engineers Conference: "The responsibility of the ice plant engineer has always been a serious one, but this year, when our nation is involved in war, your obligation becomes infinitely greater. We face the most serious food shortage that our country has ever faced—every ounce and every pound of food is vital. If we in the ice industry fall down in producing a sufficient quantity of ice to properly preserve this food supply, we shall have failed badly in our part of the war effort. There are five reasons why I think we, as engineers and managers of ice plants, face the toughest and roughest season we have faced in many years. These reasons are: (1) increase in or shifting away of the population from rural to industrial areas; (2) failure of mechanical refrigerators and the necessary replacement by ice refrigeration; (3) increase in consumption of beer and soft drinks; (4) increase in rail shipments of perishables which will result in a greater consumption of ice; and (5) requirements of the armed forces stationed in Texas. Although I would like to discuss the first four reasons in depth later, let me emphasize my fifth reason as being the most important of them all. Last year, during July, August and September 1942, the Army purchased 18,500 tons of ice. They estimate this year that they will purchase 49,750 tons, an increase of over 31,000 tons. If we project these figures over a 12-month period, we find that the army used 39,000 tons in 1942 and that they will likely use in excess of 105,000 tons for the year of 1943. Colonel Weatherred is going to discuss later today the importance of an adequate supply of ice to the army so I will not encroach upon his subject, but I would like to tell you of an experience I had last summer. Our company had a contract to furnish ice to one of the camps in Central Texas, and on one of the hottest days of the year we let the camp run out of ice. The result was that in less than an hour I had three long distance calls from different officers and was told in very definite army language that that sort of thing must not happen again, and I might add it didn't. Our company also had the contract to furnish that same camp with milk, and during a discussion with the QM officer of the camp, which at that time was, and still is, receiving only a small part of the milk they asked for, he practically said, 'Forget the milk.' In other words, they can get along all right without the milk, but ice they must have. We can afford to take no

THE
SOUTHLAND CORPORATION
DALLAS, TEXAS

chance on our repeated promise to the War Department that we can and will meet the demand of the many Army establishments in Texas."

During the war years a great many changes took place in the general organization of the company, particularly in the ice operations. In 1941 the company purchased the Ballard Ice Company in Waco. Shortly afterward the old Temple steam plant was sold, leaving two smaller, but more modern, plants.

SOUTHLAND PURCHASES CITY ICE

In 1943 Southland purchased City Ice Delivery, Ltd. of Dallas. With this acquisition, the company obtained two comparatively modern plants of 80 tons daily capacity each. The plants were located on Greenville Avenue and Cole Avenue, respectively, in North Dallas. Also included in this purchase were 20 retail ice stations, easily convertible to Tote'm-style merchandising, and a large tract of land with some small offices on Haskell Avenue which would later become the site of the general office.

The City Ice purchase brought Southland to the north side of Dallas' Trinity River for the first time. Heretofore the river had been the natural dividing line for the city's ice companies. This acquisition made Southland the largest ice company in Dallas.

In 1945 Southland's general office moved to its present address, 2828 North Haskell, in Dallas and the company's name was changed to "The Southland Corporation."

In 1944 the company made another important move. This involved the exchange of its ice plant in San Antonio with its seven retail ice stations, together with a small amount of cash, in return for two ice plants and two retail ice stations in Fort Worth. This arrangement concentrated Southland's operations in North and Central Texas.

In 1945 the company sold two more ice plants, the old Midlothian plant and the Taylor plant. However, it added a 50-ton plant located at Forest Avenue in South Dallas. Also in 1945, the general office was officially moved to 2828 North Haskell in North Dallas. On November 23 of that year the stockholders and directors authorized an amendment to the charter changing the name of the company to THE SOUTHLAND CORPORATION.

The company was now ready to begin its postwar growth. In retrospect it is uncertain whether Jodie Thompson, usually one who anticipated the future with uncanny accuracy, could imagine the opportunities and changes that lay before his company following the end of World War II.

CHAPTER 6

Jodie Thompson's personal and civic life continued to progress and develop in step with the emergence of his company as a major retailer in Texas.

His family expanded to include three sons: John, born November 2, 1925; Jere, born January 18, 1932; and Joe C. III, born August 16, 1940. Three other children were born to Jodie and Peggy Thompson, but all were to die in infancy or in their early childhood years. It was a tragic circumstance in the Thompson family life that otherwise was so full and rewarding.

A BELIEVER IN DISCIPLINE

Jodie Thompson obviously loved and respected his family. But he could be as demanding with them as with any errant employee or, as he often was, with himself. His sister, Louise Swift, remembered: "The biggest influence on Jodie's life, I believe, was discipline. I mean he never cringed from any hardship. He did not consider anything too hard for him to do, and he would expect the same from his sons. Discipline is a word we don't use much these days; each does his own thing. Not in Jodie's family. He was always a strict disciplinarian. The boys always cleaned and washed the family cars. There was never any professional car washing. The boys took care of everything. Their mother, Peggy, was treated like a queen, not only by Jodie, but it was expected of the boys, too. He treated all three of the boys the same way. He would not tolerate one word when he or Peggy said something—that was it." But Mrs. Swift recalled that there was one person who always seemed to get the last word with Jodie Thompson: "Our mother was a real matriarch. She controlled our family. Jodie would come by the house and Mama would be getting after me about something, and I would tell him about it. He would say, 'No problem, no problem at all—I will go in and get that straightened out.' He would come back in a few minutes looking like a whipped dog. She was the tiniest little thing you ever saw but he couldn't get the best of her in an argument. Mama would say, 'I don't agree with you at all,' and she would always have the last word. I believe she was the only one who ever had the last word with Jodie. But Mama really worshipped Jodie and the feeling was mutual."

The ties of family life from the previous to present and future generations were always an important factor in Thompson's life. At Christmas 1934 he wrote his mother: "Thousands of times I have passed by your window—thinking of you. Selfishly, I've stopped to talk of our pleasantries and defeats—and I can say you never failed to encourage me on to the finer and best purposes. If it has been that a small success in business has been mine, please share it with me, as most of the credit is yours. All in all, we are in this life for a purpose. It is my sincere hope that, as a father, I can help and guide the lives of our children as you have Sister's and mine. Bless your sweet heart. I love you—Jodie."

The understanding, interest and love also present between Jodie Thompson and his in-laws was exemplified by the letter Peggy Thompson's parents wrote him on April 15, 1931: "Congratulations on your wonderful promotion to president of the company. It is a lovely compliment to you. I hope you now will sit back and act the part. You have worked so hard all your life, we are wondering whether you will be able to stay in bed when the mules start out in the morning, or whether you will not just get up and lift the wagons out of the mud by sheer strength, as you have done in the past. Now, Jodie, please just sit and let the others do some of the work, and you just look important and very wise. Try to get some rest and relax for a time in the morning. Just read your paper as long as you like and don't rush out like a streak of lightning. Now, Jodie, don't think I have been too 'preachy,' just say it is 'just like a mother-in-law,' who is really interested in your welfare and that of your family. Hoping you the very best luck in your new position, and with love and kisses to each of the darling babies, in which Dad joins me. As ever . . ."

Although Jodie Thompson's devotion to family and business consumed the majority of his hours, he managed to continue his interest and involvement in civic activities.

In 1936 he was elected to the Highland Park Town Council, thus becoming one of the few men in Dallas history associated with three local governing bodies: Oak Cliff, Dallas and Highland Park. The Highland Park area is located in North Dallas. The Thompson family residence at 4217 Armstrong Parkway was situated in the heart of the Highland Park section. Thompson also continued his interest in other civic and governmental activities. In 1936 he was called to Washington to testify before a congressional committee studying the new concept of profit sharing. Jodie Thompson was the only ice manufacturer in the United States asked to relate his experiences. Each Tote'm Store manager shared in the profits of his individual store, and this idea seemed unique to the lawmakers. Thompson used this forum to present his views on an idea that would later become a standard business practice for many companies. "Profit sharing is the salvation of American industry," he told the congressmen. "It is applicable to any business and it creates the finest and highest type of worker-management relations."

THE SEARCH FOR "IDEAS"

Another facet of the Thompson character which continued to manifest itself in the '30s and early '40s was his interest in and search for the new and profitable "idea." Pinky Roberts, who had run the Sherman and Temple ice plants for Southland, stated how a trip to New York influenced another Thompson idea: "When Mr. Thompson and I were in New York City, we went into a place called Hamburger Haven. He said to me, 'Pinky, this would be the type of thing to scatter all over Texas.' He envisioned a chain of hamburger stands in every neighborhood. He was the only man I ever knew who could see 10–20 years in the future. He foresaw what eventually Burger King, McDonald's and the rest would do years before they did it. He even tried to get something started with his own Topper hamburger chain, which was separate from Southland. He ordered 10 metal buildings from Butler Metals in Butler, Pennsylvania and erected them on 10 different sites in the suburbs of Dallas. Rockyfeller and the Toddle Houses were the only other hamburger places in town. He eventually moved many of these buildings to downtown locations and had as many as 27 in operation at one time. He never got them off the ground like some of the franchise chains did later. I guess Mr. Thompson was just ahead of his time with that idea."

64

At any rate, Jodie Thompson was to find himself extremely busy with his Southland chores as World War II ended. The economic expansion of a post-war nation and the development of his own company, now renamed The Southland Corporation, seemed to be merging at just the right time. It now seemed appropriate to concentrate more on exploring the idea of neighborhood convenience stores, a concept that had temporarily been sidetracked by the company's involvement in satisfying a nation's hunger for ice.

Peggy and Jodie Thompson with sons John and Jere at Sea Island, Georgia.

1946—The name "7-Eleven" was
created for the little stores
open from 7:00 A.M. to 11:00 P.M.
and a new logo was dis-
played on the stores.

In the early weeks of 1945 Jodie Thompson devoted much time to developing an advertising program for his Southland ice store operators. In planning the campaign he reasoned that all of these stores had several common characteristics:

1. They were open-front, drive-in stores.

2. They were open from early in the morning until late at night, seven days a week.

3. They were selling ice, cold drinks, groceries and drug sundries.

4. They were giving curb service to their customers.

There was only one worrisome problem. The Southland stores did not possess a common name identification. For example, the City Ice stores still were called by that name despite the fact that the company had been purchased by Southland some two years earlier. And of course Southland's own outlets in Dallas, Fort Worth, Waco, Austin, Sherman and Temple had been called Tote'm Stores for many years. For any advertising program to succeed a common identity was needed. Since neither group was especially eager to assume the name of the other, it was finally decided that an entirely new name was required.

THE BIRTH OF "7-ELEVEN"

Thompson had been working closely with an established Dallas advertising agency in planning the co-op advertising. The Tracy-Locke Company was selected to carry out the production and placement of the newspaper, radio and point-of-sale advertising. They were also charged by Thompson with creating a new name that would identify all of these unique little stores under one common banner.

The agency deliberated, brainstormed and then came up with an idea. If all of the store operators involved in the co-op program would agree to stay open from 7 A.M. to 11 P.M. seven days a week, the stores could be called "7–11" Stores. A trademark was designed combining the good luck symbolism of the four leaf clover and the numbers "7" and "11." The suggested name was accepted by the participants in the co-op effort and the advertising program began. It proved to be an outstanding success and no one was more pleased than Jodie Thompson. Early in 1946 the change became official for Southland's convenience stores. The company's board of directors changed the Tote'm name to 7-Eleven on January 24, 1946. The modern convenience store era had now begun.

THE DAIRY EXPANSION BEGINS

The 7-Eleven convenience stores were not the only phase of Southland's operations becoming more active. The company's dairy interests also were beginning to expand after the war. In 1946 Southland bought the Crystal Pure Dairies in Fort Worth. The purchase price was $160,000 and Southland's board also set aside $50,000 to modernize and improve the property. Most of this modernization came in the form of new equipment, an obvious need for which was recalled by one of Crystal Pure Dairies' experienced routemen, J. R. Walker: "On my Crystal Pure route

I left the plant at 3 A.M. each morning. Before Southland bought the dairy we operated strictly with horses and wagons. On my first route I had a big gray horse named Charlie. Charlie weighed about 2,000 pounds. After I loaded the milk I could sleep until we got to the first customer because Charlie always knew where to stop. When I would begin to step off the wagon at a customer's home or place of business, Charlie would come to a complete stop. When I would put my foot back up on the wagon after delivering the milk, he would start up again. It took him about two mornings to learn a new customer. The first thing Southland did after buying Crystal Pure was to purchase a fleet of trucks, and we didn't have horses and wagons any longer. This was not the only improvement. Southland owned the 7-Eleven Stores and we got their dairy account immediately, which was a big boost to us. I had a hard time on my retail route at first because the other dairies would tell my grocery store customers that they should quit us because 7-Eleven was in competition with them and owned Oak Farms. I was a pretty good salesman and convinced most of my customers to stay."

Southland's Oak Farms also added to its postwar potential by beginning the dairy's first ice cream operation during the summer of 1947. Along with the commencement of ice cream production, Oak Farms established its first quality control laboratory designed to monitor the production of its dairy products.

ICE OPERATIONS GAIN

During World War II the decline of the manufactured ice business had been reversed because of two basic reasons: first, the war effort had required huge quantities of ice and, second, the manufacture and sale of mechanical and electric refrigerators virtually ceased during the war. Most of the manufacturing plants were busy turning out materiel for the armed forces and domestic goods were given either low or no priority.

After the war the nation's industrial companies began their rush to satisfy the American consumers' demand for various items such as the automobile and the electric refrigerator. As its availability increased the modern refrigerator would become one of the most popular purchases by postwar consumers. However, in the first years immediately following the war there still existed a strong demand for block ice as industry slowly began its conversion to peacetime production.

In 1947 Southland anticipated this continuing need for manufactured ice. It purchased the Texas Public Utilities Corporation, known as T.P.U. The acquisition included 20 ice plants with six retail ice stations and two locker plants, all located in small or medium size communities within a 200-mile radius of Dallas. From the standpoint of total ice plants in operation, Southland now became the largest ice operator in Texas. The purchase also proved timely from a weather standpoint. The summer of '47 proved to be one of the warmest on record and Southland enjoyed the greatest ice sales in its history.

Jodie Thompson, in welcoming the Texas Public Utilities managers to Southland, provided an insight into his corporate philosophy on various subjects. On December 4, 1947, he spoke to all Southland managers at a meeting held at the Baker Hotel in Mineral Wells. Since the T.P.U. managers were in attendance, it seemed a good time for him to elaborate (to the newest members of his corporate family) on the Southland way of doing business. A partial transcript of his remarks includes the following comments: "First, I want to welcome the new members of the Southland organization with us this morning, the T.P.U. people. We took over this operation on May 29 of this year and I have had just a slight chance to know all of you. We are delighted to have you with us at this managers' meeting.

"You T.P.U. people who have already become associated with us have heard about our profit sharing plan and some of you have looked forward to being put on some basis like that. We are proud of the fact that our company was one of the beginners in profit sharing in this part of the country. We are proud of our plan, which started back in the early '30s, because it has meant so much to the company in its development and to those who have enjoyed the profits. Beginning next year we will forego this old plan in its entirety. During 1948 we will devote the entire year to the study of more far-reaching plans. We want to develop a new plan that will take in most, if not all, of our employees. It is going to be a fine new plan, and we hope that in 1949 you will be quite proud of the basis on which you are working. I assure you it will

Although new, modern stores were being built, some older stores retained their original look, with, of course, the addition of the "7-Eleven" name.

be an excellent, high calibre plan, and one that will stay with the company for long years to come.

"Now, in order that you may understand a bit about our plans for the coming year, I want to explain what we have in mind, especially to those of you who have not dealt with budgets and operating reports before. Those of you who have been with Southland know how very important it is for us to anticipate the obligations of our company in connection with money. We have a great many requests for new trucks, new stores and new equipment that run up into hundreds and thousands of dollars. So, for that reason we have to know pretty well what we are doing because we don't owe any money, and we don't intend to. We are very proud of our operations. We are equally as proud of the work done in the T.P.U. organization, but you gentlemen have never worked with an operating report before. You have never really known at the end of the month how much money you made. Maybe you have figured what your profits have been by taking your total receipts and guessing at your expenses, but it has really been no job of yours, nor your responsibility, to keep up with your profits.

"Beginning in January you will receive a copy of your operating budget, and as the months roll by you must expect to do that well, or maybe better. Each item of expense and each source of revenue must be known to you. This report is only one page, totally unlike T.P.U. reports, if you have seen one in years past. We want you to study your Southland report and know it from A to Z.

"Now, how are you going to learn this report? It is going to take time and study. When we get older, we think our days of studying are over. You will have to study this report just like a history lesson, and I think it will develop you into becoming a better manager and you will be able to make more money for your company and more money for yourself.

"The first thing I want you to do is study this report. At all times you should know what your sales were a year ago in comparison to the corresponding month. We want you to keep up with your operations and master this report. It is something new and different, but you will enjoy it and in time it will become quite interesting to you."

ICEE BOTTLING IS FORMED

As the ice operations, the newly-named 7-Eleven Stores and Oak Farms Dairies continued to grow, Jodie Thompson decided that another store-related business offered promise for Southland. In 1947 the company opened the Icee Bottling Company at 2820 North Haskell, directly in back of the general office. Icee was established to bottle soft drinks, which Thompson regarded as a coming industry which would grow in importance. In addition, he felt the Icee operation was needed to guarantee an uninterrupted source of bottled soft drinks for 7-Eleven. The plant bottled such flavors as cola, grape, orange, lemon-lime, creme soda and root beer. As a special extra the plant also bottled "sparkling water." Clifford Wheeler, who would later become the key member of the 7-Eleven operations team, was assigned the task of running the new Icee operation. He remembered the new venture: "After the war, because of the sugar shortage, it was awfully hard to get enough cold drinks to sell in the 7-Eleven Stores. Mr. Thompson called me and told me he was making me president and general manager of a bottling company called Icee which Southland was opening. I was manager of 7-Eleven #21 on Fort Worth Avenue at the time, having joined the Stores Division after I got out of the service in 1946. I think Mr. Thompson gave me the Icee job mainly because I was a veteran and could get a sugar allocation. He asked that I first go to work for some other bottling company and learn something about the soft drink business. I went over to the Grapette bottling plant in Dallas. They told me that they had just let a man go who had been with them 20 years because their sales were so slow. I asked them just to let me work and if they did not think I was worth something, they didn't have to pay me. I stayed there two months and learned all I could, then came back over to Haskell Avenue and started running the Icee operation. We had a quonset hut on the back of the general office property, and this was our plant. We started making flavored drinks and a cola and delivered them to our stores in Dallas, Fort Worth and Waco. We were able to have enough soft drinks to sell in our stores for one and one-half years. A little while later we decided that we needed to spend our time developing the 7-Eleven Stores, so we sold our plant to Royal Crown Cola and I devoted my entire time to the stores."

A wooden bottle case is the only known souvenir of Southland's Icee Bottling Company.

Alan Dodds, Southland's first architect, redesigned the 7-Eleven emblem that went on the stores.

CHAPTER 8

S ince the recently introduced 7-Eleven name was proving to be an effective new identification device for Southland's convenience stores, Jodie Thompson decided that the architecture and design of the stores also needed updating. As the company had a professional architect on its staff, Thompson passed the assignment along to him. Southland architect Alan S. Dodds first joined the company in 1945: "As you know, all of our retail stores were constructed dock-high, as they were originally ice stores. They were all concrete and were reinforced with bedsprings, wagon rims, old axles and most any kind of shrapnel. They had more garbage in them than you can imagine. We even found an old ploughshare in a store built in Oak Cliff. No regular steel reinforcing rods were used. When we went to break up these old docks and remodel or rebuild the stores, we had a problem because of these strange reinforcements. Another great change in our store design in the mid- to late-'40s came when we went from wood cooling towers and old ammonia compressors, like we had in the ice plants, to freon equipment. The new equipment simplified the inside of the vault to the point where we could use a small blower coil rather than the outdated old system. In the days when we began building the first so-called modern 7-Eleven Stores, we could build a whole store for $6,000 or $7,000. The equipment was simple. We had one cash register, one produce stand, one scale, one checkstand, one gondola and two sections of shelving. One of my first jobs was to design the 7-Eleven emblem that would go on the store itself. We had a dozen different designs that we were considering. We wanted something big, a sign that would stand out. We put up a huge pylon, the basic design of which worked for many years, for the first time at the 7-Eleven Store on Travis at Knox in Dallas. Of course we have made many transitions from that first design. We also had to continue improvising on our basic store design as we went along. The old City Ice stores in North Dallas had green and white striped awning hanging over the store front, which rolled up and down. They also had overhead doors which were either opened or closed. One of the first things we did was develop sliding barn-door tracks for the store fronts. The doors would slide sideways and go back into a pocket on the end wall. In Dallas we had two excellent carpenter foremen, Tom Cook and Spider Phipps, who worked for us. These two fellows supervised the remodeling of the ice stations and the building of new stores. They were both good old solid country carpenters. And without that type of fellow we could have never done what we did for the money. You know, we really had no architectural plans to speak of—we sort of developed them as we went along. I know one thing, we really built those stores right—many of them are still doing business today in pretty much the same buildings we constructed 30 years ago."

MANAGING A STORE

What was it like to manage a 7-Eleven Store in the '40s? Two men who had lengthy careers as store managers were Glenn Sparks and Don Casey. Sparks began his career at a Tote'm Store in Oak Cliff in 1936, while Casey became associated with Southland in 1942 in stores accounting before serving later as a 7-Eleven store manager. *Casey:* "I started in accounting, where we kept the books on all of the ice plants, store reports and accounts payable. I went to work for $25 a week, then got a raise to $35 a week despite wage and price controls. When that became inadequate Mr. Penniman said, 'The only thing I can do to get you more money is to transfer you to a store,' so that's how I began managing a store. I managed the first new store out on Fort Worth Avenue. It was still called Tote'm then, but it was one of the first stores that received the new 7-Eleven pylon. In those days 90 percent of your business was done on the curb. When most customers would drive in, you knew what they wanted—a loaf of bread or quart of milk. We also sold a lot of coffee." *Sparks:* "For the old ice customers we had sign language. When they would start pulling in the drive, they would put up one finger for 25 pounds of ice; two fingers would mean 50 pounds. We would have it hauled out almost by the time the customer's car stopped." *Casey:* "We had our 7-Eleven Stores numbered from #2 to whatever. We never had a #13 because Mr. Thompson was superstitious about that. We had some interesting suppliers in those days. We bought our drug and sundry items from a lady supplier, Mrs. Brewster, who carried her stock in the back of a Model A. Each store gave its own order to a supplier. You personally signed each invoice and the bills were sent to the general office for payment. The first time that prices were regulated in our stores was when the Office of Price Administration (OPA) went into effect. Then we had to keep our prices in line. Before that each store would take its invoice, figure the mark-up from information furnished by the general office and determine the selling price per dozen or the unit price. One store would take the mark-up, divide by 12 and get one price. Another store might round off the fraction differently and get another price. You might buy a can of corn in one store for 27 cents and then pay a penny more or less in another store. You see, we didn't have an adding machine, or even a cash register, in the early days." *Sparks:* "I got my first cash register when I came back from the service in 1945." *Casey:* "We used cigar boxes and changers. We carried the money in our pockets." *Sparks:* "The old pay plan was that the general office took the money for the product invoices; what was left was divided between the company and ourselves, and we had to pay the help in the stores. I believe we stayed with this system until about 1947." *Casey:* "We sold up to 80 big blocks of ice per day—50- to 100-pound blocks. We would tie the ice to the customer's running board or bumper. We even had gasoline at a few stores in the early days. Many of the ideas that are popping up in the stores today, we used back in the early days. We even had Hot-to-Go items then, with our Presto-burgers." *Sparks:* "That's right. We tried a line of fast foods with microwave ovens in five stores in the late '50s, and that is the true forerunner of today's Hot-to-Go fast foods. It was Mr. Thompson's idea. He was an amazing man. He had more foresight than most people have hindsight."

Joe C. Thompson, Jr. (behind desk) at work in his office.

By the end of 1947 Southland's operations were truly diversified. There were 74 7-Eleven Stores; the ice properties, which included City Ice Delivery, T.P.U. and Southland Ice; and Oak Farms Dairies. To bring all of these various operations into one concise corporate structure, all were merged into The Southland Corporation on January 1, 1948.

On November 7, 1948, Southland's board took another action that had been contemplated, researched and desired by Jodie Thompson for some time. He felt it would be, in all likelihood, the single most important employee-related step that the company would ever make. After careful preparation a new Profit Sharing and Trust Plan for Southland employees was established, effective January 1, 1949. Bill Harper, who would later become a trustee of the plan, was with the company at the time profit sharing went into effect: "I was working with Curtis Goodwin in the accounts payable department in 1948 when we were getting down to the final plans on announcing profit sharing. Mr. Goodwin used to have a Coke every afternoon with Frank Alderdice, who was secretary of the company and responsible for developing our profit sharing program. Mr. Thompson had told Frank that he wanted to have the best profit sharing plan of any company anywhere, even Sears, Roebuck and Co. Mr. Thompson had become a friend of General Wood, the head man at Sears, and he used to quiz the general a lot about Sears' profit sharing. Mr. Thompson had Alderdice talk to the Sears people who were in charge of their program to get all the ideas that we could. We also received some help from the National Council on Profit Sharing, which had just been formed and of which we were a charter member. We were probably the first major company in Dallas with this type of profit sharing plan, where the company contributes a part of its profits before taxes and the investments of the fund are constantly revalued. The biggest difference between Southland's profit sharing and Sears' is that most of Sears' is tied up in company stock. We own some Southland stock but our fund has invested in other solid areas, primarily in the purchase of 7-Eleven Stores which are then leased back to the company at an excellent return to the fund. At any rate, the 'little people' in Southland have really benefited from this plan, and that is the way Mr. Thompson wanted it. This was one of his philosophies. He believed so strongly in helping every employee prepare for a secure retirement. Our plan also was developed so that it did not discriminate in favor of the higher paid employees. Everyone contributes the same percentage, five percent, from his salary and there is a ceiling on the amount that can be put in every year. Mr. Thompson was firm, however, about wanting the employees to make contributions toward their own retirement. By the end of 1975 the plan was paying out nearly $2 million per year to Southland retirees. That's excellent, considering the plan has only been in effect slightly more than 25 years. Mr. Thompson would have been very pleased."

JOE C. THOMPSON—THE BOSS

As Southland began its third decade in the late 1940s Joe C. Thompson, Jr. was very much in charge. His achievements were becoming somewhat draped in legend among many new Southland employees. There were so many "Mr. Thompson" stories circulating by his own 20th anniversary with Southland that they were impossible to catalogue. One person who observed Jodie Thompson not as a legend but as a human being was his secretary, Jaunell Storey, who took over the position in 1949: "Mr. Thompson was five-eleven, perhaps 165 pounds. He dressed conservatively and was exceptionally well-groomed. He wanted the employees to be well-groomed, too, and never wanted their pictures taken for publication without a coat. I was nearly scared to death when I first became his secretary, but he was always so considerate. In the morning I would be sure to get to the office a few minutes before eight so that I could have the mail opened by the time he arrived. He would always do the mail first, answering every piece of correspondence within 30–45 minutes. He threw me off a little at first because once he started dictating, he never said 'period, paragraph.' If you weren't accustomed to this, everything just ran together. He was so well-organized; he always had a clean desk by the end of the day. He always took work home at night so that he could stay current on everything. There was one thing about him, in particular: Mr. Thompson loved the store people. He was so excited every time we opened a new 7-Eleven Store. He was always 'riding the town' to visit the people in the stores and at the same time he would be on the lookout for good new store locations. When he stopped to visit a 7-Eleven Store he would always ask: 'When was the last time you saw your district manager?' If the store person said that it had been quite a while, that manager heard from Mr. Thompson the next day. He always noticed everything, especially when it came to the stores and the people who ran them. He would say that 7-Eleven's success was based on 'convenience and the person in our store who meets our customers.' Now, he could be very stern, merciless if someone tried to lie to him or fool him. But he was always fair. His faults? Well, he could be impatient on occasion. Mr. Thompson hated to waste time. If he had a visitor in his office who began to wander on about something unimportant, Mr. Thompson would get up from behind his desk and gently escort the visitor to the door in a diplomatic sort of way. When Mr. Thompson was out visiting stores or looking for locations, he did not want to waste time then, either. He never stopped for lunch. He would grab a pack of Oreo cookies and expect anyone with him to do the same. He said that it was easy to eat and walk at the same time. I think the biggest influence on his life was the Depression. He was raised to believe that you had to work hard to make a living. The hard times made him more appreciative. He never took anything for granted. He was so honest in everything he did and he never forgot to be grateful. He treated all of the employees with dignity and respect and expected everyone else to do the same. No one was allowed to mistreat an employee, regardless of the positions of the people involved. He especially went out of his way to be nice to the employees with jobs that did not pay high salaries. He wanted them to know that he was interested in them as individuals and appreciated the jobs they were doing. In everything he tried to set the example for all of us.''

Mary Lee Roberts, another long-time employee, served first as secretary to G. Allen Penniman, Sr., then after an absence of a few years returned to Southland as secretary to J. B. Langford, the corporate secretary. She recalled how Jodie Thompson did not waste time: ''One time Jaunell was ill for a couple of days and Mr. Thompson called me in to take dictation. In the first place, I was nervous because he had never dictated to me and I was not accustomed to taking dictation that fast. He knew I was frightened because every time the phone would ring (he always answered his own telephone) he would reach for the receiver with one hand and put his other hand on my

Published Monthly in the interest of Plus Selling and Profit Sharing by 7-Eleven Dairy Store Employes . . PS

FEBRUARY, 1949

Editor
STANLEY CAMPBELL

Associate Editors

W. E. CHANDLER . . . . Central Texas
AMON JEFFERSON . . . . . . Dallas
KAY LANCE . . . . . . Fort Worth
JACK McCLELLAN . . . . . Oak Cliff
EVELYN WOOD . . . . General Office

7-ELEVEN STAFF

G. ALLEN PENNIMAN

General Manager

ALFRED HUDSON . Mgr. Centex Division
W. E. CHANDLER . . . Supervisor
CLIFFORD WHEELER . Mgr. Dallas Division
AMON JEFFERSON } . . . Supervisors
MANSFORD JOHNS }
THOMAS BROOKS Mgr. Ft. Worth Division
KAY LANCE } . . . Supervisors
BILL WHITE }
B. C. GLEEN . . Mgr. Oak Cliff Division
BURL HARPER } . . . Supervisors
JACK McCLELLAN }
STANLEY CAMPBELL Adv. & Pub. Relations
MRS. CARRIE GOODMAN Mgr. Acct. Dept.
EARL MONK . . Auditor, Facts & Figures
A. R. (BOB) WRIGHT . . Grocery Buyer
HENRY BRIDGES . . Meats & Frozen Foods
BEN CARPENTER Fresh Fruits & Vegetables

. . . AND TO THE POINT!

BIG'A-MIST—One who loves not wisely but two well.

THINK

BUS'TLE—A deceitful seatful.

THINK

CRIT'IC—One who likes to go places and boo things.

THINK

FAT MAN—One who knows where his cigar ashes will land.

THINK

LIFE—An eternal struggle to keep one's earning capacity up to one's yearning capacity.

THINK

QUAR-TET'—A group of four, each of whom thinks the other three can't sing.

THINK

J. C. THOMPSON

THOUGHTFULNESS IS THE FOUNDATION OF ALL SERVICE

Thoughtfulness is the foundation of all service.

Particularly is this true in 7-Eleven service where you men are dealing so directly and personally with your customers.

Thoughtfulness.

What does it mean? To me it means thinking about your personal appearance and your personal attitude toward EACH customer. It means thinking about good housekeeping in your store. Thinking about displaying your merchandise so as to call items most favorably to the attention of your customers.

Thinking about PLUS SELLING. Thinking about your customers and their buying habits so that you'll come to know WHAT to suggest to them from day to day; and, so that you will be able to anticipate their wants when they drive in.

Thinking about the products you have for sale and the benefits they will give your customers.

Thinking about suggestions and instructions passed on to you from those who supervise Store operations. Thinking always for the purpose of improving yourself and those who work with you in your Store. Thinking about new ideas, new and better ways of serving your customers, yourself and your company.

Whenever I see an untidy Store where customers are ignored at the curb; where no effort is made toward Plus Selling; where "bad merchandise" losses are the rule and not the exception, I know that the Store is manned by thoughtless men.

Constructive thinking is the dynamo of success for the individual and for a business institution. Thoughtfulness is the foundation of all service.

Think! Then act! Constructive action in your 7-Eleven Dairy Sore follows constructive thinking as day follows night.

Think your way to your biggest and most profitable year in your association with 7-Eleven Dairy Stores.

Congratulations on the splendid start you've made, and best wishes for a grand year.

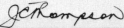

arm—he was afraid I would run away. After he finished I looked at my shorthand and started typing, and nothing made sense. I called Jaunell and she told me to read some of it to her. She started laughing and said, 'That's a separate letter. He never tells you when he's finished with one letter and begins another; he just says the name of the person to whom he's writing.' We had a good laugh about it. All of us learned to work faster, I am sure, because of Mr. Thompson. He would call Mr. Langford and tell him he wanted the average daily bank balance. When he asked for something he didn't mean he wanted it next week, he usually meant that day. There were about 10 of us in the accounting office then and we would all stop our work and start with the bank accounts. We had a lot of bank accounts—at least two in every town where we operated—and it took a lot of adding to get the average daily balance. I don't think he realized what a job it was, as often as he called for it, but it was something he had to have and he knew we would get it as quickly as we could."

In 1948 another Thompson moved into a position of leadership with Southland. John P. Thompson, a University of Texas graduate and a part-time employee of the company for many years, was named to the company's board of directors at its February 10 meeting. It was a deliberate, thoughtfully considered move by Jodie Thompson. Without question he was now beginning to prepare his oldest son for ultimate leadership of the company.

SOUTHLAND'S STRENGTH GROWS

As the 1940s closed Southland was completing the decade in a substantial position. A base for the future had been constructed and the company was in sound financial shape. Growth had been good, especially in the store and dairy operations. Store sales in 1939 had been $834,000. Ten years later annual store revenues were $9.7 million. While Oak Farms Dairies had completed its first year in 1936 with a $6,000 loss, 1949 operating profits totaled $429,000. Ice sales were naturally being affected by the booming popularity of the electric refrigerator, but Jodie Thompson had foreseen this change many years before and the company had been prepared through its diversification into the convenience store and dairy business.

At the annual board meeting in 1949 Jodie Thompson reviewed the progress of 7-Eleven by stating that being the originator and leader in the convenience store business did have some drawbacks. Since 7-Eleven was first, he noted, there were no competitors to copy when it came to operating the stores. He explained that 7-Eleven's progress depended on the trial and error method but that the company had been fortunate thus far with this approach. To better prepare 7-Eleven for the next phase of growth, the board gave approval for the hiring of additional store supervisors. It was felt that the new supervisors would assure better sales, cleanliness, checking out of customers and purchasing, and would inject new ideas that could increase the efficiency of the 7-Eleven organization.

1   From the first issue of "P.S.—the Journal of Plus Selling and Profit Sharing" for employees of the 7-Eleven Dairy Stores.

2   Secretaries for Southland executives in 1952. Seated is Jaunell Gillean Storey, then secretary to Joe C. Thompson. Standing, left to right, are Harriet Golding, Fay Newton, and Joyce Merrell, secretaries to G. Allen Penniman, Sr., Jack Harding and Stanley Campbell.

1 The expansion of the 1950s started with Texas. Austin in 1950 was the location of 7-Eleven's first concentrated expansion. Seven stores were opened in a five-month period.

2 Southland's board of directors traveled to Houston in April 1952 with G. Allen Penniman, Sr., to view 7-Eleven's newest stores. Left to right are John P. Thompson, Webster Atwell, J. Y. Ballard, Penniman, W. E. Chandler (Houston manager), J. Fred Schoellkopf, Jr., Lloyd Gilmore (Houston manager), Joe C. Thompson, Jr., William A. Sailer, and W. W. Overton, Jr.

1

2

10

By early 1950 there were 80 7-Eleven Stores in operation. The convenience store concept had proven quite successful for Southland in the North Texas area and there seemed to be no good reason why it should not work just as well in other Texas cities.

One of the first markets considered for expansion was Austin, the state capital. The company had operated "Old Number One," a combination ice plant and retail store at Ninth and Red River in Austin, since 1927. It had compiled an excellent record, selling as much as 150 tons of ice on some days and also totaling the highest daily sales volume of any retail store on many occasions. While most modern 7-Elevens usually drew their customers from a one-mile radius of the store, "Old Number One" had shoppers who drove many miles to do their buying at the unique ice plant-convenience store. Therefore Austin seemed a logical place for the first planned, concentrated expansion of 7-Eleven. Alfred Hudson, a long-time employee, was given the assignment of opening the new Austin stores. He recalled: "We opened seven new 7-Eleven Stores in Austin in five months. It was the biggest building program we had ever tried in that short a period of time, in our history. We pulled Southland people in from all over Texas to help us, such as Alton Wall, supervisor in Temple. It was quite a task. Much to our surprise, we were not accepted too well at first. We were recognized as an out-of-town corporation. We were even boycotted by the public for several months. John Thompson was my Austin supervisor then, and I can remember one time when he made a pick-up at Store #8 on South Congress and came back with only $48, which represented the sales for a full day. But we struggled along and the Austin folks finally accepted us."

Another new Austin interest for Southland was the Prewitt Creameries, which the company had purchased in 1949. Before he transferred to the store operations to aid Alfred Hudson in the 7-Eleven expansion, John Thompson had begun his full-time Southland career in the Prewitt dairy operation.

Once the Austin stores were accepted the concept of expanding 7-Eleven to other Texas markets began to gain momentum. Houston, the state's largest city, was a natural choice for the next venture. In early 1952 two 7-Eleven Stores were opened and 10 more were added soon afterward. Again, acceptance by Houston shoppers was not immediate. Southland board member J. Y. Ballard recalled: "When we added the second batch of stores, we opened them all at the same time. To open 10 stores at once was quite an achievement, but they really fell flat on their faces at first. We really had to fight for sales in Houston during those first few months until the stores were finally accepted by the community."

Although no one could pinpoint specifically why the Austin and Houston 7-Eleven Stores were slow in gaining immediate acceptance, it seemed likely that it simply required a few months for the potential customers in these two Texas cities to discover exactly where a convenience store "fit" in their daily shopping habits.

As Southland prepared to mark its 25th Anniversary in 1952, it was evident that the company had successfully managed a significant breakthrough. For much of its 25-year history it had been a regional organization mainly confined to the North Texas area. By greatly expanding its operations several hundred miles to the south and southeast it had discovered that its system

83

of operating stores worked as well in distant markets as it did near the home office. Of course most of the Southland people involved in the Austin and Houston expansion had obtained their training and experience through many years of close association with the company. These individuals understood the Southland and 7-Eleven way of operating and were able to transplant it successfully to other markets.

SUPPORT FUNCTIONS GROW IN IMPORTANCE

There were other changes also beginning to occur that indicated the company management was sensing the potential 7-Eleven expansion. Whereas general store operations were once the sole concern of management, other critical support functions now began receiving attention.

Store architecture and design, merchandising, real estate selection, training and testing of employees, and advertising and sales promotion all now began assuming added importance and stature.

STORE ARCHITECTURE

1 A Fort Worth 7-Eleven Store, 1951. Fresh produce, garden seeds and frozen meats were prominently displayed.

2 A typical 7-Eleven Store of the early 1950s.

As company architect Alan Dodds recalled earlier, the design of the basic 7-Eleven Store layout had undergone many refinements. Between 1945 and 1952 an intensive remodeling-rebuilding program had been under way. During that time the amount of floor space in a typical store was more than doubled, customer parking lots grew from five to 10 times larger, ice and milk vaults increased fourfold in size and store aisle space was greatly increased. Although the stores still maintained the basic open-front design and were not air-conditioned, some other improvements had been made. All new stores were being equipped with horizontally sliding doors for their fronts instead of the overhead doors found in most older stores. Use of the sliding doors had resulted in better store interior lighting, according to Dodds. One other notable change in the new store design was the shift of the refrigerated dairy vault from the front to the rear of the store. This switch allowed the opening-up of the store more fully than before, in turn providing greater freedom of movement to both the customer and the store personnel.

MERCHANDISING

The merchandising of the products sold in the store was also rapidly gaining in importance. Many old and some new products received increased emphasis and attention. Ice-cold watermelons, always one of Jodie Thompson's favorite promotional items, received new emphasis during the early 1950s. It was no surprise that by 1952 7-Eleven was selling more watermelons than any other retail food organization in Texas. In fact, 7-Eleven was so sure of the quality of its melons it confidently advertised that the company stood behind every watermelon with a money-back or replacement guarantee to every buyer. Sharp-frozen fresh meat, using a system that 7-Eleven claimed to have pioneered, was a new item which was merchandised strongly. 7-Eleven customers were told that the company's process of sharp-freezing fresh wholesale cuts preserved all of the meat's natural juices, flavors and food

1

elements. According to 7-Eleven merchandisers, many of those important food factors were being lost in the conventional methods of processing and marketing fresh meat. Although many in the meat industry were predicting that sharp-freezing of all fresh meat would be a general practice in the trade in the near future, 7-Eleven claimed to have the only frozen meat retailing operation of its type at this time. By 1952 the company was in the process of constructing a new meat freezing and processing plant in Dallas which would serve all of its 7-Eleven Stores. The meat operation, known as Circle T Meats, would be a member of the Southland family for several years.

Merchandising of the most popular convenience store items also began receiving more planned attention. The results of this concentration on merchandising were soon evident. By 1951 7-Eleven claimed to be Texas' largest retailer of beverages, dairy foods, bread, frozen meats and crushed ice. Annual sales of the stores (based on the '51 figures) included: 2.5 million cases of beverages; 6.5 million loaves of bread; 10.5 million quarts of milk; 250,000 pounds of coffee; 800,000 pounds of frozen meat; 1.1 million bags of crushed ice; 2.1 million pints of ice cream.

Southland processed its own sharp-frozen meats for 7-Eleven with Circle T Meats. The plant was located behind the general offices on Haskell. Later, the plant produced frozen dinners.

REAL ESTATE

Real estate was another critical area for the company. Jodie Thompson had long believed that the most important factor in the success or failure of a 7-Eleven Store was the proper (or improper) selection of the actual store location. Although the company did not yet have an official real estate department, there were many within the organization who had become experts at recognizing good 7-Eleven store locations. Jodie Thompson, G. Allen Penniman, Sr., Clifford Wheeler and all of the company's district managers were considered adept at evaluating potential store sites. According to Thompson, the best at site selection was R. T. (Bob) Storey, then a 7-Eleven district manager in Dallas. Storey commented: "What makes a good location is really a hard question to answer. There are several determining factors: the type of neighborhood, the age bracket of the people around the store, the income level, the competition and what type of competition it is. One of the main things to consider when looking at a site for a convenience store is whether the people who live near the proposed location have to pass it on the way to a supermarket. If people are headed for the supermarket for just one or two pick-up items and have to pass a 7-Eleven Store, they will tend to whip in our store first because we can save them so much time and effort. One way we would determine where a store should be located would be to get out in the neighborhood in the mornings and watch the people coming and going to do their shopping and then go back in the afternoon between 4:00 and 6:00 P.M. and see which streets the people used most to travel to their homes. You might think that they will use one particular street, but when you check you find that, sure enough, they will use another. No two locations are alike. No hard and fast rule will apply to any of them. Of course our methods are really refined and computerized now. In the old days we simply counted rooftops. It may sound outdated these days, but I would even look at things like the number of bicycles in a neighborhood. If you are in a neighborhood where things are happening, kids are out playing in the yards and there are lots of toys and bicycles around. This almost always has meant that the neighborhood is a good one in which to locate a store. If all the houses are quiet, with the curtains drawn and no children playing on the streets, then you know it is an older neighborhood and business is not going to be very good. Also, you must keep up with the builders and developers and know their thinking and plans. You have to be there before the other fellow and get the location tied down first. You cannot wait until they have all the houses built to get a good location."

PERSONNEL

The selection of store personnel was another area being updated in the early 1950s. The company had contracted with Sadler & Associates, a prominent personnel screening organization, to administer a special test to all present and prospective employees. The test was designed to measure the growth potential of Southland people. Although it was said by top management not to be the final determining factor in hiring and promotions, it was not guarded information among Southland people that heavy emphasis was given to the test results when a decision had to be made regarding the promotion of an individual. All factors considered, it seemed a useful management tool and a considerable improvement over earlier methods.

ADVERTISING

One of the most significant advances for Southland during this period involved advertising and sales promotion. In 1946 the company hired Stanley Campbell as its first official advertising manager. Campbell was an experienced professional and highly respected by the Dallas advertising community. He had been the Dallas Advertising League's Most Valuable Member in 1939 and had served as president of the league in 1941–42. He had authored several textbooks on advertising and was in demand as a lecturer on the subject. He obviously knew his business from the print media and broadcasting media to sales promotion. Trained on the production side of the advertising business, Campbell had a basic knowledge of all phases of the craft, especially in the area of copywriting. He brought a professionalism to Southland's advertising strategy and execution that had not been needed when the company was much smaller. Now a structured advertising program was unquestionably required and Campbell provided it. He brought the corporation into previously untried areas. For example, Southland was the exclusive sponsor of Washington commentator Fulton Lewis, Jr. from January 1, 1948, until July 3, 1950. Mr. Lewis' broadcasts were heard jointly in the Dallas-Fort Worth market over the top radio station in each respective city. The listening audience for the Lewis commentary was one of the largest in the North Texas area for any radio program. The Lewis program promoted a prestigious association for the company and was credited with bringing in many new dairy and store customers. Campbell's contribution in modernizing Southland's advertising strategy was best demonstrated in 1949, the year televison first surfaced in North Texas as an advertising medium. Many local advertising men were terrified of this strange new means of communicating with their customers.

7 A.M. ROOSTER

11 P.M. OWL

3

1 Stanley Campbell, Southland's first advertising manager. He was one of the first advertising men in Dallas to effectively utilize television advertising, as evidenced by 7-Eleven's "Owl and Rooster" animated TV spot. It was the first time television advertising was used by a food chain.

2 Southland sponsored radio broadcasts of Washington commentator Fulton Lewis, Jr. in the late 1940s. Southland management and 7-Eleven store managers attended one of his broadcasts from Dallas. Joe C. Thompson, Jr., is seated at center, left front.

3 Bob Stanford, the host of 7-Eleven's Dollar Derby in 1952, was one of the first television actors in Dallas-Fort Worth and quickly became a well-known personality.

Most of the advertising people chose to employ the same type of creative approach with television that they had used when writing and producing radio commercials. It was soon evident that the two were two quite different media, each requiring its own special technique. To assist Southland in using television effectively, Campbell decided to enlist the help of those advertising people who already had some experience with this new medium. He traveled to California and there, with this outside guidance, produced an animated television commercial for 7-Eleven which was to become famous wherever it was used in Texas. Campbell's 60-second TV spot introduced the "Owl and Rooster" to the Texas television audience. The owl, of course, signified 7-Eleven's late-night hours and the rooster demonstrated that the stores opened earlier than their competition. The jingle, in a chant, stressed such copy as: "Seven days a week, we open up at seven. And seven days a week, we're open 'till 11. We've got soup to nuts and that's why we sing—7-Eleven's got everything."

In 1952 Campbell involved 7-Eleven with a new television promotion called "Dollar Derby" which featured an experienced movie actor who had recently returned to Dallas after a brief career in Hollywood. The actor, Bob Stanford, was the first true television personality in the Dallas area. He was the master of ceremonies of "Dollar Derby," assisted by his wife Agnes and actor Easy Marvin. The show was rated as the most popular daytime TV show in the Dallas-Fort Worth market. It was seen four days a week, two days on a Dallas station and two days on a Fort Worth station. The show, which featured an auction of valuable items before a live studio audience, was enhanced through Stanford's unrehearsed interviews of the studio audience and skits and stunts staged by Bob, Agnes, Easy and others. Of course the live nature of the TV auction created its own type of excitement. The bidding at the "Dollar Derby" auction was done with "7-Eleven Derby Dollars." Shoppers received one "Derby Dollar" with every regular dollar purchase in a 7-Eleven Store. Five auctions were conducted during each half-hour broadcast: four for the "Dollar Derby" participants in the studio audience and one for bidding competition by telephone between a viewer in Dallas and another in Fort Worth. Stanford himself contacted both telephone bidders simultaneously and this live on-the-air competition added spontaneous excitement to the show. Major items auctioned on "Dollar Derby" included holiday weekends at the luxurious new Western Hills Hotel in Fort Worth, a Maytag electric washer, electric ironers, food freezers and gas ranges. Other auction items included smaller appliances and assortments of 7-Eleven fresh frozen Circle T meats. "Dollar Derby" was a tremendous success for 7-Eleven as far as generating sales and new customers and establishing the "little store around the corner" as a place where something interesting was always happening. This reputation, created by the combined advertising abilities of Stanley Campbell and Bob Stanford, made a significant contribution to 7-Eleven's popularity and success.

WHEELER, HEADY AND STOUT BECOME KEY 7-ELEVEN FIGURES

Also in the early '50s the careers of three Southland people, each of whom would create exceptional momentum for 7-Eleven within the next few years,

began to unfold. At the company's Christmas party in 1951 Clifford Wheeler was named general manager for all 7-Eleven Stores, succeeding G. Allen Penniman, Sr., who had left Southland to begin his own convenience store company—Pak-A-Sak—in Louisiana. Vaughn Heady, who had begun his association with Southland in January 1948 as a store manager in Weatherford, was now serving as district manager in Waco and was establishing himself as one of the company's best store operators. Forrest Stout, who had clerked with Heady at the 7-Eleven Store on Bluebonnet Circle in Fort Worth, was now 7-Eleven supervisor in that city. Vaughn Heady recalled his early years with 7-Eleven and his experiences at the Bluebonnet Circle store: "I managed the 7-Eleven Store in Weatherford until November 1948. Mr. Penniman came over and told me that he wanted me to move to Fort Worth and open a new store at Bluebonnet Circle, which was located near Texas Christian University. This is where I started working with Forrest Stout and Sam Meyer, who was later a 7-Eleven division manager in California. Our store didn't go over very well because the neighborhood did not want us there. There were several days that the store didn't run over $30. But in May 1949 we had a flood in Fort Worth when it rained 13 inches in a period of only a few hours. All of the Trinity River bottom was flooded and the entire western part of Fort Worth

1951—"Mr. 7-Eleven," G. Allen Penniman, Sr., left Southland to form his own company and Clifford Wheeler, right, was named general manager for all 7-Eleven Stores.

was under water. Most of the city water lines were shut off because the rain had seeped into them. Fortunately, we had a hydrant with good water directly in front of our store, and people would come by and get drinking water. We also knew that folks would be buying a lot more soft drinks, so when the drink trucks would come by the store we would buy everything they had. We sold all of the cold drinks we could get. From that point on the store did real well. The neighbors appreciated our being open during the flood and they continued to trade with us. The store started running about $20,000 a month and 80–90 percent of the business was curb service. The majority of the customers were women. Later, in 1949–50, I became a Fort Worth supervisor and it was during that time that we originated the modern chart meeting. We had operations meetings in Dallas with Mr. Thompson once a month but they were not called chart meetings then. We were doing so very, very well with our Fort Worth stores and were so proud of the operation that we decided to make up charts and bring them to the monthly meeting so we could show everyone how we were doing and could brag a little. We made the charts showing the sales and profit figures with all of the operating lines on them and a chart showing the sales comparisons of every store. Mr. Thompson liked them so much he told everybody to bring charts of their operations the next month. That is how our modern day chart meeting got started. We are still doing basically the same thing today. Mr. Thompson took a very active part in the chart meetings, and you had to be prepared. I remember when Alfred Hudson's stores were having a terrible time getting started in Austin. Mr. Thompson would give Alfred a rough time every month at the chart meeting. Alfred soon got them going, though, and the chart meetings became a little more pleasant for him after that.''

25 YEARS—AND 100 STORES

In 1952 7-Eleven opened its 100th store. It had taken a full 25 years for the company to reach this milestone, but the foundation was now well established. The convenience store concept had been tested and proven, the store operations system had been developed and refined and an adequate number of capable, talented people had been trained and prepared to handle the expansion beginning to accelerate. Having survived a bankruptcy; the Depression; the invention of the mechanical and electric refrigerators; equipment, manpower and product shortages during World War II; post-war inflation; and the uncertainties of pioneering a brand new industry from a zero base, Southland was now strongly prepared for future growth.

The company celebrated its 25th Anniversary with special advertising and editorial sections in seven major Texas newspapers. Advertising manager Stanley Campbell created and wrote the sections, which appeared in the *Dallas Times Herald, Dallas Morning News, Fort Worth Star-Telegram, Fort Worth Press, Austin American-Statesman, Waco News-Tribune and Times Herald* and the *Temple Daily Telegram.* Ranging in size from two to 20 pages, the special sections not only featured a review of the company's first 25 years but also spotlighted individual 7-Eleven store managers in each city. There was little doubt that the store manager was regarded as the single most important

employee by top management, especially by Jodie Thompson. Everything revolved around "the store" and every decision and action was measured carefully as to its impact on each 7-Eleven Store and the people who operated it.

7-ELEVEN STORE OPENINGS

Jodie Thompson especially believed that the manner in which a store was first opened determined whether or not it would be successful. Emphasis was placed by management on opening every 7-Eleven Store with as much excitement as possible. Bob Stanford, who had joined Southland on a full-time basis as a copywriter in 1954, was at the center of the planning and execution of many grand openings during the period when they were considered so important: "The store openings in the '50s were a pretty big deal—everybody came. I don't care where it was—Fort Worth, Temple, Houston, Waco or wherever —you got in your car and went, took off your coat, rolled up your sleeves and helped. That included stocking the shelves and whatever else needed to be done. Seems like it was always a panic. We never knew exactly when the electricity would be turned on, or the water, but somehow or other it all came together. Someone would always be going after potato chips, bread or whatever might be missing from the shelves. In Austin once we were promoting a hot dog and Coke for 10 cents. We rented the cookers for the hot dogs, and the day before the store was to open we discovered they were made for 220 volts and the store had only 110-volt outlets. Bob Peck, our advertising account executive in charge of the opening, and the man from whom we were renting the cookers stayed up all night changing the cookers to 110 volts. Then we found out at the last minute that someone had forgotten to order the wieners. Peck called Dick Boone, who is our Stanford Agency art director, in the middle of the night and Dick had to go out, find some wieners and put them on a truck to Austin so that they could be there in time for the opening. We always tried to do something special for every store. I remember our 161st store opening in 1955 at Preston Road and Forest Lane in Dallas. Thomas Mitchell, the movie star, who had been an Oscar winner, had a television show called 'Mayor of the Town.' We hired him to come down to the opening. That was the biggest and damnedest store opening we ever had. We called it Thomas Mitchell Day in Dallas. We had an agenda you wouldn't believe—going to the mayor's office, luncheon at the Brook Hollow Golf Club, dinner at Mr. and Mrs. Thompson's house, a television interview and, of course, the store opening. We even had a police escort from the time Mitchell stepped off the plane. Two days before all of this was to happen, Mitchell's agent called me from Hollywood to say that Mitchell could not come. Mitchell had agreed to appear in a Schlitz Playhouse live TV drama on the day he was supposed to be in Dallas. I couldn't believe that the mixup had taken place. I told his agent that it would take me 20 minutes on the phone to read Mr. Mitchell's Dallas itinerary to him, but that I would do it and when I had finished I wanted him to tell me again that Mitchell could not come. I read all of it and the agent said, 'Well, he has got to come.' And he did come to Dallas and we had a very prestigious and successful opening with the mayor and a huge crowd attending, but it was quite a close call."

To celebrate the company's 25th anniversary, advertising manager Stanley Campbell created special sections for seven Texas newspapers.

Gala store openings of the 1950s featured live entertainment and personalities and drew large crowds.

AN EMPHASIS ON INCENTIVES

Other factors contributing to 7-Eleven's solid progress in the '50s were the corporate recognition and incentive awards presented to its operations personnel. Jodie Thompson was convinced that division managers and supervisors responded to contests which resulted in personal financial reward and company-wide recognition. One-thousand-dollar prizes were regularly given to the top 7-Eleven division managers and supervisors. The second and third prizes were worth several hundred dollars to the runners-up. These monetary awards were certainly an incentive for all of the managers to produce the best possible results. Many of the contests were based on sales results involving specific product promotions on items such as frozen meats, sausage, cottage cheese, ice cream, apples, turkeys and Christmas trees. Jodie Thompson personally presented the prize money and bestowed the recognition to the winning managers. He firmly believed that 7-Eleven Stores were in the business of selling and those who were the top producers should be rewarded and honored accordingly.

Thompson quite often recognized employee accomplishments by publicizing an exceptional performance throughout the company. The recognition included tributes such as that appearing in a special 7-Eleven publication honoring the outstanding store supervisor of 1952. The Number One supervisor that year was Alton Wall of Temple. Thompson's tribute read: "It became obvious early in the year that Alton had accumulated enough points to be at least one of the winners, but by the first of October he was so far in front that it became very evident he would be the winner. Alton's record for the year was very fine, for he won the Supervisor's Monthly Contest five times and was the winner of the Cleanliness Contest five times during the year. This shows without a doubt that Alton was the outstanding supervisor in 1952, for not only did he produce sales in the cleanest stores in our company, but he produced these sales at the best percentage of net profit. Alton also has a better knowledge of his stores than any supervisor in the company, and this is one of the contributing reasons to his being the most outstanding supervisor in 1952." The publication in which the Alton Wall tribute appeared was dedicated to the 7-Eleven storemen: "It is through their efforts and through the efforts of those who came before them that our organization has made its tremendous growth. All of the supervisors and operating managers and the general manager of our organization were at one time 7-Eleven storemen. The opportunity for the storemen in 7-Eleven is tremendous for the growth of our company is still in its infancy. We salute the 7-Eleven storemen in 1952 and in all the years to come for their tireless efforts to produce more sales and profits for the 7-Eleven organization."

In 1953 another change directed by the board of directors proved correct and timely for a company whose expansion was rapidly gaining momentum. The board decided to provide more authority to individual division managers in all areas of their operations. Personnel selection and training, buying, merchandising and store operations were delegated almost entirely to the local division manager. It was a necessary change brought about by the need for on-the-scene authority and by the generally rapid growth in the scope of

7-Eleven operations. In a word, this new policy provided autonomy to the division managers. The decentralization of control also gave the division managers the freedom to plan and operate on their own. It was quite a vote of confidence in the 7-Eleven division managers as a group and the eventual results of this decision proved its wisdom.

7-ELEVEN VENTURES FROM TEXAS

The next year—1954—brought another decision with even more far-ranging importance to 7-Eleven's future. After the success of the Austin and Houston expansion Jodie Thompson believed that 7-Eleven should consider establishing stores outside of Texas. In November 1953 he asked Clifford Wheeler and John Thompson to make a market survey of the southern and southeastern areas of the United States with the objective of selecting prime cities for possible 7-Eleven expansion. They were asked to visit New Orleans, Mobile, St. Petersburg, Miami and Jacksonville in particular. Wheeler and Thompson reported back from Florida that the cities of Jacksonville and Miami seemed to offer the greatest potential for 7-Eleven. Jodie Thompson immediately flew to Florida for a look at the area and agreed with their assessment. David Neale, one of the first employees to be chosen for 7-Eleven management through the new Sadler test program, was chosen to open the Miami stores. Ed Pack, an outstanding store employee in Waco, was selected to open the Jacksonville market. The first store in Florida opened May 15, 1954, in Miami.

Jodie Thompson had established the Florida operation separately for a unique reason. He felt that all three of his sons, John, Jere and Jodie, would be equally capable of managing and operating a retail-oriented company. He was cautiously skeptical of having one son work for another. Since John, the oldest, was developing extremely well in the management structure of Southland's current operations, it seemed logical that this arrangement should continue. Jere, the second son, after completing his military obligations as a naval officer, was now prepared to begin his own business career. Again applying the principle of keeping the three sons' responsibilities and opportunities separate, Jodie Thompson viewed the Florida stores as the proper vehicle for Jere to develop and manage. The ownership of the Florida venture was first in the hands of various company directors and a number of key Southland employees. In 1961 certain Southland shareholders, who questioned whether the Florida arrangement was an opportunity that should benefit all Southland shareholders, instituted legal proceedings. Before trial, the matter was resolved by consolidating all 7-Eleven Stores, including the Florida outlets, into Southland.

7-ELEVEN IN FLORIDA

7-Eleven opened a total of five stores in Miami and Jacksonville, respectively, during 1954. Again, as had been the early experiences in Austin and Houston, the initial customer reaction to the stores was mixed. There were no convenience stores operating in Florida at the time 7-Eleven was introduced into the state. 7-Eleven represented an entirely new retailing concept totally different from what Florida shoppers had come to expect from the old "Mom and Pop" grocery stores or the large supermarkets. Even the state's other grocers, soft drink bottlers and bakers did not completely understand this little convenience store. It was hard for them to conceive how a relatively small store which charged a few pennies more for providing a service—speed and convenience of shopping—could possibly expect to make it on its obviously lower volume. Even after the stores became profitable and well-accepted it was still difficult for the Florida food industry to comprehend 7-Eleven's attraction. One grocery supplier stopped by one day in 1957, after the Southeastern operation had grown to nearly 20 stores, to tell Miami manager Neale, "You know, David, I don't think you all are going to make it in Florida." Neale personally reflected on the beginnings of the Florida experience: "When I first moved to Florida, I really wasn't a zone manager or district manager, I was just manager. I had only two stores to begin with. My office was in the back room of that first store. Floridians had never really seen a convenience store before. The first store was on a lot 110 feet deep and we put the store back 60 feet from the street. The merchants from all over the area came to see the idiots who would put their store on the back of the lot instead of the front. Everybody thought you had to be up on the street. Of course we used the pole sign so people could see us, but it wasn't long before we had people copy us, which they still do. With its warm weather and casual lifestyle, Florida was a natural for 7-Eleven and it wasn't long before people really accepted us. Mr. Thompson had determined in the early '30s that we were becoming a mobile society. He realized that the new society represented a lifestyle built around the automobile. You didn't walk to the store any more; you went in the car. This was the reason we set the stores on the back of the lot. I do think that proper site selection also has been especially important in 7-Eleven's growth in Florida. About twice a year Mr. Thompson would come down to personally approve the store sites we had found. I would always have 10 or 12 locations to show him each time. He had more business sense than anyone I've ever met and it was such a pleasure to learn from him, especially on the finer points of picking the right location for a store. The beach is such a factor in selecting sites for Florida stores, especially in areas like Daytona and Miami Beach. The closer you get to the ocean, the more people travel in that direction. We may draw customers to a beach store from as far away as 15 miles instead of the usual half-mile or so. This was a super advantage for us and helped to make the Florida operation succeed."

Another 7-Eleven manager who moved from Texas to Florida during this first expansion outside the home state was Sam Meyer. He had begun his career with Southland in 1948 working with Vaughn Heady and Forrest Stout in the Bluebonnet Circle store in Fort Worth. Meyer said of the Florida move: "7-Eleven and the convenience store idea were just great for Florida. In fact, it wasn't long before we had competition begin to move in on us. I was manager of the Tampa area, which covered the entire middle belt of Florida, including Orlando and down the west coast to Fort Myers. We had been in Florida only a few years when the Li'l General Stores began to come in very strongly. I wrote a letter to Mr. Thompson telling him about how strongly

1 7-Eleven's first move outside Texas was to Florida in 1954. David Neale, one of the first employees to be chosen for management through a new testing program, opened the first Florida store in Miami.

2 After serving two years as an officer with the U. S. Navy, Jere W. Thompson returned to direct 7-Eleven operations in Florida.

3 The idea for 7-Eleven's storefront banner originated in Florida. The paper banner on the store's canopy was a built-in focal point for monthly promotions.

1

2

3

competition was developing. He wrote back, and I would like to quote from his letter because it was so perceptive and helpful: 'I've heard of your impending competition, Sam. We're expecting them in every market. In the long run, there will be stores like ours all over Florida. The greatest test is in the operation, the organization, and in your own interest and ability. You are entrusted with the original idea. As you know, Southland invented the convenience store idea. We've been in the business a long time. We have more stores than U'Totem, Cabell's, Lone Star, American Service, and the Atlantic Company combined. Of course, the other companies will hurt us to some extent, but on the other hand, they will help keep us on our toes. Remember that the company with the best organization is always the winner in the end. Your organization is a reflection of you—whether your office functions, whether your stores check short, etc. Our competitors cannot match your experience. Don't let any of this competition worry you in the slightest. Just keep right on working, thinking, and within a few years we will go down in the books of retailing in a way that will make you proud.' As usual, Mr. Thompson was right on target."

The timing of the Florida expansion proved favorable. The state itself was about to receive a tremendous influx of new residents who in turn would create a consumer boom for most of the state's retailers. The warm weather and leisure lifestyle also were exceptionally compatible with the convenience store merchandising product mix. All in all, Jodie Thompson's choice of Florida for 7-Eleven's first expansion outside of Texas seemed exceptionally fortunate.

Besides the positive developments in Florida, significant events were occurring in Texas. A milestone was reached in 1954 when 7-Eleven operating profits were more than $1 million for the first time in the stores' history. The satisfaction and confidence derived from these results triggered a prediction at the May 1954 board of directors meeting that the company would have 600 7-Eleven Stores in operation by 1960, quadruple the 150 stores then in operation.

A WILLINGNESS TO EXPERIMENT

Another new Southland enterprise opened its doors in 1954. Always searching for the different "idea" that offered profit potential, entrepreneur Jodie Thompson determined that the growing retail hardware business might be a possible successful diversification for the company. Again the venture was pursued with the attitude of "if it has potential we'll give it a try—until we find out we are wrong." M. P. (Pete) Exline, Jr. was selected to manage Southland's new 88 Hardware Stores. He remembered what happened: "We were living in Brady, Texas, when Jodie called and said that when he had been in Houston recently he had seen an open-front drive-in store that was selling hardware. He wanted to know if I might be interested in piloting an open-front hardware store experiment in Dallas. I had run a hardware store in Brady for nine years. The first seven years were profitable, but then we had a real drought that almost closed down the town. So I said 'yes' to Jodie's request. I went to Houston and spent several days with the owner of the hardware

Southland's first—and only—88 Hardware Store.

store. However, what Jodie had not noticed was a complete appliance section in the back of the Houston store with radios, televisions, refrigerators, kitchen ranges, etc. I came on back to Dallas and reported to Jodie on my trip. We decided to try it without major appliances. First we started exploring for a location. The company had an ice house on East Main in Grand Prairie next to a 7-Eleven Store. We closed the ice house and converted it into Southland's first and only 88 Hardware Store. We called it '88' because the store hours were from 8 A.M. to 8 P.M. We opened up in August 1954. We had been open only about six months when another hardware store opened across the street. They handled the same things we did, but they offered credit. I remember that one time we had a swing set for $18.88 and our competitor was offering the same set for $21.95. People would come in our store and want to buy a swing set on credit and I would have to tell them that we couldn't do it. One customer went across the street, bought one from our competitor and put the swing set on top of his car. As he passed my store he gave me a big wave of his hand. Things kept going from bad to worse and we closed the store after it had been open for 18 months.'' Southland and Jodie Thompson did not hesitate to explore a potentially rewarding idea but if it did not succeed

DALLAS, TEXAS   PUBLISHED BY THE SOUTHLAND CORPORATION   JANUARY, 1956

Southland FAMILY

OPENED BY MISTAKE

OPENED BY MISTAKE

Firm Celebrates Its First 'Error'

"OPENED BY MISTAKE," 7-ELEVEN CLOSES

Much publicity has been devoted to 7-Eleven's store openings. But this month, the company was in the spotlight because of a store closing.

One of the company's newer stores, in the Fort Worth suburb of Richland Hills, was closed at 11 a.m. on January 4. The article at right, reprinted from the front page of the Dallas Times Herald, tells why.

Above, erecting a sign announcing the closing, are Vaughn Heady, northern division manager; Junior Baldwin, Fort Worth operations manager; Jesse Minatra, assistant manager; and Roy Stancliff, manager.

The closing, widely publicized in newspapers and on television, served notice to everyone that the drive-in food store business is no pushover — "even the experts make mistakes."

A 7-Eleven Food Store in the Fort Worth suburb of Richland Hills closed at 11 Wednesday, traditional closing hour for the firm's 180 stores.

But, for the first time in 7-Eleven's 28-year history, the closing came at 11 a. m.—not 11 p. m. And the store will not re-open Thursday morning.

As Store Mgr. Roy Stancliff locked the doors, workmen erected a large sign bearing a simple explanation: "Opened By Mistake."

"We have had 28 years of experience in choosing store locations, but we really made a mistake on this one," said Clifford Wheeler, 7-Eleven president. "We're just going to walk off and leave it."

The store was opened on Aug. 11, 1954, after contractors set a new company record by completing construction in 27 working days.

Since the opening, Mr. Wheeler said, the store has continued to set records — of the wrong kind. All efforts to turn it into a profitable operation have failed.

Originator of the drive-in grocery idea, 7-Eleven has had expert advice in selecting locations for the 75 new stores which the company has built during the past three years. Company officials have conferred at length with executives of other large firms, and the University of Texas School of Business has made detailed studies on the subject.

"Sometimes even the experts can be wrong," Mr. Wheeler commented. "There is no foolproof formula we can use in selecting locations."

Although 7-Eleven officials expressed regret at the closing of the store, they made it clear that the company is not exactly out of business. With 179 stores in cities all over Texas, 7-Eleven is still the state's largest grocery chain in number of outlets.

they also were unhesitating in admitting their mistake and moving ahead elsewhere.

This attitude of admitting mistakes included unprofitable 7-Eleven Stores. Vaughn Heady recalled: "When I was district manager in Fort Worth I found a store site in Richland Hills. It looked like an excellent location. I talked it up; Mr. Thompson came over and looked at it and it looked so good to him he brought the entire board of directors to see it. They all liked it so well that they thought I should buy more property, so I went back to the owner and bought 25 more feet. The store never did run over $5,000. We tried for two years every promotion and give-away we knew, and nothing worked. When we closed the store we erected a big sign on the parking lot. It read 'Opened By Mistake.' We got a lot of national publicity out of the closing. Then we made another mistake. The store was closed for two or three years and the area built up around it, and it still looked good, so we went in and opened it again and operated it for two more years at a loss. Finally we sold the property. Interestingly enough, six or eight years ago we opened a store north of that location that didn't appear to be any better in the first few months but later did fine."

Southland, while experiencing occasional failure, also was recording its share of successes. Without question one contributing factor in the growth of 7-Eleven was the ability of the stores' merchandising to change with the times. The needs and desires of customers for specific products and services seem to undergo basic changes every generation, mostly spurred by techno-logical advances or lifestyle rearrangements. In the mid-'50s 7-Eleven capital-ized on the popularity of television by installing TV tube testers in the stores, along with a large supply of various tubes. The do-it-yourself testers were an immediate success. 7-Eleven soon acquired the reputation of the little store which had everything, including the TV tube testers, newly installed key-making machines and, somewhat later, money orders. In due time 7-Eleven would become the second largest seller of money orders in the U. S., trailing only the U. S. Post Office. Forrest Stout, who was merchandising manager for the Texas stores in the mid-'50s, recalled that the emphasis on keeping up with changing customer desires came from Jodie Thompson himself: "Back in those days, almost every Monday morning Mr. Thompson had a meeting in his office consisting of John Thompson, Clifford Wheeler, Vaughn Heady, Herbert Hartfelder and myself. I look back now and know that these meetings were probably one of the greatest things that ever happened to me—that I was able to meet with Mr. Thompson two or three hours every Monday. It was the nearest I ever came to a college education. Back in those days he and Mrs. Thompson would vacation in Jasper Park, Canada, with General Wood of Sears and other men who operated large companies. He would come back with so many ideas it would take us a year to put them all in effect. Mr. Thompson would tell us, 'Everything you do should be better than last time. Don't go along in the same rut. Even if you change back to something that you were doing two years ago, it would be better than making no changes.' A lot of things we are doing now we were doing back then. He was always pushing us to try new things. That was something Mr. Thompson really wanted—something different. Try this, try that. Try it on a small scale and if it works, then put it on a larger scale."

The cover of the company's employee publication for January 1956 featured a well-publicized "mistake."

107

1

2

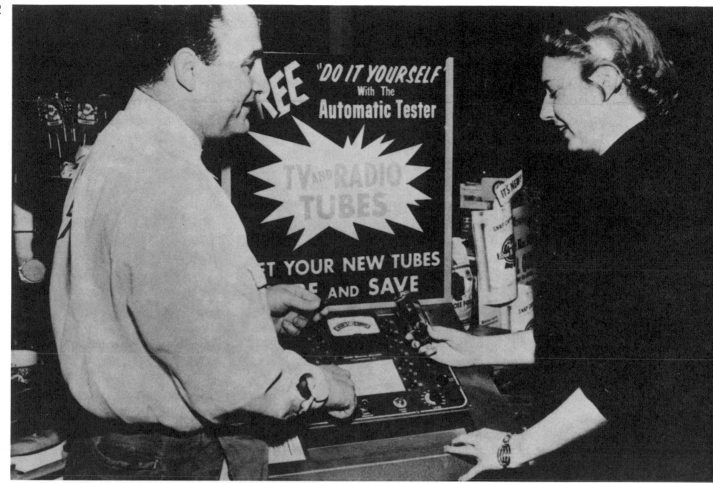

3

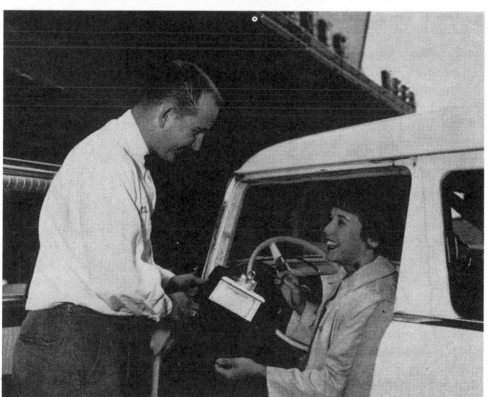

1   In-store displays became important in the early 1950s.

2   In the mid-fifties, do-it-yourself tube-testing machines were installed in the stores and sales of television tubes grew.

3   Money orders were available at 7-Eleven, with the added bonus of curb service. 7-Eleven was surpassed only by the U. S. Post Office in money order sales.

OAK FARMS MOVES AHEAD

The 7-Eleven store operations were not the only active Southland operation in the mid-'50s. Oak Farms also was active and progressing. In 1955 the dairy installed the first liquid sugar system in Dallas, thus eliminating the use of bagged sugar and materially improving the quality of various products. An important acquisition which expanded the dairy outside of the North and Central Texas areas for the first time was the purchase of the Shamrock Ice Cream Company in Houston. Maurice Palmer, a veteran Southland dairy executive, was assigned to operate the new Oak Farms plant in Houston. Oak Farms trucked milk from Dallas to Houston for more than a year before acquiring Lone Star Creamery, the city's oldest independent dairy, in 1956. An immediate expansion program in Houston by Oak Farms increased the capacity of the old Lone Star plant to 30,000 gallons of milk daily and one million gallons of ice cream annually. The expansion was necessary because of the increased dairy business developed by Southland in the Bayou City. Almost overnight Oak Farms became one of the largest dairy operations in Houston. The dairy soon expanded into other Texas markets through the purchase of the Anderson Ice Cream Company in Temple and Consumers Ice Cream Company in Port Arthur in 1956.

Oak Farms also was moving ahead in the development of its dairy products and corporate image. Under the direction of its president, H. E. Hartfelder, Trim Line low-fat products were introduced and milk was offered in gallon jugs for the first time. The Oak Farms carton also was redesigned with an oak leaf and acorn motif.

The accomplishments of Southland's dairies were becoming more widely recognized outside of the state. In 1956, Ex-Cell-O Corporation of Detroit, manufacturer of Pure-Pak equipment which automatically fills and seals paper cartons, conferred the Leader of Industry Award on Oak Farms. A bronze plaque was presented to Hartfelder "in recognition of outstanding progress in dairy management." The award followed an extensive modernization program in Oak Farms' Dallas plant, which had doubled its capacity. New equipment was installed in every department of the plant—receiving, testing, pasteurizing, homogenizing, filling and loading. Milk was now processed more rapidly and the entire processing operation was completely modernized.

The progress of Oak Farms, even before the Dallas plant modernization and the Houston expansion occurred, was noted at the 1955 board meeting, where the dairy was commended for its growth from three routes in 1936 to 196 routes 19 years later. Also, from a beginning of one small plant, the dairy now operated two manufacturing and eight distribution branches.

ICE STILL IMPORTANT

The third division of the company—ice—was not dormant either. In July 1955 Southland acquired the state's largest ice plant, Southern-Henke in Houston. Paramount Ice Company in Dallas also was purchased by Southland

1

1 1954—H. E. Hartfelder, then president of Oak Farms, was recognized for outstanding dairy management and Oak Farms was named a Leader in Industry.

2 Oak Farms promoted sales of cottage cheese with a recipe booklet.

3,4 New developments for Oak Farms Dairies in the 1950s included a new low-fat line called Trim, the introduction of gallon jugs of milk and a fresh new look with an oak leaf and acorn motif.

110

2

3

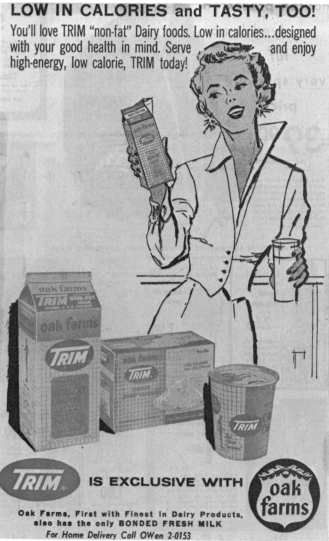

4

in the same year. By 1957 Southland had become the largest ice company in Texas. The company's ice plants were scattered from Lamesa in West Texas to Sulphur Springs in the eastern part of the state and from Sherman in the north to Houston and Austin in South Texas. Southland's ice volume, despite the electric refrigerator revolution, was still respectable, numbering in the tens of thousands of tons every year. The ice division's operations were headed by Frank Alderdice, Bob Collett and Burl Smith, all experienced icemen. The ice division had a variety of customers. It provided much of the railroad car ice for the yards at Dallas, Fort Worth and Houston. Ice also was sold to such diverse users as shrimp boats operating in the Gulf of Mexico, oil refineries in their processing of petroleum products, chicken packers, private clubs and public restaurants and, of course, to Southland's own 7-Eleven Stores. However, there was no doubt that the ice business had experienced a general decline. At one time there had been 38 ice plants operating in Dallas. In 1957 only seven remained and Southland operated three of the seven plants. Although ice had dropped significantly in importance to Southland because of the 7-Eleven and Oak Farms growth, Jodie Thompson did not hesitate to remind listeners that the company's successful move into convenience stores and dairies had been financed by the profits from Southland's original business, ice.

A COLD WEATHER TEST FOR 7-ELEVEN

There was little argument about where the company's forward thrust was going in the late 1950s. The profitable 7-Eleven Florida operations clearly illustrated the potential for convenience stores. However, there was one troubling consideration in all of the discussions about where to expand the 7-Eleven concept next. Texas and Florida were both sunbelt states, with the accompanying warm climate. Many popular convenience store items, such as soft drinks, beer, ice cream and crushed ice, were hot weather staples. Although the demand for these products was assured in areas where the weather cooperated most of the time, what would happen to a convenience store chain which ventured into a cold weather area? It was a difficult question to unravel since no convenience stores existed outside of the South. Events were soon to provide an answer and the results would influence 7-Eleven's growth probably more than any other single event. Clifford Wheeler, general manager of 7-Eleven, remembered what happened when the decision was finally made to test the colder climates: "In 1956 John Thompson and I were going to an American Management Association meeting in New York. When we got to the Washington, D. C., area air traffic was heavy and the plane circled about 45 minutes before landing. We looked down and saw so many good locations that we began to get excited about the potential of the D. C. market for 7-Eleven. John had been stationed near there while he was in the service, so he was already familiar with the possibilities. When we came back to Dallas we asked Mr. Thompson to let us survey the area. We then went up to do this and Mr. Thompson joined us after a few days. After we rode by some of the possible locations he became very excited, too. We were concerned, of course, about whether our business would be successful in the colder climate. However, what happened in Washington proved that it did not matter. The very first winter we were there the city had a foot of snow

The first 7-Eleven Store in the Washington, D. C. area was opened in 1957 in Falls Church, Virginia. At right is J. O. Turley, next is Jack Wooldridge, and at left are two unidentified store employees.

in one 12-hour period. Everything was completely paralyzed. John Thompson came up to join me the next morning after the storm, and I remember we had to wade in snow almost up to our knees to get to the hotel. We started out looking at stores the next day and we were able to visit only about three. However, our stores were located in densely populated areas and the people could wade through the snow to our stores to get groceries. What we saw really made us enthusiastic. In just 18 months we were able to open 20 stores in the Washington area.''

Southland management had fully realized the risks involved in moving to a colder climate far removed from the company's Texas base of operations. With a headline reading "ARE YOUR FINGERS CROSSED?", the following article had appeared in the September 1957 edition of *The Southland Family:* "The success of our Washington, D. C., stores is almost beyond conception of what it means to the future of our company. No one is smart enough to predict whether or not we will succeed in the Washington market. It is the first time, we believe, in the history of retailing that a chain organization or an individual from the South or Southwest has tried to show the people in the East how to sell merchandise. We don't know whether the open-front store will work or not in the colder climate. We don't know whether the people will want to buy at the odd hours or whether they will find our stores convenient. We don't know if they will pay the prices we charge. We don't know a lot of things. We do know it is a big jump and it takes courage. It takes a willingness to risk failing, which a lot of people don't have. We don't like to make too many mistakes, but we are big enough to make a few. If we succeed in Washington, the whole eastern seaboard is open for our company. Did you know that there are more people living in greater Washington alone than live in Houston, Dallas and Fort Worth, where we have more than 200 stores? Just think what an opportunity this is. Only 30 miles away is Baltimore, an even larger city. From there we go into Philadelphia—still larger—and then into New York. It is almost too much to contemplate. We will keep you advised. In the meantime, keep your fingers crossed.''

J. Y. Ballard, a member of the board, added a postscript to that snowstorm and what it proved to the company: "Some of us had worried that our stores would not be successful in a cold climate. After that snowstorm hit the Washington area we sold the stores out to the walls. The managers were so busy most of them slept in the stores for several days. People in Washington discovered 7-Eleven because we were there when they needed us. This really proved that our little convenience store could make it in a cold climate and, in my opinion, it was the making of the company.''

THE FIRST SOUTHLAND SALES CONVENTION

Throughout his life Jodie Thompson never stopped looking for the new "idea." Therefore it was appropriate that the theme for 7-Eleven's First Annual Sales Convention was "Ideas." The convention proved to be a unique event. It was held December 3–5, 1957, at the Baker Hotel in Mineral Wells, a North Texas resort city. It was the first modern sales convention that the company

1 At 1955 management meeting are, left to right, Stanley Campbell, J. Y. Ballard, Jack Rodecap, Joe Ballard, Tommy Brooks, Webster Atwell, Jim Temple, Bob Stanford, A. S. Dodds, Jim Cole, William A. Sailer, Vaughn Heady, Joe C. Thompson, Jr., O. K. Irvine, Bob Collett, John P. Thompson, Bernard Langford, Frank Alderdice, W. W. Overton, Jr., Forrest Stout, W. F. Leonard, Clifford Wheeler, J. Fred Schoellkopf, Jr., H. E. Hartfelder, and Joe C. Thompson III.

2 7-Eleven's first sales convention took place during the company's 30th year in 1957 at the Baker Hotel in Mineral Wells, Texas. The convention theme "IDEAS" was illustrated on a special printed program.

had ever attempted. The meeting was billed as "an all-out effort to extract as many new ideas as possible on every phase of our operation so as to assure the continued growth and expansion of 7-Eleven."

The idea for holding the convention in the first place had sprung from a remark made by J. D. Shook, a store supervisor in Austin, to Jodie Thompson. Shook had observed, "Wouldn't it be great, Mr. Thompson, if we could bring all of our 7-Eleven people together and exchange ideas on everything affecting our business?" Thompson thought Shook's suggestion had merit and the first convention soon became a reality.

Participating in the three-day brainstorming session were supervisors, office managers and division managers. Business sessions of the convention centered on six subjects. The subjects, each with a panel chairman, were: (1) Personnel, John Thompson; (2) Operations, Clifford Wheeler; (3) New Ideas and Methods of Selling and Buying Produce, Jere Thompson; (4) Store Decorations and Merchandise Displays, Forrest Stout; (5) Opening New Stores and Helping Sick Stores, J. C. Thompson; and (6) Sales Promotions and New Items, Vaughn Heady.

The panels were composed of from four to six members with each participant presenting ideas for improvements and better operations. Everyone attending the convention was encouraged to contribute his or her own ideas and to ask questions of the respective panels.

The first convention was judged successful for several reasons. Besides the various ideas that were discussed, an unusual concept was introduced. Bob Stanford, the company's new advertising manager, created a special show for the convention which combined the best elements of showmanship and salesmanship. Stanford's carefully planned presentation was professionally written, staged and acted. Its impact on the audience was substantial. Through entertainment the ex-movie actor and television personality demonstrated that 7-Eleven business and show business were indeed compatible. This combination was later to prove important in creating a personality for the little neighborhood 7-Eleven Stores.

NEW STORE PROMOTIONS

Stanford also was still quite active in creating new store opening promotions. However, new 7-Eleven Stores were opening so rapidly now that it was becoming increasingly difficult to invent a new promotional idea for each one. In fact, the emphasis was gradually beginning to shift away from individual store openings to special events which publicized all of the 7-Eleven Stores in a given area. For example, during the 1956 Texas League baseball season 7-Eleven sponsored baseball appreciation nights at the Dallas and Fort Worth stadiums. In each city 7-Eleven provided customers with tickets—either free of charge or at reduced prices—and also sponsored a show at each park which included a Dixieland band, dancers, singers, comedians and impromptu entertainment by various members of the baseball teams. In Dallas singer Vaughn Monroe entertained more than 7,000 folks at Burnett Field.

Other promotions included a 7-Eleven carnival at the company's six Arlington, Texas, stores. Customers were invited to register for gleaming new bicycles which were awarded at special nighttime ceremonies. Mystery boxes, gift-wrapped packages featuring a variety of merchandise, were sold for $1 each. The boxes were guaranteed to be worth more than a dollar and some, containing watches, binoculars, wallets, jewelry and carving and salad sets, were valued much higher.

The whole purpose of events such as the Arlington carnival was to mark 7-Eleven as the little store where something interesting was always happening. However, Stanford did continue to prove that well-conceived publicity could still generate excitement at the by-now-routine 7-Eleven store opening. In January 1957 the "world's longest hot dog"—a six-foot wiener in an eight-foot bun—was featured at the grand opening of a new Dallas store. The bun, baked for 7-Eleven by the Golman Baking Company, required 30 pounds of dough —enough for 500 normal-size hot dogs. Publicity events such as this always provided adman Stanford with a special kind of personal excitement, including unexpected crises that always seemed to occur in staging the stunt. In the "longest hot dog" promotion, one of the big buns disintegrated before it could be delivered. When another bun was finally ready it was discovered that no six-foot wieners were available, so two shorter wieners had to be spliced together. With these difficulties overcome the "long dog" went on display, with newspaper and television coverage duly recording the event.

A SPECIAL MILESTONE

On June 18, 1958, 7-Eleven celebrated a very special store opening. Store supervisors and division managers, along with the Southland corporate staff, gathered at the home of Mr. and Mrs. Jodie Thompson on Armstrong Parkway in Dallas to commemorate the opening of the company's 300th 7-Eleven Store. The highlight of the program was remarks by Thompson stressing the opportunities and challenges that lay ahead for building an even greater and more expanded 7-Eleven operation. He noted that the pattern for food distribution was continually changing. He explained that in 1948 there had been a total of 5,485 families for every supermarket. In 1958 the ratio had declined with only 1,760 families for each supermarket. He recalled that just 10 years earlier thousands of small "Mom and Pop" grocery stores had been operating in neighborhoods across America. By 1958 the supermarkets had made tremendous inroads on the corner store. However, there was one notable exception to the trend toward supermarket retailing. The drive-in type of food and dairy store, offering its customers not only grocery products but convenience and speed of shopping, had survived the onslaught of the supermarket and was thriving. Thompson stated that "this new shift toward convenience store shopping is not only evident in Texas, Florida and Washington, D. C.; it will be evident throughout the United States in the years to come." He concluded that the pattern for food distribution in the United States promised that both the supermarket and the drive-in type of store would co-exist and prosper. In his opinion they would both be equally important in serving the future needs and wants of the American consumer. Thompson added his own personal

117

prediction that his three sons, John, 32, a vice president and member of the Southland board; Jere, 26, soon to move to Florida as head of 7-Eleven operations there; and Jodie, 17, about to enter the freshman class of The University of Texas at Austin, would all live to see the company achieve another milestone—the opening of the 5,000th 7-Eleven Store. At these words there was a huge roar of good-natured laughter from those attending the 300th store celebration.

CHAPTER
11

Jodie Thompson's continuing involvement in various responsibilities outside the company did not slow as Southland began its rapid growth during the '50s. In 1950 he was named president of the prestigious Cotton Bowl Athletic Association. In 1957 he was appointed to the Board of Regents of The University of Texas System, an honor that confirmed a lifetime of interest in higher education. He also served as a director of the State Fair of Texas and the Republic National Bank in Dallas. He participated in Texas Republican party politics and served as Dallas County finance chairman for the Dewey-Warren campaign in 1948. He was heavily involved in church activities, especially in fund-raising projects.

THE IMPORTANCE OF FRIENDS AND FAMILY

Besides his civic interests and the powerful devotion to his family and the fortunes of Southland, Jodie Thompson managed to maintain friendships with the people he had first met and known many years before. One of his closest personal associates through the years was Dallas banker and Southland board member W. W. Overton, Jr., who recalled his friend: "I think I first began to appreciate what kind of man Jodie was when my father died. It was a great personal loss to me and I was grief stricken. Jodie was the very first person to come to me and offer his sympathy and condolences. He probably never knew how much I appreciated his words of comfort. After that I began to understand what a friend this man really was to me. Of course he was quite an unusual person. He had a smile and manner about him that could charm any group or individual. He always had an earnest desire to please. Even if he were not pleased, he always made it a point to smile and be as pleasant as possible. He had an intellectual mind and he was always seeking out new ideas and solutions to problems. He was such a hard worker that we had trouble ever convincing him to take off and relax. I would try to get him out on the golf course or down to East Texas for some fishing, but he always seemed to get restless and would begin wondering about whether or not he was neglecting the company. He never took a golf lesson but he did play and he could have been a good golfer, even though he had no real interest in it. He was very civic-minded and was active in almost all worthwhile activities. There is no doubt that he helped to build Dallas into the city that it is today. He always liked *quality* in everything, whether it was people, his business or anything he did."

Jodie Thompson seemed to realize the most personal joy from his family. The tragic loss of three small children seemed to make the three surviving sons that much dearer. He could be a demanding and exacting father. He expected all three boys to work and, more importantly, to learn the convenience store, dairy and ice business as he had "from the stables to the office." Although there were no longer any stables to clean, there were still dairy trucks to wash and 7-Eleven Stores to be swept and clerked. John, Jere and Jodie responded by doing whatever was necessary. It was understood throughout the company that no easy chore would be assigned because one of the boss's sons was involved. Jodie, the youngest, was typical in his job experience with the company. He remembered the work and his father: "I started working at Oak Farms when I was about 12 years old. I caught the streetcar which ran behind the house. I rode it all the way to downtown, through town and across the viaduct to the dairy. Dad paid me 30 cents an hour. He didn't tell me what my salary was until I had been working for a couple of weeks, I guess not to discourage me. I thought I was getting paid a lot more than that. I was carrying out the trash, moving boxes and anything they wanted me to do. It was interesting work.

The Thompsons with sons Jere, left, and Jodie, right, at Armstrong Parkway home in Dallas.

I worked for the stores for three or four summers and then went back to the dairy. Dad was a firm believer in starting kids off working at an early age. He never let any of us loaf during the summer. That was the last thing we were ever allowed to do, and he spent a lot of time thinking about the best way for us to spend each summer. Believe me, he knew exactly what day school was out and he also knew when it started again. It was a special treat to get to go to camp or to Jasper Park Lodge in Canada with the family.

"There was a tremendous age gap between Dad and myself—almost 40 years. But like I say, he knew what was going on in my life. He knew how I was doing in each subject in school and when we were together I could tell he was thinking about me—he wasn't thinking about business. He was a wonderful dad. He was relaxed and yet at the same time very intense. I spent some time with him at the office, but it was generally on Sunday. After church we would go over to see my grandmother, "Bummy" Thompson, at Cliff Towers and then come back by the office. Dad was devoted to his mother; he was devoted to his friends as well as his family. He cared more for people than anyone I have ever known. He would lie awake at night trying to figure out how he could help people, especially the people who worked for the company. He would really be proud of what has happened with profit sharing."

THE STORES AND THE DAIRIES

Although Jodie Thompson's concern for the welfare of each employee was obvious, he also set high standards for their performance that often stimulated a high degree of competitiveness between various Southland divisions. The classic contest to meet his demanding goals usually occurred between the 7-Eleven Stores and Oak Farms Dairies. The stores and the dairies, though cooperating closely on many joint sales promotions through the years, were always striving to out-perform the other in reaching sales and profits objectives. The net result of this intra-family competitiveness was that each of the two divisions—stores and dairies—probably performed better and achieved more than it otherwise would have without the Thompson-imposed pressure to outdistance the other. Obviously this bottom-line result was exactly what Southland's president had in mind when he encouraged the competition.

However, the relationship between stores and dairies certainly was not without its positive aspects. The two Southland divisions worked closely together on many sales promotions which helped attract customers to each. For example, in May 1958 an extensive ice cream promotion called "Mystery Flavor, Mystery Trip" was kicked off jointly by Oak Farms and 7-Eleven. It was expected to set new ice cream sales records for 7-Eleven. The highlight of the special promotion was an unusual customer incentive, a 10-day trip for two via KLM Royal Dutch Airlines to anywhere in the world, plus $50 a day spending money. To win the trip a customer had to submit an original name for a special mystery ice cream flavor which was being given away free with every Oak Farms ice cream purchase. The mystery flavor, contained in a special four-ounce carton, was a mixture of coconut, butterscotch and pineapple. The ice cream promotion was successful in attracting customer interest and producing the desired sales results for Oak Farms and 7-Eleven. The mystery flavor was named Trop-i-Cal.

Thompson carried the theme of competitiveness on outside of the business, too. Bruce Furrh, presently division manager of Southland's Midwest Farms Dairies in Memphis, was involved in some of the extra-curricular competition: "I remember that at a certain time of year—late March or April—everyone from management at the company would go to Mr. Thompson's ranch near Cayuga. He would assign all of us to teams as 'cowboys.' We would work on the cattle, branding them and whatnot. After the cattle were taken care of everybody got a little trophy or loving cup. Mr. Thompson would pass them out with inscriptions reading 'world's slowest cowboy,' 'world's fastest cowboy,' etc. Of course the winning team members got a little bigger trophy than the losers. John, Jere and Jodie were right in there with the rest of us wrestling those cattle all day long. We always had a good time, with a lot of good fellowship, but some of us felt that we were ready for the rodeo circuit after that day at the ranch."

Furrh also had sharp recollections of Thompson as a businessman and individual. "Mr. Thompson was interested in every business we had; whether it was large or small did not matter. He always did everything he could to help each one of us in our own part of Southland. When I was a sales manager for Oak Farms in Dallas we served the old St. Paul Hospital (which was then downtown) on a rotating basis with three other dairies. It was ours one month; then it rotated over to our competitors for a month each. Once when it was our month to serve the hospital the routeman in charge of it came in my office and told me that we were not going to get the cream business that month at St. Paul. The sister who made the dairy assignments had decided to keep one of our competitors' cream because they served it in a Tetra-Pak. Since cream was one of our best items, I went to see the sister and explained that it was our turn to get all of their dairy business that particular month, which included the cream portion of it. She said, 'I am going to use the other dairy's cream and nobody but the Pope can change my mind.' Since I knew that Mr. Thompson was a great believer in and supporter of St. Paul's, I went to see him and told him of our situation. He gave me that great smile and said, 'She's a fine young lady. I think she'll change her mind.' I went back over a few days later and she told me, 'You've got the business, and I should have said that nobody but the Pope—or Mr. Thompson—could change my mind'."

THE EMPHASIS ON "WORK"

Jodie Thompson was still maintaining quite a pace. His 7-Eleven president, Clifford Wheeler, recalled the Thompson routine in the late '50s: "We used to work all week; then on Saturday morning, after we had the money counted and deposited, we would get in cars and go looking for 7-Eleven store locations. Mr. Thompson was usually with us, or we might even go on a Sunday and take the family along. He had a favorite expression, 'Please do this in your leisure time.' To him Saturday afternoon and Sunday were our 'leisure time' to do the things we didn't have time for during the week. He worked just as hard, or harder really, than anyone else. When we were out looking at locations he wouldn't take the time to stop and eat lunch. I walked into my office one morning and there was a sign hanging on my wall which said 'Perfection.' I still have the sign in my office. I had an idea Mr. Thompson had put it there and after a few months he came in one morning and said, 'Did you notice your sign?' I told him that I had noticed it the first day and had been striving for it. That all may sound corny these days, but it really had an effect on me and I did perform better. One time he had a similar idea. He used red scotch tape and had 'TNT' put up on every store front door, every office and even one on my bathroom mirror at home. I guess he got someone to go around to all the stores for him and put them up, or he might have even done it himself. He had Lillian, my wife, put it up in my bathroom. We had a meeting the next morning in his office and he wanted to know if we boys saw the 'TNT' signs. We told him we had, but didn't know what they meant. He said, 'It means Today Not Tomorrow.' Everything important should be done today as far as he was concerned. He was always doing things like this to us. He kept us on our toes and our brains functioning. He always wanted to be ahead of our competitors and we usually were. Funny thing, though, all of the successful 7-Eleven Stores were the ones he called 'my stores.' All of the rest somehow belonged to me."

Thompson's business philosophy made a profound impression on many Southland people, in particular his son John, who was developing his own leadership style as a company vice president in the latter 1950s: "Dad's philosophy was to serve the people and serve the people better. He believed very strongly in this. Naturally he was always interested in making a profit. To that end he always talked about profit-related items, such as controlling expenses. He always tried to impress upon us the value of a dollar and how hard it was to make. When I was a child, I can remember that he worked very long hours. It was usually after seven o'clock in the evening when he

got home. Many, many times we had dinner without him. Of course he always worked on Saturdays and Sundays until the last few years of his life, when he started taking off on Saturday to go to his ranch. He believed that if you worked longer and harder than your competition, you couldn't help but out-perform them.''

A NEW INPUT OF TALENT

Although the elder Thompson was devoting as much time and energy as he had in earlier years to the company's operations and development, there was little doubt that important management changes were beginning. One factor that demanded a fresh input of managerial talent was the sharp growth in Southland's size. In the early days of organizing the company, undergoing an unexpected receivership, enduring the Depression and coping with the war years, the company had survived primarily through the dominance and guidance of Jodie Thompson. Now, with the operations spread over Texas, Florida and the East Coast, there was a definite need for additional management depth. Southland's board, at the urging of Jodie Thompson, had recognized this reality by providing far greater autonomy to 7-Eleven division managers. The concept of decentralization had worked out well and had fostered more rapid development of local division management. It was now evident that the company's expansion was requiring an even faster development of future management. Fortunately, many of Southland's top executives were continuing their career moves upward during the 1950s. H. E. (Herb) Hartfelder and Clifford Wheeler were presidents of Oak Farms and 7-Eleven Stores, respectively. In January 1958 Vaughn Heady was placed in charge of all Texas 7-Eleven Stores. At about the same time Forrest Stout was selected to manage merchandising activities for the Texas outlets. In 1957 Oak Farms hired M. T. (Tom) Cochran, Jr., a former executive with the Eskimo Pie Company, and named him general sales manager of Oak Farms. Two of the Thompson sons, John, who was now a vice president and board member, and Jere, who had left Texas in 1959 to direct 7-Eleven operations in Florida, were both starting to figure significantly in the company's management structure. Other individuals in key jobs, as the expansion started building, were Maurice Palmer, Houston manager for Oak Farms; safety expert W. F. Leonard, who was receiving consistent national recognition for his work in employee safety programs; 7-Eleven store operations veteran Tommy Brooks; produce expert Ben Carpenter; Bob Stanford, advertising manager; Howard Greene, assistant advertising manager; Stan Radominski, Florida stores advertising manager; H. R. Brasuell, Monroe-Texarkana supervisor for 7-Eleven; Ralph Shaw, Oak Cliff supervisor; Amon Jefferson and Burl Harper, Dallas area supervisors; Delano Womack and Billy Ruffeno, Houston supervisors; L. D. Chappell, Dallas area supervisor; Bob Storey, Dallas area district manager; Alfred Hudson, Austin district manager; Bob Wheeler and C. O. (Tex) Beshears, Circle T Meats; W. E. Chandler, Houston district manager; Floyd C. (Buck) Spruce, Houston supervisor; George Reaves and John Hilbun, Oak Farms managers in Waco and Beaumont, respectively; Bob Spencer, production supervisor for Oak Farms; Bruce Furrh, sales manager for Oak Farms in Dallas; and Burl Smith, Oak Farms manager in Austin.

The basic nucleus of an expansion-minded management, able to function in the new atmosphere of growth and autonomy, was in place as the decade of the '50s came to a finish. There also had been a few changes in the makeup of the company's board of directors, again signaling the beginning of new directions. One influential member, William A. Sailer, who had joined the board in 1936, died in 1959. J. Fred Schoellkopf, Jr., a member of a highly respected Dallas family, came on the board in 1944 and was still serving. H. E. Hartfelder was a new addition to the Southland board, being named a member on April 15, 1959.

CHAPTER 12

In the 1950s Southland's major convenience store competitor in Dallas was Cabell's, Inc., operator of the Cabell's Minit Markets and Cabell's Dairies. Much of Cabell's history paralleled that of Southland. The company had been founded by two brothers, Ben and Earle Cabell, in 1932 in the midst of the Depression. Ben Cabell had been driving an old Buick automobile which he decided was about ready for permanent retirement. He had removed the motor from the car and used it to power the original Cabell's dairy plant. At first there were no Minit Markets or even home delivery of dairy products. The Cabell brothers operated just one lone ice cream shop located at 4017 Commerce Street in Dallas. The brothers, faced with a depression-scarred economy and limited consumer spending, were aware that only a few nickels were available for the purchase of a Cabell's ice cream cone. So they reasoned that the company with the best product and the best service would get the biggest share of those nickels. To add to the product and service appeal the Cabell boys applied the clincher that was to build their ice cream business into a multi-million-dollar company: the brothers began giving their customers two dips of ice cream for their nickel in a special double-dip cone. The response to the double-dip idea was overwhelming and the concept soon became a standard merchandising method in the ice cream business everywhere. In 1940 the Cabell brothers opened their first drive-in food store, similar in design to Southland's 7-Eleven Stores.

On Saturday, February 7, 1959, the purchase of Cabell's, Inc. by Southland was announced by Earle Cabell, president of Cabell's, and John Thompson, then executive vice president of Southland. It was agreed that Cabell's would retain its highly regarded name on the 66 Minit Market convenience stores, its two milk plants and one ice cream plant. The Minit Market stores were located primarily in the Dallas area, with other outlets in Fort Worth, Longview, Tyler, Waco, Odessa, Midland and Austin. Cabell's Dairies had milk processing plants in Dallas and Tyler and an ice cream plant in McKinney, covering a 30-county area of North and East Texas.

Commenting on the Cabell's acquisition, John Thompson said that he was "pleased to welcome into the Southland family the prized name of Cabell's, which has won many friends through decades of leadership in the field of dairy products and through the Cabell's Minit Markets."

Earle Cabell and Jodie Thompson were contemporaries, having attended elementary and high school together in Oak Cliff. The challenge of elective politics now attracted Cabell. His father and grandfather had both served as mayors of Dallas and Earle hoped to become the first third-generation mayor in the city's history. After one losing campaign to a long-time incumbent, Cabell was elected mayor in 1961. He served in that position until his election to the United States Congress in 1964.

As the 1950s ended Jodie Thompson believed that Southland's achievements during the decade had laid the foundation for the company's long-range future. Perhaps most importantly, 7-Eleven had successfully expanded its convenience store formula outside of Texas to Florida and the East Coast. The already widespread 7-Eleven Texas operations had been considerably bolstered by the addition of Cabell's Minit Markets. Southland's dairy division had received a similar boost from the addition of the top-quality Cabell's milk and ice cream. Besides these positive developments, a growth-oriented management team was coming together at Southland with John Thompson, Herb Hartfelder, Cliff Wheeler and Jere Thompson the most visible supporters of the concept of even more rapid expansion.

1

2

3

As of December 31, 1959, there were 490 convenience stores in operation: 274 7-Eleven Stores in Texas, Louisiana and on the East Coast; 151 7-Eleven Stores in Florida and 65 Cabell's Minit Markets. The 500th store opening was scheduled in early 1960 in the Meyerland section of Houston.

It was with confident anticipation that Southland's board of directors and management readied themselves for the new decade. However, the powerful lifestyle changes occurring across the landscape of America were to alter even the most optimistic assessments of the company's future. A nation was on the move and the little company which originated the convenience store concept on a wooden ice dock in Oak Cliff many years before could hardly foresee the effect this movement would have on its own destiny.

1 Where the double-dip ice cream cone originated— Cabell's ice cream shop, Dallas, Texas. Cabell's introduced the double-dip cone, sold it for only a nickel in 1932 and survived the Depression to become a successful business.

2,3 In 1959 Southland acquired Cabell's Dairies, opposite, and Cabell's Minit Markets, above.

A 7-Eleven Store in the 1960s.

CHAPTER
13

The changes in America which began with Henry Ford and the Tin Lizzie accelerated spectacularly in the 1960s. As the big cities became more congested the gradual movement into the suburbs became a swarming explosion of growth. Between 1960 and 1970, 70 percent of America's population increase occurred in the suburbs.

Many factors contributed to this unprecedented migration from the inner cities to the outer perimeters. Most families simply wanted more space in which to live and raise their children. Only the suburbs could offer the combined promise of easy access to the good jobs provided by city-based industry and the breathing space afforded by an uncongested landscape. Another contributor to the attraction of the suburbs was the tremendous improvement in the nation's roads and highways that began in the 1950s. The government's Highway Act of 1955–56 committed $33 billion to build the largest and most modern network of roadways ever conceived. This development of a national interstate highway system virtually guaranteed that the automobile would continue as the primary method of transportation in America. It also made the lure of suburban living even more powerful as commuting time from home to work was reduced substantially.

The majority of families and individuals who joined the rush to the suburbs were relatively affluent. Most were homeowners but there were also many who opted for the plush, modernistic apartment houses just beginning to appear in suburban areas. These new suburbanites soon discovered that their altered living patterns created the need for a service relatively unimportant to clustered city residents. The service was "convenience," the conserving of one's own personal time through a more effective use of the minutes spent on the routine matters of daily living. Of course a major feature of suburbia was the emphasis on leisure activities of all kinds. Backyard cooking, evening neighborhood get-togethers involving children and entire families, trips to nearby recreation facilities, even home maintenance and required yardkeeping all combined to accentuate the value of one's available time. The need to conserve personal time also was especially evident to the individual who lived in the suburbs and commuted by automobile to a job back in the city. This unproductive time expended in moving back and forth on the freeways quite naturally subtracted from the remaining minutes and hours left over for necessary chores or leisure activities. So, for both those who worked and those who played, "convenience" became a desired service for the new inhabitants of suburbia. With this need for convenience obviously growing along with the creation of every new suburban area, the country's largest operator of convenience-oriented stores surveyed the trends of New America.

Southland's management liked what it saw. The opportunities for convenience store expansion appeared staggering. With the movement into the suburbs becoming ever more rapid, the time seemed right to tap this new consumer demand for faster, more convenient shopping. People wanted, needed and were beginning to expect that convenience stores would be available to support their new suburban lifestyles. Southland and 7-Eleven began to prepare for a surge in corporate growth that hopefully might keep pace with this demand.

SOUTHLAND PREPARES FOR GROWTH

The company now began readying itself for a more rapid expansion. At the board of directors meeting on February 26, 1960, a thorough study of the existing corporate organization was authorized. The study was expected to help the board in establishing long-range company goals, projecting organizational needs and developing systematic plans to accomplish growth objectives. This effort was deemed necessary by the board "if the company is to increase its dairy operations 10 percent per year and double the number of convenience stores within five years." In conjunction with the study other actions were taken to prepare for the imminent expansion. The company's first official personnel department was established for the general office and the store and dairy divisions. An employee morale study was assigned to the new department as its priority mission. Another board decision was a movement into the revolutionary new information system being embraced by businesses throughout the nation—computer accounting.

Specific store expansion plans set by the board included a goal of 102 stores on the East Coast by the end of 1960, a substantial increase over the number then in operation.

One of the eastern areas 7-Eleven charted for immediate development was the Tidewater region of Virginia, which included Norfolk, Hampton and Virginia Beach. To enter these new markets required transplanting 7-Eleven employees from older existing areas. H. R. Brasuell, who joined the company in 1950, was a typical example: "I knew that the company was considering the idea of expanding further on the East Coast outside of the Washington, D. C., area. John Thompson asked me to come over to Dallas from Monroe, Louisiana, where I was in charge of 16 stores. I never will forget that day. I walked into his office and he said, 'H. R., what would you think about going to Norfolk, Virginia?' I said, 'Where?' I told him that I had never been there and could scarcely even locate it on a map. Shortly after, John and I met in Washington and we toured the Virginia area together. When the time came for me to move in 1959, my wife and I had butterflies about going. She was pregnant and I told John I couldn't go until after the baby was born. I just went up for a couple of weeks to get the contracts for the construction of the first stores handled. After the baby was three weeks old, we moved for good. We started out with one store in Norfolk, one in Hampton and one in Portsmouth. The first store opened in Norfolk on December 7, 1959. We did all the usual things like circulating our handbills and taking a big ad in the newspaper. Many local people said that a little store like 7-Eleven would never make it. For one thing, the Health Department rules said we could not have an open front. Although they were very skeptical, they finally agreed to let us open the first store on an open-front basis just to see what would happen. After we opened they looked us over and consented for awhile, but shortly thereafter they came back and said we had to close our store front or put an air curtain across the front. We decided to close the front and that's the way we built future stores. We also gave curb service at first, but the Virginia customers didn't know what to make of this service. About 1961 we discontinued curb service. The Tidewater area itself amazed me. We were exactly two feet above sea level and some of the area always seemed to be under water. There were bridges and canals all over and I had trouble getting around. It was a 75-mile

Bill Harper, left, trained for two years to head Southland's data processing department, established to use the company's new RCA 301 electronic computer installed in 1963. Standing is Jim Scott, RCA representative.

trip between the stores at Portsmouth and Hampton, and I made this trip twice a day. My toll fees were $5 a day to visit the three stores. Virginia really became a great 7-Eleven area. They loved us and we loved them. At the time I was transferred from Virginia to Atlanta, about 1966, we had 95 stores open and eight under construction."

7-Eleven was making progress in other East Coast markets, too. In May 1960, comments from the various Eastern Division managers reflected this positive mood. From Ralph Shaw in Baltimore: "We are receiving many gratifying comments from our customers, our sales are increasing daily and we are enthusiastic about the future of 7-Eleven in Baltimore." From L. D. Chappell in Washington: "We have opened 42 units in 30 months in the Washington Division. We expect to have 46 units open by June 1. We do not have any more special grand opening promotions because they are no longer necessary." Philadelphia also had experienced the 7-Eleven phenomenon. Between April 22 and June 3, 1960, five stores were opened in the Philadelphia area, with negotiations for other sites well underway. Without question the eastern seaboard was endorsing the 7-Eleven style of convenience shopping.

SOUTHLAND'S 33RD BIRTHDAY

On July 11, 1960, Southland celebrated its 33rd birthday by selling 133,573 pints of ice cream, an average of 566 pints per store. The ice cream birthday sale offered a pint of ice cream for a penny with the purchase of a pint at the regular price, and the customer response was virtually a stampede.

7-Eleven's president, Cliff Wheeler, highlighted the birthday celebration by announcing an expansion goal of one store for every 7,500 residents in Texas. In Dallas and Houston alone this would require at least 100 7-Eleven Stores in each city. A full page two-color newspaper advertisement in Texas newspapers thanked 7-Eleven customers for their patronage. It read in part: "How well have we succeeded? The verdict is yours—the public's. We feel that the overwhelming public acceptance which has made possible our expansion into so many neighborhoods is proof that we are performing a service which you want and need. For 33 wonderfully enjoyable years, our sincere thanks to you."

On October 26, 1960, Wheeler was elected to Southland's board. He was only the third new director elected to the board in more than 20 years. Jodie Thompson, in announcing Wheeler's election, said that he was named "because of his outstanding leadership during the company's greatest period of growth." Thompson noted that during Wheeler's management of 7-Eleven operations the convenience stores had: (1) expanded the Texas operation from 100 to 300 stores, to become the state's largest food merchandiser in total number of outlets; (2) established a new division on the East Coast, where 90 new stores had opened in the past three years; (3) grown into Texas' largest retailer of milk, ice cream, soft drinks and ice; and (4) enlarged the size of the newer 7-Eleven Stores to 2,400 square feet of floor space.

SUPPLIERS—A KEY TO 7-ELEVEN'S SUCCESS

How best to merchandise and promote the products available at 7-Eleven was a continuing priority for Thompson, Wheeler and other members of the 7-Eleven team. Buying procedures were constantly being updated and this naturally meant that some familiar products began to disappear from the store shelves. The new 7-Eleven buying system was designed to eliminate products that moved slowly while increasing stocks of the more popular items. This distribution system required the help of a valued group of individuals and companies that had been crucial to 7-Eleven's growth and success all along —its vendors and suppliers.

In the years before sophisticated methods of product distribution were developed it was up to the individual supplier, or grocery supply firm, to keep each 7-Eleven Store amply stocked. Many a bread supplier, dairy or soft drink distributor had received a panic telephone call from a 7-Eleven manager or supervisor regarding an "out" on a particular item. It was then up to the supplier to run a "hot shot" delivery to ease the pain of a lost sale or an angry customer. Without the help of these loyal and capable suppliers, 7-Eleven simply would not have been able to adequately serve its customers.

In upgrading distribution procedures there was much discussion of opening a warehouse to serve the needs of the 7-Eleven Stores in Texas. Much of the store merchandise was purchased through grocery wholesalers, and Pete Exline, who had started with Southland's 88 Hardware Store venture, recalled the buying and distribution system in the late '50s and early '60s: "After the 88 Hardware Store closed, I came into the company as a grocery buyer for the Texas Division. Every town was buying from a different grocery house. It was a darn mess as far as coordinating the buying. I tried to talk Jodie into building our own warehouse, but the board turned it down because they were not interested in buying trucks, building a warehouse and carrying inventories. We started doing business primarily with one particular wholesale grocer who had agreed to take on most of our 7-Eleven business. Its board of directors eventually became dissatisfied with our arrangement in Houston for some reason and decided not to serve our 7-Eleven Stores there. I guess it was just more difficult to service a small store as compared to a supermarket. Anyway, when they cut us off in Houston we had to scramble to find a supplier. We finally got another firm there to take on our stores. I also finally found a warehouse in Temple to take on our Austin, Waco and Temple accounts. It was just a constant struggle to keep the stores stocked properly, our business was growing so fast. Just seeing all of the vendors who had products they wanted to sell through our stores was no simple matter. I originally set up Thursday as vendors' day. It got so hectic that I started seeing the vendors every day except Wednesday, when I would go to Houston and see the vendors there. I guess that one of my biggest projects was establishing one price book for all the Texas stores. At one time would you believe that we had seven different price books for our stores in Texas? Even after we consolidated the books we still had separate price pages for Dallas, Houston, etc., but at least we had them all in one book."

NEW MERCHANDISING TECHNIQUES

Other new merchandising improvements were introduced, including changes in the arrangement and displaying of merchandise and an updating of point-of-sale techniques. One particular point-of-sale innovation introduced by David Neale's Florida stores involved putting up a paper sign on the canopy of each 7-Eleven Store. The out-front banner, usually measuring 36 to 40 feet in length, began serving as the focal point for the individual store's monthly product promotion. Bob Stanford's advertising department, which by now had become a full-service in-house agency bearing Stanford's name, originated the copy phrases which were used on the storefront banners. Whether it was "Our Shotgun Shells Are for the Birds" or a simple sign that said "Money Orders Sold Here," these canopy messages provided an extra advertising exposure to several hundred customers per day.

Much of the emphasis on the changes in merchandising technique came from Jodie Thompson's usual procedure of seeking out expert counsel when undertaking new directions. On the recommendation of his friend General Wood, chairman of Sears, Thompson had hired an ex-Sears merchandising expert, Herbert F. Murphy, to study 7-Eleven's merchandising methods and submit recommendations. Murphy, a Sears vice president and member of its board of directors, pioneered development of the company's new statistical

133

research and analysis program. In simple language, the system dictated that the store should concentrate primarily on the products and the brands which customers preferred most. Murphy also made an in-depth study of store operations, working closely with Vaughn Heady of 7-Eleven and Joe DePasqual of the Cabell's Minit Markets. Murphy and the two Southland operations executives personally visited many 7-Eleven Stores. From these visits came specific recommendations regarding improved personnel training and customer traffic movement and additional new merchandising concepts.

William J. Brown, a Dallas retailing executive and close associate of Jodie Thompson, was another contributor to a change in Southland's merchandising technique. He suggested that a study be made of soup sales in the 7-Eleven Stores. It was found that Campbell offered 23 soups, of which 7-Eleven stocked—or attempted to stock—20. Statistics revealed that 11 of these soups accounted for 85 percent of total soup sales. 7-Eleven quickly discontinued nine slow-moving flavors and stocked more of the 11 top sellers. Result:

Campbell soup sales were up 19.23 percent the first month after the system went into operation.

OTHER OPERATIONS REMAIN ACTIVE

Other Southland operations besides 7-Eleven were aggressively expanding as the new decade began. Southland Ice was installing new blast freezing equipment which increased its Waco plant's daily capacity from 30,000 to 72,000 tons, making it the largest cold storage operation in Central Texas.

In the dairies Oak Farms was actively increasing its production capabilities. The capacity of the Temple ice cream operation was doubled in the fall of 1960 to accommodate a growing demand for Oak Farms products in the area. The expansion was made necessary primarily because the dairy had secured an old-time Southland customer, one that had meant much to the company's growth approximately 20 years before. The United States Army was in the process of significantly expanding its Fort Hood facilities near Temple. The Army had chosen Oak Farms to supply both ice cream and milk to post exchanges, commissaries and mess halls at the huge military base, home of the First and Second Armored Divisions. It marked the first time that a single dairy had received milk and ice cream contracts for all three outlets. Besides the increase in Temple's operations, San Antonio was also proving to be a rewarding market for Oak Farms. Its sales performance won a new Ford Galaxie for the San Antonio branch manager, W. W. (Woody) Fuller, who was named as the dairies' Most Outstanding Manager of 1960.

AN UNEXPECTED DEVELOPMENT

The first year of the 1960s ended with the total number of 7-Eleven Stores leaping to 591, a 20 percent jump in only 12 months. With the dairies and ice divisions also moving ahead, the initial phase of Southland's expansion seemed right on schedule. However, a new extremely serious and unforeseen development had surfaced which represented not only a personal tragedy but theoretically posed a challenge to the company's future. While visiting North Carolina on an inspection of store sites Jodie Thompson noticed that an unusually large growth had appeared suddenly on his neck. Upon returning to Dallas he visited his physician. Subsequent tests confirmed that the growth was malignant. Thompson had always been so vigorously active that the news not only saddened but also shocked everyone who knew him. There was no question that he was a seriously ill man. However, with determination he now gathered his strength to fight the malignancy with the same energy and strong will that had delivered his once desperate company from bankruptcy. His family, friends and associates rallied to him as he began his personal struggle. During his daily working hours at Southland it remained business as usual. He knew what the final result of his illness might be and he began his own careful planning for that eventuality. To that end the man who had so masterfully conceived, planned and executed much of his company's success now thoughtfully considered what would lie ahead for Southland if he were no longer able to lead.

1,2 Merchandising in the early 1960s saw increased use of the store-front banners and billboards for the dairies.

3 A new produce item—the Thompson Melon—appeared in 7-Eleven Stores. Joe C. Thompson, Jr. had tasted the melon, grown in Israel, during a 1960 trip to London. He dried the seeds on the windowsill of his hotel room and brought them home to Texas, where he planted them at his ranch. The Texas Research Foundation at Renner ordered some seeds, too, and grew the melons. Unfortunately, they didn't go over in the stores. In those pre-air conditioning days, they quickly ripened in the warm stores. The aroma of over-ripe melons was too much for both clerks and customers!

*1961—John P. Thompson was named president
of The Southland Corporation.*

CHAPTER 14

In 1960 a Southland Creed appeared in the company magazine. Although its author was not credited, there is little doubt that Jodie Thompson contributed all or part of its wording. It summarized his philosophy of the company which he helped begin in 1927. It read:

A SOUTHLAND CREED

WE BELIEVE that the most important asset of Southland is its people—in every plant, office and community, wherever they work and live.

WE BELIEVE that the well-being and security of the employees are dependent upon the soundness and security of Southland; that to keep our company sound and secure, the people of Southland have an obligation to make the most effective use of their skill, effort and time on their jobs.

WE BELIEVE that all of the people of Southland must recognize our joint responsibility to the owners of the company, to the public we serve and to our nation as a whole.

In recognition of these beliefs, and of the company's responsibilities to employees, we pledge:

- That every employee will be treated fairly, with consideration and respect, and that we expect all who supervise the work of others to treat those under their direction as they themselves want to be treated.

- To pay wages and provide employee benefits that fairly reward employees for their skill, effort and time.

- To weigh all decisions with full regard for their effect on the well-being of employees.

- To try to provide stability of employment to the greatest possible extent.

- That the complaint of any employee will be listened to and handled with fairness and promptness.

- To provide employees every possible opportunity for self-improvement and advancement with the company.

- To provide good working conditions—a safe, clean, friendly work place and proper facilities to help the employee do his job effectively.

To many Southland employees raised in the sobering climate of a Depression, these idealistic, honest words held much meaning. The interchanging flow of common interests between a company and its workers still ran strongly in organizations such as Southland. The cynicism that would plague the relationships of many employees and their companies in later years was virtually non-existent. In the early '60s, at least as far as Jodie Thompson's company was concerned, loyalty was as much a corporate asset as the hundreds of 7-Eleven Stores, the dairy plants or the ice trucks.

There was little doubt that the Depression had dramatically influenced Jodie Thompson's business philosophy. He believed that to survive one must work. To more than just survive but also to prosper, one had to work much harder than his competitors. His belief in hard work, mixed with an entrepreneur's willingness to develop a new idea if it offered a possible profit, was the foundation on which he had constructed his company. He always had been an innovator, but he had shrewdly tempered this eagerness to experiment with a solid conservatism, again traced to the economic wounds endured as a participant in the Depression.

THE COMING TRANSITION

Now, as he suffered with the demands of his illness, he thoughtfully planned the coming transition for his company. On March 8, 1961, there were two meetings which signaled the beginning of an orderly transferral of corporate responsibility. At the board of directors gathering held that morning Jodie Thompson was elected to a newly-established position—chairman of the board. At the same meeting a young man 35 years old, who had been associated with the company from his elementary school days, was named as Southland's new president. That evening, at a dinner so carefully arranged that specific table assignments were made for each of the 278 guests, the passing of leadership from one generation to the next was completed. Dallas' elegant Chaparral Club was the setting for a dinner honoring the company's newly-elected president. At the dinner, hosted by Southland's officers and directors, the guests dined on Boeuf Roti and drank champagne as a prelude to the scheduled remarks of board chairman Jodie Thompson. His personal secretary, Jaunell Storey, remembered that he prepared no formal speech for the dinner. He chose to speak without notes about the company and its new president, John Thompson. He spoke movingly about John as a son—but more significantly as a Southland employee. He reviewed and evaluated his oldest son's performance as an employee and contributor to the company's growth much as an impartial observer might have done. Those attending the dinner recalled the insight and perceptiveness shown by the father in seeing the son precisely as most employees also saw him. It was a moment tinged with obvious sentiment, yet maintaining the businesslike atmosphere necessitated by a serious change in corporate responsibilities. The audience included employees from almost every position in the company, from offices to dairy plants to 7-Eleven Stores. For Southland it represented a "family" gathering. And it seemed quite appropriate that Jodie Thompson would gather his Southland family around him to explain and discuss the important changes that had taken place that morning. The end result of the dinner was to bring the Southland group even closer together, united behind their new president. The future of the company appeared undisturbed by this profound change in leadership.

TRIBUTES TO A LEADER

On May 15, 1961, Jodie Thompson entered Baylor University Hospital in Dallas after a sudden worsening in his deteriorating condition. On Sunday, June 11, he died at the age of 60. The newspapers in various Texas cities reported and editorialized on his passing. From the *Dallas Morning News:* "Joe C. Thompson, who died in Dallas Sunday, played a chief role in the development of a new concept of retail food merchandising. The 60-year-old businessman transformed the ordinary corner ice house from an ice dispensary to a multi-million-dollar drive-in grocery enterprise. Under his leadership,

Joe Thompson Dies In Dallas at Age 60

DALLAS, June 11 (AP).—Joe C. Thompson, 60, board chairman of the Southland Corporation who was credited with helping put this country's first drive-in food stores into operation, died Sunday.

The Dallas business executive entered a hospital after becoming ill several weeks ago.

As board chairman and former president, he headed a multimillion-dollar corporation which has more than 300 stores in Texas and 105 on the East Coast.

Southland Corporation subsidiaries include 7-Eleven Food Stores of Texas, Oak Farms Dairies, Circle T Meats, Cabell's Dairy, Cabell's Minit Markets and Southland Ice Company, the parent firm for which Thompson first went to work after his graduation from the University of Texas in 1922.

(The corporation operates nine Minit Markets and 39 7-Eleven Stores in Fort Worth and Arlington.)

Survivors include his wife and three sons, John Thompson of Dallas, Southland Corporation president; Jere Thompson, president of 7-Eleven Stores of Florida, and Joe Thompson Jr., a University of Texas student.

Rosary will be recited at 8 p. m. Monday at the family home here. Requiem mass will be celebrated at 9:30 a. m. Tuesday in Holy Trinity Catholic Church, where Thompson was a member. Burial will be in a Dallas cemetery.

Associates recalled Thompson, planning to be married shortly, advanced an idea in 1924 for Southland Ice to start selling iced watermelons—the first ever offered Texas customers. Sales boomed and at the end of the summer young Thompson was $2,300 richer.

He became secretary-treasurer of the firm by 1927 and that same year helped put into effect another employe's suggestion for Southland Ice to start selling milk, bread and eggs. These sales at 21 outlets are said to have made them the first drive-in grocery stores.

Southland Ice continued to branch out, but the 1929 depression brought setbacks and the company went into bankruptcy. Thompson headed a group of Texas business men who bought the properties in 1934.

More stores were added. At first they were called Tot'em Stores. The name was changed to 7-Eleven Stores in 1945. Meanwhile, the parent Southland Corporation branched into the dairy

JOE C. THOMPSON.

business in 1936 and now says its Oak Farms Dairies branch is the largest independent dairy in the state.

Southland established Circle T Meats, offering quick-frozen and packaged meats, in 1954 and the Cabell Dairy and Minit Markets became part of the system in 1959.

Thompson also was a director and former president of the Cotton Bowl Association, a director of the Republic National Bank of Dallas and the State Fair of Texas, a regent of the university and a former Dallas and Highland Park city councilman.

1 The Fort Worth Star-Telegram and the Associated Press reported the death of Joe C. Thompson.

2 A photo of Joe C. Thompson, circa 1960.

a few dozen ice houses in Dallas became the seeds from which the present chain of 7-Eleven Stores and Cabell's Minit Markets sprang. Thompson was always a dapper 'idea man.' One particular idea came to him in 1927 from an ice house manager, the late Uncle Johnny Green. He suggested that milk, bread and eggs, as well as ice, be sold through the ice houses. And from the old man's idea and the young Thompson's vision, a new word touched the tip of the consumer's tongue: 'the drive-in grocery'."

From the *Oak Cliff Tribune:* "Jodie Thompson was another Oak Cliff boy who made good. Maybe we stretch the point to call him Oak Cliff for he was born in Waxahachie and had been a long-time resident of Highland Park before death claimed him last week at age 60. Under Thompson's shrewd administration, Tote'm Stores, predecessor to 7-Eleven, became a business phenomenon. When he was interviewed as Oak Cliff Chamber 'Man of the Month' several years ago, he attributed his success to 'one of those happy business accidents.' The Southland Corporation today is a huge, successful enterprise born of ingenuity, drive and perseverance. To his three sons and his Southland associates, Jodie Thompson has left a thriving business. He left his mark in Oak Cliff and we shall miss him."

From an editorial in the Waco, Texas, *News-Tribune:* "The death of Joe C. Thompson in Dallas took from the American scene one of the most imaginative and energetic merchandisers of this century. His career was a textbook example of what the free enterprise system is all about. And his generous use of his own time and money in unselfish ways to advance the causes of local self-government and higher education also was in the classic pattern of the successful man with a public conscience. In the years of growth and expansion, his firm came to own hundreds of drive-in establishments and to be used as the pattern for thousands of others. It is probably an understatement to say that Jodie Thompson had more impact than any other one individual on the shopping habits of America during his lifetime. Nor did Jodie Thompson quit learning and pioneering when he became successful. He was fond of telling how, on a pleasure trip to California, he observed drive-in groceries selling money orders. He came home and installed the service in his own widespread chain of stores at a most satisfactory rate of profit. Whether this year's graduating classes turned loose any young men in the Jodie Thompson mold we will learn later. The probabilities are that they will be showing up rather promptly as they have in increasing numbers in recent years. The real question is whether the freedom to use their imaginations and energies to benefit themselves and their fellow citizens will be preserved. Without that freedom to succeed, with the corollary freedom to fail, there wouldn't be the kind of society we live and flourish in. That is why Mr. Thompson worked as hard at his civic and local self-government responsibilities as he did at merchandising. His example is a shining one indeed."

Another tribute to the memory of Jodie Thompson was presented by Preston A. Weatherred at the 71st Annual Convention of the Southwestern Ice Association, meeting in Austin, Texas, November 13, 1961. Weatherred said, in part: "As we open our hearts to the memory of Jodie Thompson, numerous and various facets of his brilliant and successful life crowd for recognition. Jodie was so fine and so effective in so many of his relationships and undertakings, that selection is indeed difficult. And, too, words are, after all, such poor messengers as we seek to express the honor we desire to extend. Jodie was a man of few words. He would, if he could, sharply limit the number of words I should use, even now, as we pause to give expression to the loss that has come to his loved ones, to us, to his friends and his associates, in a score of great and fruitful fields of endeavor. 'Fruitful,' possibly, is the word that Jodie would like for me to use here in retrospect, in our endeavor to appreciate the value and meaning of his life and career. I was a close observer, in fact, in many respects his mentor, as his career unfolded step by step, from the days when I first knew him as a bright, friendly boy, a recent graduate from his beloved University of Texas. In these early days he was nominally a bookkeeper, but such a bookkeeper no one has ever seen before or since. From the very beginning, Jodie Thompson expanded manyfold the usefulness of any assignment in his many civic and business undertakings. Truly his career is exemplification of the opportunity for success and happiness afforded by this, his country. And Jodie loved, in truth, idolized his country.''

1 Jere W. Thompson was elected a director and vice president of Southland in late 1961.

2 The first air-conditioned 7-Eleven Store, Dallas, Texas, 1961. Air conditioning gave another "new" look to the stores.

2

CHAPTER 15

After his father's death Southland's new president, John Thompson, moved deliberately but with confidence. He possessed his own ideas about future directions for the company. Three significant moves made before Jodie Thompson's death were to greatly aid him in managing the sensitive transition. H. E. Hartfelder and Clifford Wheeler, both excellent and seasoned executives, were named vice presidents of Southland and R. G. Smith, manager of the general accounting office, was elected controller for the firm. John Thompson remembered: "After Dad died I brought Herb Hartfelder over to the general office from Oak Farms. Herb asked me what kind of company we were going to run and I told him I wanted to expand as quickly as possible. At that time we had Mr. Herbert F. Murphy working for us on a consulting basis. Mr. Murphy was one of the bright lights in the company's expansion. While visiting with him one day I told him about our success on the East Coast and how great it was for us. I asked him what we should do about building on this success. He told me that we should do exactly what Sears had done and was doing in the Los Angeles market, where they were so well accepted. He said, 'Take the ball and run with it. Build all the stores you can, as fast as you can. Do not be careless about it, but put all of the muscle at your disposal in capturing this market.' So we decided to do just that and our expansion was underway in earnest."

Herb Hartfelder added: "When Mr. Thompson died, we were a $100 million company. One of the first resolutions John and I made was to aim for $1 billion in sales within 10 years. It represented a lot of expansion but that was the direction in which we wanted to head."

To further strengthen the management team Jere W. Thompson, who headed 7-Eleven's Florida operations, was elected a vice president and board member in late 1961. Jere had followed in the family tradition, graduating from The University of Texas at Austin with a degree in business administration. A popular student, he had followed another Thompson family example by serving as student manager for the Texas Longhorn football team. His father and two brothers all had held or would hold that same position for Longhorn athletic teams at some point in their years at the University. Following his elevation in the company's executive ranks, Jere was assigned to continue his supervision of the Florida stores as well as to oversee 7-Eleven's entry into the North Carolina market.

AN EMPHASIS ON PREPARATION

Jodie Thompson had carefully planned for the time when his sons would assume leadership positions in the business community. He was determined that they would be able to perform well no matter what direction their careers might take. He was particularly aware that an ill-prepared son in a critical Southland management position would quickly undermine employee morale. So the senior Thompson saw to it that all of the sons worked and learned. When the time came for the new generation to replace the old, the Thompson sons were ready and totally familiar with the operations of the company. Louise Swift, Jodie Thompson's sister, watched the educational process employed with the sons: "Jodie realized that John was going to be head of the company some day and needed to be coached especially well. Being the oldest, I suppose, John was his pride and joy. He would dictate these long letters to John when he was at the University, and I remember one day he seemed to be especially frustrated and he leaned back and said, 'Sister, do you think John pays any attention to these letters—do you think he ever reads them?' I said, 'No, I don't think so now. He is living in a world all his own. But I don't think there is a word that is wasted. Years later he will say, "My daddy said this, and my daddy said that." ' I told him that he and I were still saying things that our own daddy, who was a tax commissioner and statistician for the Dallas Power & Light and Texas Power & Light companies, had said to us. At the time he said them they meant nothing to us. The older you get the smarter your father gets. You have always heard that. Not when we were young, but as we grew older, Dad grew smarter and smarter. To this day I am still repeating things he told Jodie and me."

Mrs. Joe C. Thompson, Jr. and son Jodie at Southland's 35th anniversary celebration, July 11, 1962.

In December 1961, six months after his father died, John Thompson was able to direct "A Message of Importance To All Employees" which included these comments: "By the end of 1961, we will be operating almost 700 stores in nine states and the District of Columbia plus all of our dairy, ice and frozen meat operations. The economy of the country looks good to us at this time, and certainly our company is more than fortunate to be operating in some of the fastest growing areas in the whole United States. We are all looking forward to 1962 being our biggest and finest year ever, and certainly the outlook over the next several years is extremely good. I believe that our company affords all of us an excellent opportunity for security and advancement, and I promise on the part of management that we will work hard toward this goal and I know we can count on your help."

When Southland's new president reviewed the year he was able to see progress in several areas. Perhaps the most important new development was the successful experimentation with closed-front, completely air-conditioned stores. The old open-front stores, with such an uncomplicated open access, were certainly as effective as ever from a convenience standpoint. However, many businesses were now moving rapidly to the installation of air-conditioning because of customer—and employee—demand. Clerking in an open-front 7-Eleven Store in Houston or Miami in July was indeed a rather warm experience. So, to improve the working conditions for the store people and to provide another customer service, the air-conditioning of the stores began. Despite scattered concerns about losing sales because of a less convenient, closed-in look, the air-conditioning seemed to help rather than hurt sales.

Several acquisitions also occurred. Goble Dairyland Products in Wichita Falls, Camellia Ice Cream in Houston and Pure Ice Company in Austin were purchased and integrated into the Southland operations.

One other change in the board of directors occurred in 1961. J. Fred Schoellkopf, Jr. resigned as a director and his son, J. Fred Schoellkopf III, was named to succeed him.

The year concluded with the transition smoothly accomplished and Southland continuing to expand. Although 1961 had been eventful, the following year was to prove even more so. For in 1962 the company was to radically increase its growth rate.

144

CHAPTER
16

W hile the lifestyle revolution generated by the automobile and the suburban migration gathered even greater momentum in the '60s, another revolution occurred in the food industry.

The gigantic supermarket, a one-stop shopping point for grocery shoppers, had virtually eliminated the once dominant "Mom and Pop" neighborhood stores. The modern supermarket, with its large size, wide variety of foods, self-service system for shoppers, sales on a cash-and-carry basis and many non-food items, offered far more than the old corner grocery store. Because of its large purchasing power and more efficient administration, it was simply able to provide groceries at a lower cost than the one-family operation. The supermarket evolved, as did the convenience store, through customer demand and a changing lifestyle.

As the supermarkets accelerated the demise of the "Mom and Pop" stores, the convenience store found itself with another void to fill. Not only did customers respond to their own need of saving more personal time by choosing convenience stores for their fill-in shopping requirements, but also they began thinking of these modern markets as a replacement for the old neighborhood grocery store. It was an extremely bullish situation for a young industry still being delivered into the retail world. Southland, the founder and largest convenience store chain, viewed this additional positive development for what it was—a golden business opportunity.

7-ELEVEN ENTERS NEW MARKETS

To capitalize on these highly favorable trends, the decision was made to expand 7-Eleven operations into new market areas. The company's entrance into Colorado, Arizona and New Jersey was made by purchasing small existing companies and converting the outlets to 7-Eleven Stores. The acquisition of the Minit Markets in Arizona added 24 stores, Colorado's Scotland Pride Dairy and Scotty Stop Stores brought 11 stores and E-Z Way Stores, also in Colorado, provided another seven units to the growing number of 7-Eleven Stores appearing in many parts of the country.

On the East Coast four Minit Markets in New Jersey were acquired. Geographically it was the farthest north that the company had ever ventured. However, the population concentrations in the New Jersey area were impossible to ignore.

About this time other top management changes were made to allow more concentration on expansion. In August 1961 Herb Hartfelder was named executive vice president and Jere Thompson moved from Miami to Dallas as head of all 7-Eleven store operations.

Former 7-Eleven president Cliff Wheeler was assigned the responsibility for researching, negotiating and coordinating development of new areas for Southland. Wheeler became a key contributor to 7-Eleven's expansion program. He recalled: "After Mr. Thompson passed away in 1961 our new area development was so gigantic. John had been made president and Herb became executive vice president, and Jere was brought into the corporate office from Florida and put in charge of the 7-Eleven Stores. I was relieved of store operations responsibility and put in charge of our new area development. It seems like that was when our big expansion really

*The architect's original illustration for the colonial store design,
which became the standard for stores on the eastern seaboard.*

started. I was able to devote my full attention to new areas while Jere was concentrating on continuing to develop areas in which we were already operating. In my new job I was on the road about 80 percent of the time, but this was absolutely necessary if we were to expand 7-Eleven quickly into these new markets which offered so much potential to us."

1962: A CRUCIAL YEAR

In many respects 1962 was one of the most crucial years in Southland's history. It was the first full year of the administration of John Thompson, the company's new president. During this time the transitional period following his father's death was completed. The sorting out of new priorities and directions was accomplished smoothly and without incident. A new top management team was formed, a commitment to expansion and growth was regenerated and improvements were instituted in various phases of the company's operations.

In addition to entering new areas such as Colorado, Arizona and New Jersey for the first time, Southland further expanded in the populous East Coast markets where the stores already were known and accepted. A new 7-Eleven store exterior design, more compatible with the colonial architecture often found on the eastern seaboard, also was introduced during the year. The colonial store soon became the standard architectural concept for new eastern stores.

It was a year when a new director, Walton Grayson III, was added to Southland's board. Grayson, an attorney in the law firm of Atwell, Grayson and Atwell, had long been active in handling various legal matters for the company.

The year also was marked with a continuing dedication to worthwhile interests outside Southland, especially in the field of education in general and The University of Texas at Austin in particular. The board of directors authorized a contribution of $50,000 to the University in memory of Jodie Thompson. The donation was given to help establish a Joe C. Thompson Conference Center on the University campus. Many Southland employees also added their personal contributions to the conference center fund.

Another important milestone occurred in 1962 when a 7-Eleven television advertisement was chosen as one of the two best retail store commercials created in the United States. The award was presented to Bob Stanford, 7-Eleven's advertising manager, at the American TV Commercials Festival and Forum at the Waldorf-Astoria Hotel in New York City. The winning commercial featured 7-Eleven's famous watermelons with a "sing-along" theme. The 7-Eleven TV spot was the only entry from any southwestern-based company which reached the finals of the nationwide competition. It was high recognition for 7-Eleven and Stanford and the first of many such awards.

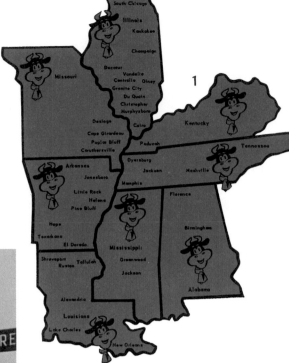

1   The first dairy expansion outside Texas. Southland acquired Midwest Farms with a territory spanning the Mississippi from northern Illinois to southern Louisiana.

2   The Midwest Farms home office and ice cream plant.

3   Midwest Farms' division office and ice cream plant was once the home of Fortune's ice cream parlor, "the" place to meet in Memphis in days past.

CHAPTER 7

Perhaps the most noteworthy development during 1962 did not directly involve 7-Eleven. During that year Southland decided to expand its dairy operations significantly beyond its successful Oak Farms and Cabell's divisions. There was no doubt that the potential for dairy expansion existed. The company possessed a talented group of knowledgeable individuals thoroughly skilled in dairy management who could help accomplish this expansion. One of these was M. T. Cochran, Jr., vice president and general manager, Southland Dairies Group. "Why did we decide to expand our dairy operations? I would have to say that the decision was reached by John Thompson and Herb Hartfelder after they assumed the leadership of the company following Mr. Thompson's death. Their horizons were unlimited. The opportunity came to buy Midwest Dairy Products, a firm headquartered in Memphis but with operations from Illinois to Louisiana to Arkansas to Alabama. This represented our first dairy expansion outside of Texas. This was the first step toward John and Herb's desire to expand our dairy business. Once the first acquisition was made, other dairies began coming to us and things began developing rapidly from that point." Herb Hartfelder, the company's premier dairyman, remembered: "Soon after I moved from the dairy plant in Oak Cliff to the general office of Southland, we purchased Midwest Dairy Products. It was owned at the time by the City Products Corporation in Chicago, and its principal stockholder was a man named Bill Sinek. John and I talked to him about buying the company, but he was dubious. Midwest was definitely for sale, but although several people had expressed interest in purchasing it, Mr. Sinek said that when they got to Chicago they did not have any money in their pockets. He told John and me: 'If you two boys from Texas want it, you better have some money in your jeans when you come to see me.' We did manage to have a check for $1 million with us when we went to see him and I think this convinced him that we meant business. The Midwest Dairy was scattered from DuQuoin, Illinois, to New Orleans to Birmingham. We made a few immediate changes. At the time we bought Midwest Tom Cochran was running the dairies, Oak Farms and Cabell's. We told him: 'Congratulations, you are now running Midwest, too.' He got an apartment in Memphis and stayed over there until he got it reorganized."

JACK HOUSE REMEMBERS

One of the Midwest Farms' key executives was Jack House, who remained with Southland when the acquisition was completed. House recalled the Southland-Midwest negotiations from another viewpoint: "Our first experience with Southland was when they contacted William J. Sinek, who was the head of City Products. Sinek was trying to sell Midwest to the Pet Dairy Company. It was really funny around Midwest—we knew that the company was going to be sold but we just did not know who would end up buying it. City Products was anxious to sell Midwest so that they could get into the clothing business. How it happened I don't know, but John Thompson and Herb Hartfelder got in touch with Sinek and began to talk about Southland making the purchase. Both John and Herb knew my father-in-law, Harry Strong, who was president of Midwest at the time. It was amusing—one time Mr. Strong and I were on the Pet Dairy plane flying around to see the various Midwest locations in Shreveport, Little Rock and so forth. And Basil Companionette, one of our people, was flying with Tom Cochran, John Thompson and Herb Hartfelder in a Twin-Beech looking at other Midwest properties. Their plane was going one way and ours was going the other, but we never crossed paths. Mr. Strong said many times that he thought we would have a much better potential with Southland. He

1

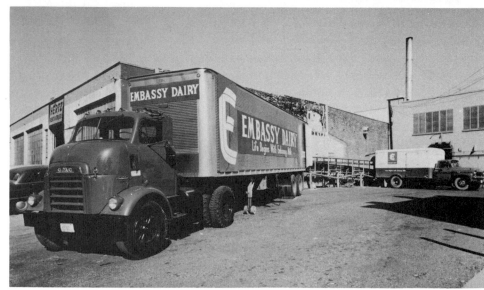

1 With the addition of Velda Farms in Miami, Southland dairies entered the Florida market.

2 Embassy Dairies, Washington, D.C., joined Southland in 1963.

liked the idea of a dairy company having a natural outlet for their products through retail stores like 7-Eleven, which already were a part of the same company. Midwest never had anything like that and it really made sense to us. He recommended to Mr. Sinek that we go with Southland and that, thank goodness, is the way it turned out. Midwest, at the time that Southland bought us, had something like six or seven production plants and 30-odd branches scattered all over the countryside. Midwest's sales were about $20 million per year, which was about equal to what Oak Farms and Cabell's did. Midwest probably sold about twice as much ice cream as Oak Farms and Cabell's, but the Texas dairies sold about twice as much milk. I was personally very happy about our new relationship with Southland, but I did have an interesting introduction to the company. Everybody at Midwest always kidded me because I played golf all the time. I seriously had the feeling that if you wanted to sell a guy something and went into his office you had the desk between you. But on the golf course you could talk and relax and have a better understanding of each other. I always have had the theory that you could talk golf in the office and business on the golf course. At least it works better for me. The day that the transaction with Southland was completed Mr. Strong and I had lunch in Memphis with John, Herb and Tom. Mr. Hartfelder asked the question: 'Mr. Strong, I know you say that Jack is a very capable man and can do a lot of things, but why do you pay him less money than you pay Basil Companionette?' Mr. Strong said, 'Simple. He sneaks off and plays golf.' That was my auspicious start with Southland.''

150

THE DAIRY EXPANSION GAINS MOMENTUM

Midwest was not to be the only important dairy acquisition for Southland in 1962. Although the first important step in the expansion of dairy operations, it represented only the first beginnings of a major new direction. Herb Hartfelder, who was at the center of the Midwest negotiations, recounted: "I had been very active in the dairy business. I guess I knew practically everyone of importance within the industry. I had long been involved in our state organization, the National Dairy Council and on the executive committee of the International Milk and Ice Cream Association. We knew just about everybody in the business. From the standpoint of dairy acquisitions, when we first bought Midwest this was a signal to the entire industry that we were interested in the growth of our dairy operations. Since we had set a precedent with the way we handled the Midwest acquisition, people within the industry who had dairies suffering financial problems (some of which I already knew about) soon began to come to us. They wanted to see if we might be interested in acquiring their particular dairy. Most of the operations we eventually bought were in financial trouble and our future really lay in bailing them out and making a profit—which we had a good track record of doing."

Walton Grayson III, the lead legal counsel on most of Southland's dairy acquisitions and a newly-elected member of the board of directors, recounted what happened after the Midwest purchase: "We acquired Midwest in about April 1962. Because of the knowledge of this acquisition within the dairy industry or through the publicity it generated, other prospective sellers suddenly started approaching Southland in substantial numbers. Following Midwest we were approached by the owners of a small dairy operation in Ardmore, Oklahoma. We bought it and it still operates as Cooper Farms. We were then contacted by a group of dairy farmers, a cooperative in Florida. They had purchased a dairy operation in Miami called Velda Farms from Arthur Vining Davis, the famous and wealthy businessman. Mr. Davis had built a beautiful plant outside of Miami to process pineapples which he planned to raise nearby. The attempt to raise pineapples was unsuccessful, and the plant was converted into a dairy operation. Little had been done to improve the facility by the dairy cooperative, and the operation was in bad financial condition. One of the biggest problems while we were preparing documents for closing the acquisition was that frequently we had to stop our work and help solve Velda's operating problems. The Velda acquisition was the first time I had worked closely with Southland's capable dairy controller, Elsie Gage. Velda was so badly organized that we even came to the point where we had to search for the certificates of title to all of the dairy trucks. Nobody could find the titles and after looking for a day or two, we found them in the tool chest of the chief mechanic. He had gotten them from the office to go down and buy new licenses for the trucks and simply forgot to return them to the office after he bought the plates. Believe me, Velda was an interesting experience. But it turned out to have great potential and became one of Southland's best dairies."

ELSIE GAGE: A KEY PARTICIPANT

As Grayson mentioned, Elsie Gage, the controller for the Southland dairies, played a critical role in the acquisitions. It was her responsibility to replace an acquired dairy's accounting methods with Southland's proven system. She had first started with the company in 1936, just prior to the opening of the original Oak Farms plant. She added her recollections of the new activity in dairy operations: "Midwest, of course, was our first acquisition outside of Texas and I spent several months over in Memphis with Tom Cochran getting their accounting transferred over to our system. As the other acquisitions followed I would go with Walton Grayson, who was doing the legal work, and usually with Morris Haliburton to do the accounting work. Morris and I used to tell Walton that he was a slave driver because he made us stay up every night until midnight or later getting figures for him. Walton always said that one of the funniest things he ever saw was the time during one of our acquisitions that Morris was working with the adding machine at 2 A.M. He had been playing with that machine like a man possessed all day. All of a sudden the machine started smoking and practically melted right before our eyes. We all three looked at each other like the end of the world was at hand, as it almost was since we needed the figures by the next morning. Anyway, we had a lot of fun and it was all very enjoyable. You didn't consider titles and positions and things like that—there was just a job to be done and you did it. We never had any problems getting along with the personnel when we bought the various dairies. They were all good, hard-working people and in every case they were truly glad that we had bought them. Southland had so much to offer and most of them realized the benefits almost immediately."

A RESPECT FOR TRADITION

Grayson added: "In the acquisitions we made, the people who worked for the various dairies had a great loyalty to their company and to the local management. They were really delighted when they found out Southland wasn't going to change the old established name of their dairy. To the extent we could, we kept unchanged the business relationships they had developed in the communities. We tried to maintain the same banking arrangements, suppliers, etc.—and where feasible, the management even kept the same titles and positions. We didn't go in and change everything under the old saying, 'a new broom sweeps clean.' In many instances though, their personnel were pretty generalized and had not had the advantage of having available specialized staff experts in such areas as plant equipment, vehicles, scheduling and so forth. When the appropriate person from our staff came to help solve a problem, they really appreciated it. They knew they had a problem and needed some outside assistance to find a solution. Also, in all cases, Southland's fringe benefits, especially profit sharing, offered so much more that they were truly delighted to join the Southland family.

The momentum in major dairy acquisitions continued into 1963 with the purchase of Embassy Dairies in Washington, D. C., and Delvale Dairies in Baltimore, Maryland. Another smaller firm, A&M Dairy in Greenwood, Mississippi, also was added and merged into the Midwest operation.

CHAPTER 18

As the Southland dairies began to blossom, 7-Eleven continued its own rapid growth. New 7-Eleven Stores were built in Kansas City, Missouri, and Salt Lake City, Utah. The Speedmart, Inc. chain of eight convenience stores in El Paso also was added and on October 3, 1963, in Midland, Texas, the 1,000th 7-Eleven Store was officially opened. By the end of 1963, 1,052 stores were doing business in approximately 250 cities and towns across America.

The expansion of the 7-Eleven store operations far removed from Dallas' corporate headquarters was altering many of the firm's old concepts and traditions. As the total of 7-Eleven Stores increased, so did the number of employees working for the company. One of the primary reasons for 7-Eleven's early success and acceptance had been the intimacy of the company. In the old days when it was located mainly in the North Texas area Jodie Thompson had known every one of his store managers personally. He regularly visited each of the stores to see for himself what was occurring within those four walls. Now he was gone and so was the intimateness that had sprung from a smaller, more compact operation. It was simply not possible for John Thompson to know personally the 1,000-plus store managers and other thousands of employees working in the stores. Besides the physical impossibility of accomplishing such a feat, the energies of the new management team were properly focused on the longer range goals of rapid expansion and the required financing of this growth. Although John and Jere Thompson, Herb Hartfelder, Cliff Wheeler and the rest of the Southland top management still "made" 7-Eleven Stores on a frequent basis, there simply was no way to expect that the old style of personal contact with each store manager could continue. In its place, as the company expanded, the concept of divisional autonomy began to flourish. Already sanctioned by the board of directors as early as 1953, local autonomy now became an absolute necessity as the stores began to multiply numerically and geographically. This autonomy meant that the store managers who once funneled comments and ideas almost directly to Jodie Thompson and his own closest associates now communicated with their own supervisors and, in many cases, division managers. Since autonomy allowed the local divisions to make buying, merchandising and operational decisions based on their own respective conditions, action could be taken on individual situations far more rapidly. Of course this decentralization of operations carried with it an accountability for the profit results in each division and area. The geographical alignments for the stores seemed to be shaping up well and the acceptance by customers was almost universally positive. The Texas Division stores were now under the leadership of Vaughn Heady. Following Jere Thompson's return to Texas as head of all 7-Eleven store operations throughout the country, David Neale assumed responsibility for the Southern Division stores. The Mountain Division stores in Colorado, Utah and Arizona were led by A. T. (Red) Robbins; the Eastern Division stores were assigned to Forrest Stout. By 1963 Stout was a 15-year veteran with 7-Eleven and a good example of how management's autonomy theory was to prove so effective. As not only an outstanding operator of stores but also thoroughly accomplished in the merchandising aspects of the convenience store business, he proved an excellent choice for the eastern area. Stout was in Houston when the call came to move east: "I had moved to Houston in 1961. Kay Lance was the manager in Houston then, and they divided the area into two divisions. Kay had one group and I had the other. Since Kay was already there he naturally picked the best group of stores and gave me the poorest group. I sort of took this as a challenge. I told Kay that I was going to make as much money with my group in March as he did and I would beat him outright in April. He said that if I did that he would quit. Sure enough I did it—and by golly, he quit.

Southland management, spring 1963. Front row, left to right: David Neale, M. M. Palmer, M. T. Cochran, Jr., H. E. Hartfelder, John P. Thompson, Jere W. Thompson, Clifford Wheeler, Vaughn Heady, Forrest Stout. Center row, left to right: R. G. Smith, J. B. Langford, Sam Meyer, T. R. Collett, C. O. "Tex" Beshears, Delano Womack, J. T. Loughney, Neil Williams, R. L. Moore. Back row, left to right: Harley Gobel, Jack House, Bruce Furrh, Ford Madison, Cecil Lewis, Basil Companionette, Bob Spencer, L. B. Smith, W. J. "Buddy" Hunt, Jack Hartfelder.

Later he came back with the company in another area of the country. There was a hurricane named Agnes which hit the Houston area that year. It was disastrous for many people. There were six or eight 7-Eleven Stores completely under water. We called all of our supervisors in and together we cleaned up the Texas City and Lake Jackson stores. We managed to have one or two of the stores in operation the next day. The company sent trucks from Dallas loaded with groceries and, because we had to throw away all the ice that was under water, they also sent a large van of ice. We sold everything in one day. People needed food to eat and cold drinks and milk to drink until the water was safe again. The people appreciated our getting back in business again so quickly and many of them continued to trade with us. We were in the midst of having a wonderful year in Houston when John Thompson called on Labor Day and asked me if I wanted to move to Washington, D. C. I said I was sure I would but would like to look it over first. My son was a senior in high school and supposed to start school in Houston on Thursday. We flew to Washington on Wednesday and my son stayed in a motel and enrolled in school in Virginia. My family and I moved to Washington for good on September 17, 1962. The Eastern Division then had 151 stores and the managers were H. R. Brasuell, L. D. Chappell, Delano Womack, Ralph Shaw and Billy Ruffeno. About a year later we decided to reorganize the Eastern Division because it was growing pretty fast and we set up the zone structure for the first time. The decision to set up zones was another step in decentralizing our operations for greater local control. We had a big meeting in Williamsburg, Virginia, to announce our new organization and invited people from the Dallas office and Florida, and I must say that everybody came. When I first moved up here I was working directly under Jere Thompson and both he and John worked very closely with me. Also, I had Bob Storey in charge of real estate, and he can pick locations and knows real estate better than anyone else in our company. John and Jere gave us completely free rein and they both encouraged us to grow as fast as we could. They gave us full autonomy and support and did not hold us back on anything. We kept working hard and kept growing and the profits kept up with us."

ORGANIZATIONAL CHANGES

The Southland organizational chart was also growing. Although autonomy was the key to growth in the field, a larger, more sophisticated support staff was necessary to complement the booming operations expansion. The chart on the following page illustrates the organizational structure in July 1963.

STAFF FUNCTIONS GAIN IN STATURE

Obert K. Irvine, Southland's chief engineer, was an example of the corporate office group which was called upon to support all aspects of the company's operations. Irvine started to work with Southland in 1948 after Jodie Thompson heard him deliver a speech to the Southwestern Ice Manufacturers Association and subsequently offered him a job as the firm's chief engineer. He remembered: "I wore all of the engineering hats at Southland for many years. I was the supervising engineer for all divisions, including buying all of the equipment that went into the stores, dairies and ice plants. I suppose our toughest time came when we had an ammonia explosion at the Waco ice plant and then, just three weeks later, the entire Cabell's plant at Tyler burned down. The explosion in Waco caused a fire that burned through the roof and caused a lot of damage to the equipment. We still don't know what caused the Cabell's fire but it completely gutted the plant, and it had to be rebuilt from the ground up. It was a struggle, but we did not suffer too much from these losses. When Southland acquired a new plant we always checked it out very carefully. When we bought dairies we would go in and evaluate the engineering and utility sections. When we bought stores we would also go in and thoroughly check the refrigeration. Mr. Joe C. Thompson was always interested in properly maintaining the dairy plants, the 7-Eleven Stores and the equipment in them, and he raised us all to act accordingly. I was driving to Houston with him one day and on the way out of town we passed right by the Oak Farms plant in Oak Cliff. There was a little wisp of black smoke coming out of the smokestack. He stopped the car and said, 'Irvine, you go in there and see that they adjust those boilers so that they will burn the gas more efficiently.' So I went in and regulated the air flow on the boilers, stopped the smoke and we went on to Houston. After Mr. Thompson died the new management, John, Herb and Jere, took the same interest in maintaining our equipment properly at all times—I am sure that Mr. Thompson must have influenced them in that way also."

The Southland Corporation Organizational Chart
July 1963

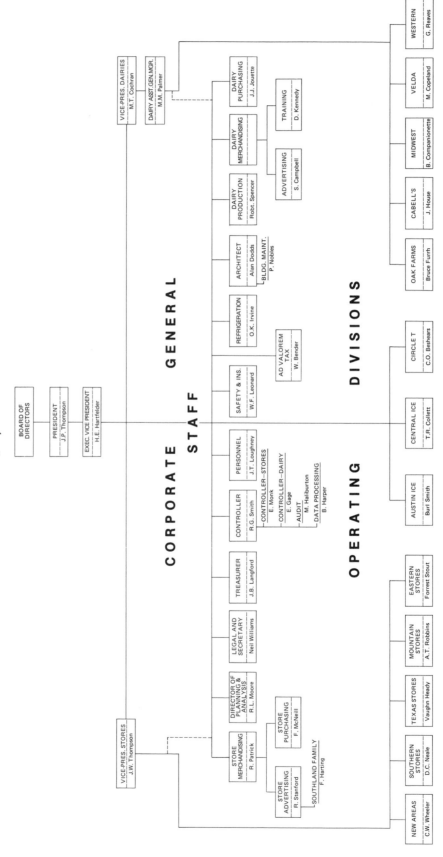

CORPORATE GENERAL STAFF

OPERATING DIVISIONS

BOARD OF DIRECTORS

PRESIDENT
J.P. Thompson

EXEC. VICE PRESIDENT
H.E. Hartfelder

VICE-PRES. STORES
J.W. Thompson

VICE-PRES. DAIRIES
M.T. Cochran

DAIRY ASST.GEN.MGR.
M.M. Palmer

STORE MERCHANDISING
R. Patrick

STORE ADVERTISING
R. Stanford

SOUTHLAND FAMILY
F. Harting

STORE PURCHASING
F. McNeill

DIRECTOR OF PLANNING & ANALYSIS
R.L. Moore

LEGAL AND SECRETARY
Neil Williams

TREASURER
J.B. Langford

CONTROLLER
R.G. Smith

CONTROLLER—STORES
E. Monk

CONTROLLER—DAIRY
E. Gage

AUDIT
M. Haliburton

DATA PROCESSING
B. Harper

PERSONNEL
J.T. Loughney

SAFETY & INS.
W.F. Leonard

AD VALOREM TAX
W. Bender

REFRIGERATION
O.K. Irvine

ARCHITECT
Alan Dodds

BLDG. MAINT.
P. Nobles

DAIRY PRODUCTION
Robt. Spencer

DAIRY MERCHANDISING

ADVERTISING
S. Campbell

DAIRY PURCHASING
J.J. Jouette

TRAINING
D. Kennedy

NEW AREAS
C.W. Wheeler

SOUTHERN STORES
D.C. Neale

TEXAS STORES
Vaughn Heady

MOUNTAIN STORES
A.T. Robbins

EASTERN STORES
Forrest Stout

AUSTIN ICE
Burl Smith

CENTRAL ICE
T.R. Collett

CIRCLE T
C.O. Beshears

OAK FARMS
Bruce Furrh

CABELL'S
J. House

MIDWEST
B. Companionette

VELDA
M. Copeland

WESTERN
G. Reaves

THE IMPORTANCE OF TRAINING

An important step in adequately coping with the growing need for qualified personnel occurred in October 1963. Five new Southland employees were selected to take a two-week store manager training course—the first formal training class in 7-Eleven's history. The young storemen, under the direction of instructor Dale Belcher, underwent a two-weeks training period. They divided their time equally between the classroom and working a shift as a clerk in a nearby 7-Eleven Store. Modest as it was, this beginning effort represented another necessary advance in the process of meeting the demands brought by expansion.

At a 1963 management retreat at the Little Sandy Hunting & Fishing Club in deep East Texas, Jere Thompson, vice president and general manager of the Stores Group, confirmed the new emphasis on the thorough training of personnel by saying: "All the way up and down the line training is our most important single responsibility. While we cannot yet announce the new area locations for our stores, I can tell you that our planned expansion is big and important. A year from now we will have 7-Eleven Stores open in many areas where we have no stores today."

These words were hardly an overstatement. Within a year Southland was to make an acquisition which would bind the quickly multiplying 7-Eleven Stores from one coast to the other and, in the process, add a totally new dimension to the little store around the corner. In the meantime, however, another critical question facing the growing company was how to go about refining an essential ingredient for any national company's success—its image.

As 7-Eleven grew its merchandising and advertising strategies became more organized and carefully planned. The merchandising function benefited from the addition of three talented new marketing men, Ben Holland, Bob Patrick and Dick Turchi. Holland joined Southland in 1961 as merchandising manager for all of the company's stores in Texas. Patrick came some months later from the Jewel Tea Company in Chicago to assume the position of corporate merchandising manager. In 1963 Patrick recruited Turchi, another Jewel Tea alumnus, to be the assistant merchandiser in the Texas stores.

The company's flexible merchandising policies had always been structured to keep up with changing customer needs. This attitude had begun with Uncle Johnny Green's positive response to his customers' requests for milk, eggs and cold drinks to go along with their ice purchases. In the '30s the Tote'm Stores had offered curb service and created a new style in neighborhood shopping for staples, canned goods, ice cream, salt, cookies, candy and, in season, ice-cold watermelons. In the '40s, frozen foods, fresh fruit and vegetables, health and beauty aids and picnic supplies were popular items. The company entered the ice cream business for the first time in the 1940s and also marketed its first private label products. In the '50s, selling everything from "soup to nuts," 7-Eleven had added TV tubes, money orders, magazines, sunglasses, garden seed, shotgun shells, wine, postage stamps, hula hoops and keys "made while you wait." Now the '60s were bringing even more adaptation to shifting customer desires. Hot coffee, cold sandwiches and popcorn were among the items beginning to appear in some stores. Without question this constant willingness to change and keep up was creating its own positive image for 7-Eleven.

THE PERSONALITY STORE

The little store was perceived by its customers as being alive with activity. It seemed to be consistently surprising the shopper with a new product or service besides offering the usual selection of popular convenience items. It was becoming the "neighborhood" store where an interesting promotion was always occurring. 7-Eleven was gaining an overall reputation of possessing a unique personality quite different from its big brother—the supermarket.

Kids seemed to feel more at home in a 7-Eleven because it was close to their own size. It did not overwhelm them as did the massiveness of the giant market. There was no high ceiling or numerous aisles where a child might become confused. The candy rack was handy and in easy sight of even the smallest youngster.

Teenagers and young adults endorsed the 7-Eleven informality of shopping. The working person found it handy for cigarettes, coffee or a fast sandwich. Mothers also were discovering it for miscellaneous needs such as last-minute school supplies or cookies for a lunch box. The 7-Eleven groove was being located and endorsed by its various publics and this image was becoming more positive and solid as the stores increased in numbers and locations.

Much of the credit for creating 7-Eleven's happy face belonged to Bob Stanford, the company's advertising manager. In 1958 Stanford, with his assistant Howard Greene and staff artist Dick Boone, formed the Stanford Agency. The agency functioned as an in-house advertising company servicing the Southland account on an exclusive basis. The assignment was unusual from one standpoint: 7-Eleven was the first and practically only convenience store chain to use paid media advertising. From his extensive background in show business Stanford had long believed that the public not only expected to be informed by advertising, it also wanted to be entertained. So he set out to create a different type of retail advertising. By the mid-'60s the advertising awards scattered about the agency were proving that his theory had been correct. Stanford's entertainment formula rested primarily on humor. He remembered: "It is simply great that Southland invented an entirely new concept—convenience stores. Then it was up to us to help our management develop a personality for these stores. I think we were able to develop a great personality for our little 7-Eleven Store because Mr. Thompson, the Thompson sons and the rest of our top people gave us the freedom to do and say some pretty outrageous things in our advertising. People are always asking me, 'How can you get away with that?' I tell them that we have that freedom and as long as we keep their confidence the management will let us go on just about anything. We have always tried to use humor whenever possible. We like for people to think of us as the little store that can smile at itself. You remember when we had the two watermelon seeds talking—that was a fun thing to do. People would come by the store and ask, 'Is that the watermelon with the two seeds in it?' They were in on the fun thing."

The watermelon commercial Stanford referred to featured him as the narrator and *The Southland Family* editor, Frank Harting, and Leon Rabin as the two watermelon seeds. The copy read:

Frank Harting, editor of The Southland Family, *whose distinctive voice soon became identified with 7-Eleven radio commercials.*

BOB:	(SHIVERING) WE NOW TAKE YOU DEEP DOWN INSIDE A WATERMELON. THE WATERMELON SEEDS ARE TALKING.
LEON:	(SHIVERING) I'M FREEZING TO DEATH, FRANK.
FRANK:	STOP TALKING ABOUT IT, LEON.
LEON:	HOW DO THEY GET THESE 7-ELEVEN MELONS SO DOGGONE COLD?
FRANK:	THEY GOT A COLD VAULT IN EVERY STORE THAT GETS RIGHT DOWN THROUGH THE RIND. DOWN HERE TO THE MIDDLE.
LEON:	SHUT UP AND DO SOMETHIN'. . . . LET'S BUILD A FIRE.
FRANK:	A FIRE IN A WATERMELON? . . . . THAT'S SICK.
LEON:	WE'RE DESPERATE. . . . WE GOTTA GET OUT OF HERE.
FRANK:	LET'S HOLLER AND BEAT ON THE SIDES.
LEON:	GOOD IDEA.
LEON & FRANK:	(YELLING AND BEATING ON THE SIDES OF THE MELON) HELP, HELP, GET US OUT OF HERE!
BOB:	FRIENDS, THE SEEDS IN THE WATERMELONS IN THE COLD VAULTS AT YOUR 7-ELEVEN STORES ARE FREEZING TO DEATH. IN THE NAME OF HUMANITY, PLEASE BUY ONE OF THESE FULLY GUARANTEED WATERMELONS AND LET THOSE SEEDS OUT OF THERE.

Stanford continued: "Our 'Strange Things' campaign was another great series for us—the ads that tell you the strange things that happen when you shop at 7-Eleven. They were so popular all over the country. The concept was so unusual that we had second thoughts about even running the commercials, but then we decided to try them in one area and they took the city by storm. All in all, I guess the 'Strange Things' spots were some of the best we ever did. As I said before, it is that freedom we have been allowed. It is hard for other people to understand it. We have always dared to try that other path.

Bob Stanford, advertising manager, left, and Tom Loughney, labor relations manager, performed in a sales meeting skit.

We never did become Number One by imitating someone else; otherwise, we would be Number Two. Mr. Thompson always dared us—dared us—to try something new and different."

THE NEW VOICE OF 7-ELEVEN

In the process of introducing the "Strange Things" commercials Southland and Stanford discovered a new performing talent. Frank Harting, editor of *The Southland Family* and former public relations executive for General Motors, suddenly found himself an important element in the emerging 7-Eleven personality. Harting was as surprised as anyone by his newfound role. He said: "My making of TV and radio commercials was a complete fluke. In about '63 or '64 Bob Stanford came barging into my office and said that one of the actors scheduled to do a radio commercial for him that day had become ill. He asked if I would take his place and do the spot. I sort of begged off, but he insisted. He told me just to come down to the recording studio and give it a try. We went to the studio and he handed me a script. I got the cue and opened my mouth and started reading. After we finished Bob said, 'Let's play it back.' When he did everyone in the studio just laughed, whooped and hollered. It was so bad and my voice was so funny sounding, that everyone simply cracked up. Up until that point I always thought my voice sounded just about like everyone else's. But now people tell me I have the most distinctive radio voice they've ever heard. Then they just laugh. Of course I have always enjoyed doing the commercials. I guess it was just a happy accident."

As 1963 closed, 7-Eleven's image with its various publics was strongly positive. And sales, profit and dividend figures achieved during the year confirmed Southland's tangible progress. The '63 record included:

$202,524,477	Total revenues (first time to exceed $200 million)
$2,585,717	Net earnings (best in company's history)
$888,112	Cash dividends to the 514 shareholders

There was another development coming on quickly that would greatly affect the company's future. Southland was preparing for its first venture with a business system soon to revolutionize American retailing—franchising.

161

1 The acquisition of Speedee Mart took 7-Eleven to California and into the franchising business.

2 A social gathering of the Speedee Mart/7-Eleven management team.

CHAPTER
20

In the late 1950s, following the successful introduction of 7-Eleven Stores to Florida and the East Coast, Jodie and John Thompson discussed the possibility of entering the California market. The idea was carefully studied and exploratory visits to the West Coast were made by various Southland people. However, the decision was made not to move west at that particular time. There were two basic reasons for deciding against a western expansion. For one, labor costs were considerably higher in California compared to the company's experiences elsewhere. And, as far as entering the West Coast market through an acquisition, most of the successful convenience-type chains there consisted of stores which were individually franchised. The franchising system was totally unfamiliar to Southland, which owed its success to close company supervision of its stores.

Thus the idea of taking the 7-Eleven concept west was tabled. However, in the '60s California became impossible to ignore. The state was growing enormously in both population and economic clout. John Thompson decided to reopen the company's interest in California. He recalled: "In the fall of 1963 I went out to California to watch the Dallas Cowboys play the San Francisco 49ers. I spent the next two weeks driving all over the West Coast, up as far as Seattle. I came back and told Herb Hartfelder that we just had to go west. We had previously looked at the Speedee Mart stores, a chain of more than 100 convenience stores all located in California. We really did not know much about franchising and Speedee Mart knew it better than any other company. All of their stores were franchised and they also had a very good organization with some very high-calibre people. After a series of meetings with Mr. Henry Boney, president of Speedee Mart, we finally acquired the stores. Speedee Mart gave us the know-how and expertise that we needed in franchising."

The acquisition of Speedee Mart provided Southland with a wealth of positive factors. It gave the Texas-based company penetration in the swiftly developing West Coast market. It also provided Southland with an immediate expertise in the operation of franchised stores. And, perhaps as important, Speedee Mart possessed a management team which glowed with talent and promise.

THE SPEEDEE MART STORY

Speedee Mart had experienced a brief but interesting history. Ted E. Glover, operations manager for Speedee Mart, remembered: "Mr. Henry Boney, prior to organizing a corporation, went to Dallas and visited convenience stores, primarily the 7-Eleven Stores. I had a small family grocery market in San Diego at that time but Mr. Boney and I had been friends for a number of years. At one time we had been in the supermarket business together. He came back from Texas very excited and enthusiastic about the potential of the convenience store business. He asked me to join him in establishing a corporation and we formed Speedee Mart in April 1956. It took us about six months to draw the plans and outline the program. We had decided on franchising as the way to operate the stores, so we formulated our own original franchise agreement. We decided to go the franchise route because of our past 'people' experiences in the grocery business. As we ran and operated our own businesses, we would occasionally run into an employee who was a bit more than just your average worker. He was one who seemed to have a deeper interest in our business as well as in his own job. We felt that these people

were few and far between. These were people who could have been successful in their own businesses. Most of them lacked the opportunity to work for
themselves because they simply did not have the financing necessary. If we
could provide them with finances and a place to do business, then they could
put their own enthusiasm and interest to work for themselves as well as for
us. And so this was really our concept of franchising and we worked it out
that way. The man who franchised our first store placed another mortgage
on his home and took the money that he received from that transaction and
put every penny of it into his store. Just two and a half years later his net worth
was somewhere in the neighborhood of $90,000. We opened our first store
in November 1956 in San Diego and it was a great beginning. The second
store that we opened was in a low income area and it created some problems
for us. I guess you must have a system of checks and balances. Number Two
balanced us from the standpoint that we now had a problem store to go with
our first successful store. This was an excellent learning experience for us. Our
third store was the tie-breaker and it was very successful, even doing better
than the first one. About a year or so after we started Speedee Mart, Jodie
and John Thompson had come out and talked to us about introducing 7-Eleven
into California, but they didn't want to get into the franchise business. Later,
in about 1959, I visited Dallas and talked again to John Thompson. He told
me then that he was interested but he just didn't feel that Southland could
ever relinquish the local control they had over the operation of the 7-Eleven
Stores. I explained to him that you did have *some* control even if you did not
have all of it. I also explained that if you had all of the control you would not
be able to give the franchisees the opportunity to grow and do a lot of things
for themselves. Although John and Southland still were not interested then,
we heard from them again in the fall of 1963. This time we both began to
talk seriously. We were desirous, of course, to sell because we were under-
capitalized, number one. We did have a lot of assets but they were pretty well
tied up. Number two, in establishing a business that grows very rapidly, it can
sometimes grow so fast around you that you begin to lose track of what is
happening. Then one day you begin to wonder: what would happen if the
lights went out for you one night and you didn't wake up in the morning? This
is where Mr. Boney and I found ourselves. Our wives couldn't operate the
business. We did have some excellent people but whether or not our wives
knew enough to operate the company and take care of these people, we
simply did not know. We decided that we probably would be better off if we
sold Speedee Mart to Southland. After we were acquired I had the title of
assistant to the division manager. Sam Meyer, from 7-Eleven's Florida operations, became our new division manager. My particular job was trouble-
shooting—keeping the management informed of situations where we had an
unhappy owner or perhaps an internal problem. I was so pleased that Southland wanted my services. They said later that it was the first company they
had ever acquired where they asked *all* of the people to remain with Southland
following the acquisition. I felt good about that because as operations manager
for Speedee Mart it was my responsibility to choose our key employees. Many
of our Speedee Mart people now have gone on to bigger jobs at Southland
and have been redistributed all over the company. I guess we did have quite
a staff."

164

MEYER ASSIGNED TO CALIFORNIA

Sam Meyer, who had spent 16 years with the 7-Eleven Stores in Texas and Florida, was given the task of overseeing the Speedee Mart operation. It was a sensitive assignment as the California firm was no small company. With 126 convenience stores and four supermarkets, it represented Southland's largest single acquisition to that date. Meyer recalled what happened: "Actually, we knew that Mr. Jodie Thompson had been looking at California for a number of years. John, Jere and Bob Storey had made two previous trips looking at locations in California and had come across the Speedee Mart chain. They were quite taken by it—it was such a jewel. After Mr. Thompson's death John picked up the ball from there and continued to visit the West Coast. He became personally acquainted with Henry Boney and Speedee Mart and made the decision to try to acquire them. After some lengthy negotiations from the middle of December 1963 to March 1964 we were able to close the deal. I really never had much contact with John Thompson until that point in time. I must say that I was very impressed with this young man and his ability to negotiate in tough situations without losing his temper. He seemed to sense exactly how to keep things on an even keel. John finally closed the deal on March 16, 1964. Speedee Mart became such a great challenge to us because it was our first entry into the franchising business. At the time John was doing the negotiating, I was spending my time getting acquainted with their people, trying to understand them and their problems. John wanted to proceed cautiously with Speedee Mart after we acquired them so as not to disturb their successful operation. I was the only 7-Eleven operations person brought out here to the West Coast. John wanted me to be patient and to learn their business. The Speedee Mart employees really loved Henry Boney and I didn't want to affect that loyalty by coming in and changing everything overnight. Rather than moving into his old office, I operated out of the meeting room for a year. I think everybody started wondering, 'When is Sam going to move into Mr. Boney's office?' I put it off for a full year. However, once I moved into his office I completely changed the decor, the desk, everything. By that time everything had pretty well settled down and I knew what I was doing. We also went slowly in changing the name of the stores. We did, however, want to introduce the 7-Eleven name to the West Coast. We decided to drop the 'Mart' part of the name and call the stores 'Speedee 7-Eleven.' When you think about it, if you have an ad on radio or TV and say 'Speedee 7-Eleven,' 'Speedee' becomes an adjective. After awhile we finally dropped the 'Speedee' entirely and they became simply 7-Eleven Stores."

DICK DOLE REMEMBERS

An example of the new talent added to Southland through Speedee Mart was S. R. (Dick) Dole, who would later become the company's vice president for franchise operated stores. Dole recalled the acquisition: "I was an assistant vice president of Speedee Mart in charge of our stores in San Jose when we were acquired by Southland. We were running about 30 stores in northern California. I was excited about it because, well, we didn't know a thing about Southland except that they just literally had the biggest company in the whole world—to us, anyway. I think they had about 1,400 7-Eleven Stores at the time. As far as we were concerned that represented nearly all of the convenience stores in the world outside of California. We thought the new arrangement would really offer us a chance to grow, and we were right. There were two things that were most impressive to me after Southland took over. First, they moved Sam Meyer to California to take charge of the organization and he was the only person to 'invade,' so to speak, the Speedee Mart domain. Sam was such a sensitive person. He officed out of the meeting room in the division office. All of the Speedee Mart people were impressed that he wasn't coming in like some bigshot with all of the answers, trying to take over and change things overnight. All Sam did was just visit, learn, listen and comprehend. Every morning he had a very long telephone conversation with Jere Thompson, who was back in Dallas. Of course no one had any idea what he was saying, so there was a little suspense. The only really major change Sam made at first was the switch in accounting procedures from a cost-type accounting that we used in Speedee Mart to a retail-type accounting, or the Southland system. The second thing was that, overall, we were so impressed with the Southland people. I guess there was one Southland man I remember in particular. I got a call from Dallas one day from O. K. Irvine. He told me that he was Southland's chief engineer and that he was coming out to California to see me. He said that he wanted the two of us to meet with the president of our utility company. Of course to arrange an appointment to see this man was quite a task. It was also something the Speedee Mart people would never have thought of doing—visiting with the president of the utility about our rates. I asked Obert, 'Just specifically what do you want to see him about?' He said, 'I'm going to get your utility rates reduced.' And I said, 'Now won't that be fine. You are going to talk to the president of the largest utility in California and reduce our rates, huh?' I thought I was talking to some oddball on the other end of the line, not ever having met him at all. Well, to make it short, on the date we set he came into my office and said, 'Hi. I'm Obert Irvine. You must be Dick.' I just nodded my head. We got in the car and all the way over I'm saying to myself, 'This is going to be interesting.' We arrived at their building and were ushered into the president's office. It was the largest office I had ever seen in my life. It had two of everything: two desks, two tables, two couches. The first thing Obert did was to take off his hat and put it on the couch. He sat down and got right to the point with the president. Very politely he said, 'Sir, may I tell you something? We're from Texas, and we're not a bit pleased with the utility rates your company is charging our little stores out in this part of the country. What I want to know is—why?' Then he started into this technical jargon with all sorts of codes and other fancy terms. It was obvious that only he and the president of the company could understand it. In fact, the president didn't even understand it and could only apologize to Mr. Irvine for not knowing. He immediately called in all of his top engineers and even they could not answer all of Obert's questions. Obert had the stage for over an hour with these people and absolutely challenged their entire utility system and the way they were charging our stores. When he was through he had saved us about $20,000 a year, which was some kind of money, at that time, for our small group of stores. Of course it was great that the utility company took the time to listen to him and then react the way they did. That was my first acquaintance with anyone from Southland on a real nitty-gritty basis. I was terribly impressed with this man because he came in and really did a job for us, right off the bat."

TRAINING: A SPEEDEE MART SPECIALTY

While Southland was having some impact on Speedee Mart, the reverse was also true in specialized areas, such as training. The California company had developed and was continuing to refine an outstanding training program for its new franchisees. The two men responsible for developing and conducting franchise owner training were Palmer Waslien, an ex-physics instructor, and Lew Maddox, who had been associated with the Boy Scouts of America before joining Speedee Mart. Lew Maddox remembered Southland's new emphasis on training and how it has evolved: "I worked eight years for the Boy Scouts, organizing camps, training, etc. I wrote a lot of material for them. In my opinion the Boy Scouts have the best training techniques of any organization I know, especially in the area of teaching skills. When I started with Speedee Mart this background helped considerably. In my opinion our new franchise owner gets a fantastic training program. It has evolved from the time Palmer Waslien put a cash register on top of a desk, in the early Speedee Mart days, through the five-day classroom program that we established in the mid-'60s and the five-day classroom, five-day in-store training in the early '70s, to what we now give a franchisee today—a concentrated 15 days of instruction and on-the-job training. We used to do so much in the classroom, telling the new franchisees—'These are the things you should do: you should smile, you should give change properly and so forth.' Of course there are certain advantages to this kind of mock-up situation—when you make a mistake you can laugh it off and do it over again. The old-style training with the mock-up was effective, there is no question about that. We have evolved far past that point in our training methods today, using videotape playback to demonstrate and review real-life situations. However, even in those days I think we still had the best training program."

Palmer Waslien, who originally developed Speedee Mart's training program, also recalled: "I was with Speedee Mart and developed the first training school in 1959. It consisted of a cash register and four boxes of groceries. I would talk to the new franchisees about the philosophy of being in business for yourself. We would all just sit on the sofa and talk about the philosophy of operating one's own store. By 1961 we had a training school that featured gondolas stacked with groceries—a typical 7-Eleven Store in miniature. When Southland purchased Speedee I developed several charts to show the way our gross profit improved from the time we really started our training school. This was presented to the Thompsons and they said, 'Of course, that is a very important facet of our business.' Right after the deal was consummated in May 1964 they asked me to come to Dallas to observe the training facilities they had here. I was supposed to spend several weeks going through it but I could take only a week of it. I told Jere Thompson, 'You really ought to close it down—it is doing more harm than good for the employees.' Well, they did close it down immediately, although I really didn't expect them to do it so quickly. Jere then told me he wanted me to come to Dallas and start a

Southland training school. I went back to the drawing board in LaMesa and drew up a plan for Southland's program. I came back to Jere with it and I asked him what he had in mind as far as the cost of the program was concerned. He said he would like to begin with a budget of $50,000, which was no small sum. I told him I might as well pack my suitcase and go back to LaMesa. I said, 'If we can't spend $250,000 between now and the end of the year, there is no need to mess around with it.' He said that it would take the approval of the board of directors but Jere, especially, believed so strongly in the value of training that the board agreed to it and our training program was on the way."

Dick Dole commented on Speedee Mart's innovative training concept: "We had probably the first and only complete prototype of a convenience market ever used in training franchisees. It was located in the basement of a shopping center in which we operated a store. That's right, we actually built our own 'training store' with a regular sales counter and actual-size gondolas. We had the gondolas stacked with produce and groceries and other products. We also had bins on the walls with all kinds of merchandise in them. A franchise owner-trainee would choose a particular bin and then go through the entire process of checking it out. We made sure that there would always be something tricky in it—like an item that was not taxed. Back in those days we had nothing to sell but bread, milk, cigarettes, soft drinks, beer and a few groceries. Today it is a lot more sophisticated, with fast foods and all, but the basic concept is still the same in our training program."

WESTERN-STYLE ENTHUSIASM

Besides giving Southland penetration into the exploding West Coast economy, the Speedee Mart acquisition introduced a special West Coast style of enthusiasm to Southland. Dick Dole explained: "Most of the Speedee Mart people were super-enthusiastic and livewire individuals. I would credit much of this spirit to Ted Glover but there are other factors, too. In the first place, the West Coast tends to be maybe a little more liberal in its lifestyle than Texas. Not that it is good or bad, but a true-blue Californian is usually a little louder and less inhibited than a fairly conservative Texan. But regional differences aside, Ted Glover really was the key. He was such a dynamic person, with a smile on his face all the time. He was always so enthusiastic. All of us who worked for Ted learned that the franchisee was the most important man in the company—he was the man running the store and it was our job to keep him motivated. It was Ted's job to keep us fired up the same way. Enthusiasm has always been my style, and it had to come from Ted Glover."

A TYPICAL FRANCHISE OWNER

Southland also inherited an able group of franchise owners with its new operation. Typical of the Speedee Mart owners were Nick and Eva Furticella, who franchised a store in Costa Mesa, California. They recalled: *Eva:* "Prior to the time we became a Speedee Mart franchisee in 1961, we had an A&W Root Beer stand in Arizona. We came to California to visit a cousin who talked

1 The first convenience store franchisee in the United States was Kenny Brooks, right, with Ted E. Glover, vice president and general manager, Speedee Mart, Inc. San Diego, November 1956.

2 The early "training store" for franchisees in LaMesa, California. Lew Maddox, at left in dark suit, was Western Division training manager.

us into staying. Since we decided to settle here, we had to find something to do. We heard about this Speedee Mart convenience store chain operation and it seemed interesting. We looked into it and met Mr. Lew Maddox. He was the one who sold us our store." *Nick:* "Lew Maddox was the first man we came in contact with. That is one man I will never forget. He will always have a place in our minds. We went through the company's training school under Palmer Waslien. He is another one that we respect so much. Of course it helped that we had been in the grocery business previously. Prior to moving to Arizona we had operated a family grocery store in Gary, Indiana, so we knew quite a bit about the food business." *Eva:* "When we saw the store in Costa Mesa we fell in love with it. We have been very happy with it ever since. We have been in the same shopping center since the beginning, although they have built us a new store building. Since Southland bought Speedee Mart there have been great improvements in every way to our benefit. We have been the most fortunate of franchise owners, also because of the fine people who work in our store. Our newest employee has been with us three years and the others five and eight years. We work as a team and everybody is happy. That's what helps any franchise operation to succeed."

THE BASIC FRANCHISE AGREEMENT

Southland's basic franchise agreement was relatively simple. After the applicant received approval and company-sponsored training, Southland then leased or subleased a ready-to-operate, fully stocked 7-Eleven Store to the new franchise owner. In return the franchise owner paid for all business licenses and permits and was required to invest an amount equal to the store inventory plus a nominal cash register fund. The inventory was usually financed by 7-Eleven to some extent. Southland's share in the gross profits of the store represented the charge to the franchise owner for the license to use the 7-Eleven system and trademarks, for use of the premises and equipment and for continuing services provided by Southland. These services included merchandising, advertising, bookkeeping, store audits and preparation of financial statements. Southland bore all property taxes and building, utility and equipment costs.

Each 7-Eleven franchise owner paid all operating expenses including: payroll, sales and inventory taxes, inventory and cash variations, supplies, certain repairs and maintenance, and other controllable in-store expenses. In the event the franchise agreement expired or was terminated, Southland repurchased the franchise owner's interest in inventory and other assets in the business.

The franchising method of operating 7-Eleven Stores in California proved so successful that it soon spread to other new operational areas, in particular the Northeast and Midwest. Without question the turn to franchising proved to be a crucial breakthrough in 7-Eleven's rapid expansion.

170

CHAPTER
21

As 1964 ended the Speedee Mart infusion of stores and talent was not the only sign of Southland's accelerated expansion. Total revenues surged to more than $274 million and net earnings exceeded $3.6 million. Also, the year closed with 1,519 7-Eleven Stores in operation, including the new Speedee 7-Elevens.

Southland's momentum carried over strongly into 1965. During that year another assortment of "firsts" was recorded. Some of the achievements were more meaningful than others, but all had their own particular importance. During 1965: 7-Eleven began construction of its first store in the Chicago market; the first 7-Eleven to be completely carpeted was opened in Salt Lake City; a real estate department was begun and site selection procedures established; for the first time in its history the company printed a formal annual report (covering 1964) for its shareholders; and Southland's '64 performance cracked the *Fortune* magazine annual ranking of the nation's 50 Largest Merchandising Firms, announced in '65, by edging in with a ranking of 49th. It was Southland's first appearance ever in the *Fortune* rankings.

During the year there were significant purchases, acquisitions, sales and even the formation of a new division, Southland Chemical. The Circle T Meat Company, which had been established in 1952, was sold to a Dallas businessman. Southland's dairy divisions continued their own expansion with the purchase of established properties. The addition of Adohr Farms in Southern California and the Spreckels-Russell Dairies in San Francisco gave Southland strong dairy sales penetration on both coasts, the Midwest and Southwest.

THE HOME DELIVERY CHALLENGE

The Adohr Farms purchase presented Southland with an especially interesting challenge. Although Southland had some experience with the home delivery of dairy products, Adohr was heavily weighted with residential routes. Jack House, general manager of Cabell's Dairies in Dallas at the time of the Adohr purchase, was assigned the responsibility of managing Southland's new California dairy. House recalled: "We had a very interesting time in California. It was entirely different from anything else Southland had ever experienced before in the dairy business. Adohr had about 250 home deliverymen but their routes were really two-sided, so they really had 500 daily routes going six days a week. There was no doubt that we were in the home delivery business to stay. We soon discovered that many of the Adohr routes were losing money. Of course that's always been Southland's strong suit on the dairy side, taking a loser and making it into a winner. We decided the only way to turn the situation around would be to lop off or bring together some of the routes. We finally managed to combine quite a few of the routes. Just sitting down with the maps of the various routes and combining them was not the biggest problem. Our number one problem was that every dairy customer in Southern California wanted his milk every morning at exactly 7:00 A.M. Anyway, we did manage to combine many of the routes and that slowed down the losses. And, somehow, we made a lot of seven o'clock stops. Another thing we were not attuned to in California was that the home deliveryman was not a salesman, he was an hourly paid employee. We really were not paying him for selling but just for delivering. If a customer complained the deliveryman really didn't care all that much. We finally figured out that the only way we would ever become really profitable with these routes would be to turn the routeperson into a distributor, which, in reality,

1

2

3

would make him an independent businessman. During the first year we reduced our number of routes from 500 to 300 and began putting the distributorship plan into operation. It was a delicate thing, but the idea took hold and the route people who remained really liked the idea of being their own bosses. It is an understatement to say that this distributor arrangement has worked out very well for Adohr and Southland."

THE ADOHR HISTORY

Adohr Farms was typical in many respects of the dairy properties being added to the Southland family. Adohr had been established by Mr. and Mrs. Merritt Adamson in Southern California in 1916. The Adohr name originated from Mrs. Adamson's first name—Rhoda—being spelled backwards. Over the years it had acquired an excellent reputation and was often called "America's Model Dairy." An extensive advertising campaign to find "Adohr-able Babies" had resulted in favorable publicity and increased customer acceptance. The dairy's milk came from the Adohr Dairy Farms located near Los Angeles, a 650-acre assortment of modern corrals, feeding lots, milking barns and fields of irrigated alfalfa. Five thousand Golden Guernseys, the largest such Guernsey herd in the world in 1965, were quartered on the farm. The primary asset Adohr added to the Southland dairy operations was a solid reputation in a growing market. However, Adohr's profitability had suffered in recent years. Profitability, or the lack of it, was a common trait among many Southland dairy acquisitions. The company was establishing a definite pattern of selecting high-visibility, respected regional dairies operating in less than profitable circumstances. Then, with a fresh viewpoint, assistance when necessary in specific areas and sometimes an injection of capital, Southland was able to accomplish a turnaround.

HARBISONS JOINS SOUTHLAND

Another Southland dairy purchase in 1966 followed much the same trend. Harbisons Dairies in Philadelphia had served the eastern areas of Pennsylvania and neighboring states for more than 100 years. Its credentials were impressive and completely first-rate. Its capable president, Robert Harbison III, had been raised in the family business and was a nationally respected dairyman. Although not facing the severe profitability troubles of other new Southland dairies, Bob Harbison regarded the acquisition by Southland as a new opportunity for his firm to expand its impact.

AN IDENTIFICATION PROBLEM

Southland's fairly sudden growth into a national dairy brought the company an identification problem. Oak Farms, Cabell's, Midwest Farms, Velda Farms, Adohr Farms, Spreckels-Russell Dairies, Embassy Dairies, Delvale Dairies, Cooper Farms and now Harbisons Dairies all had their own distinctive, highly recognized names—and equally familiar logotype identification on the packaging of their dairy products. There was simply no commonality whatsoever among the various dairies, especially as far as visual identification was concerned.

1 Southland dairies management meeting, December 1964, Inn of The Six Flags, Arlington, Texas.

2 Adohr Farms, acquired in 1965, put Southland into home delivery in a big way. Adohr's extensive home delivery business in California is one of the largest in the country.

3 The century-old Harbisons Dairies of Philadelphia joined Southland in 1966.

173

Southland management believed there was a need to establish some sort of family relationship among the dairies. America was still very much a nation on the move with thousands of families moving daily to new areas. It made sense that when a satisfied Harbisons customer in Philadelphia moved to Los Angeles, it might be helpful if he or she realized Adohr Farms also was a member of the same corporate family with the same high standards of quality.

The dairies' identity tangle caused much discussion. Various options were considered. There was conversation about changing all of the individual dairy names and products to one common brand, such as Southland or Oak Farms. This idea was discarded because customer loyalty usually focused on the local dairy name, which in most cases had taken many decades to establish. If the name identification could not be altered, then a logical alternative seemed to be the development of a new look in the product packaging which might visually combine the dairies into one instantly recognizable family. After much thought this direction was approved. The New York industrial design firm of Frank Gianninoto and Associates was commissioned to create a "New Image" graphic look which could be adapted for use on all Southland dairy packaging. H. E. Hartfelder, Southland's executive vice president at the time, led the company's move to bind the dairies through a new visual identification. He recalled: "With the acquisitions we had rather suddenly accumulated quite a collection of dairies. We decided to continue utilizing the local names because a good bit of money had been spent on advertising them in each of their respective markets. We felt we would realize residual benefit by keeping the established names. However, we had all these various designs of cartons and different colored trucks. We had nothing cohesive to really indicate that we had become a national factor in the dairy industry. In fact, at that time we thought we were perhaps the fourth or fifth largest in the business, but nobody knew it. We discussed the situation and decided that the retention of the individual names would be a great idea but perhaps we could do something to tie everything together. None of the designs on any of our cartons was worth a darn. They were old, they had been in service 20 years or so. They were all of local origin and really nothing that we could carry forward from one place to another. John and I had a discussion on it and decided we would look around and see what we could do about hiring an outside consultant who might give us a central design. Then we could use our individual names and still have a national motif, so to speak. We had watched several dairies in other markets go through a similar program some five years before. They had used a New York firm, Frank Gianninoto and Associates. Before hiring Gianninoto we interviewed several other top design firms— really researching the whole thing pretty thoroughly. Finally we made the decision to hire Gianninoto because of their experience and we entrusted them with coming up with the idea. They did create several outstanding designs and we picked what turned out to be our current dairy logo. But it was still a big decision for us to go ahead and make a change that drastic. It represented quite a substantial expenditure—new printing plates for all of the dairy cartons, repainting 2,500 trucks, etc. However, we decided to do it and do it all at once. And we decided that, with the money we were spending, we had probably better spend some additional money and see if we couldn't attract some national as well as local attention to the change. We decided to have a big bash in each one of our dairy areas and really make it an event—with the press invited, as well as local bankers, chamber of commerce officials and civic leaders. We especially wanted to invite our local dairy customers in each market so that we could introduce them to the new design. Well, we did it and it took us about a year to get around to all of our dairies. It proved very successful and was a highlight in the dairies' history. It tied the thing together. The "New Image" program interested all of our Southland dairy people. It created a whale of a lot of enthusiasm and it was well worth the effort and the expense."

THE NEW DAIRY DESIGN

The Gianninoto firm created a flowing three petal design which combined simplicity with elegance. It presented an abstract, modernistic look that insured instant recognition in whatever context it was used. The packaging of the various dairy products was color-keyed: red, homogenized milk; blue, low fat, skim milk and cottage cheese products; green, buttermilk; brown, chocolate milk; yellow, orange drink; and so forth.

Southland's Stanford Agency helped introduce the dairies' "New Image" through an advertising campaign built around the phrase "Looks delicious—tastes beautiful." As Herb Hartfelder mentioned, it also was decided that each individual Southland dairy would receive its own personalized introductory program to announce its "New Image." It was necessary that customers in each respective market understand that nothing had really changed except the look of the dairy packaging. The old established name was still the same; only the carton design was new.

To properly introduce the changeover an extensive public relations program was conceived. Southland dairyman Tom Hill, sales manager for Midwest Farms, was temporarily reassigned to coordinate the details of the "New Image" introduction in each major marketing area. The formula usually included a VIP reception for local city officials, a press conference for area media and a complete briefing by John Thompson, Herb Hartfelder and M. T. Cochran, Jr. concerning the reasons for the image change. Prior to the public introduction, employee meetings for dairy and 7-Eleven store personnel were held to explain the importance of the dairies' new design.

The overall results of the city-by-city blitz were excellent. Besides accomplishing the primary objective of formally introducing the packaging change, another unanticipated benefit accrued. Many of those attending the "New Image" meetings discovered the identity and scope of Southland for the first time. Civic officials, the news media, area businessmen and others were brought into contact with Southland executives for their first close-up look at a company previously unknown to a sizable number of them. A common experience which occurred during the "New Image" meetings was for an invitee to express surprise when told that Southland also owned 7-Eleven as well as the local dairy.

1

2

The centerpiece of the introductory activities in each city was the new design itself. Its public acceptance was instantaneous. In discussing the design Mrs. Doris Gianninoto said, "We made sure that the design had charm and feminine appeal. All food packaging should be pleasant and attractive to have in the kitchen or on the breakfast table. It should 'belong' there—like bright crockery, fresh curtains or a growing plant on the windowsill."

The world premiere for the new design was staged by Midwest Farms in Memphis in June 1967. The overwhelming success of the Midwest program was surprising even to the Southland officials involved. The "New Image" format used at Memphis became the model for the other cities and dairies involved in the changeover. The total "New Image" project was to eventually extend to all Southland dairies, with the exception of Cabell's, over a two-year period. The original success in Memphis was duplicated without exception in all areas. And, quite unexpectedly, the entire exercise had not only united the Southland dairy family, it had established the company as a diversified, aggressive corporation moving forward in all areas of food retailing.

1 A nationwide promotion—market by market—introduced the new Southland dairy design. Velda Farms division manager Mason Copeland initiated the program in Florida.

2 John Kellum, manager of operations for the Southland Dairies Group, has a prized collection of milk bottles from far and near, which includes samples of the Southland Dairies' early containers.

3 The Southland Dairies family of products, 1967–68.

177

THE
SOUTHLAND
CORPORATION

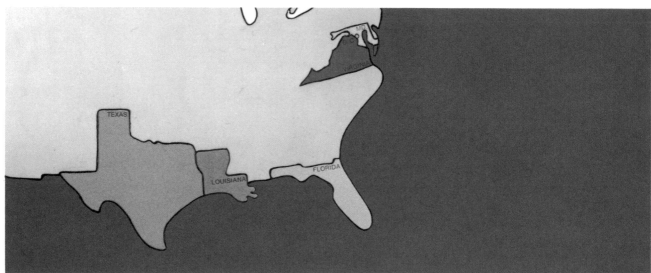

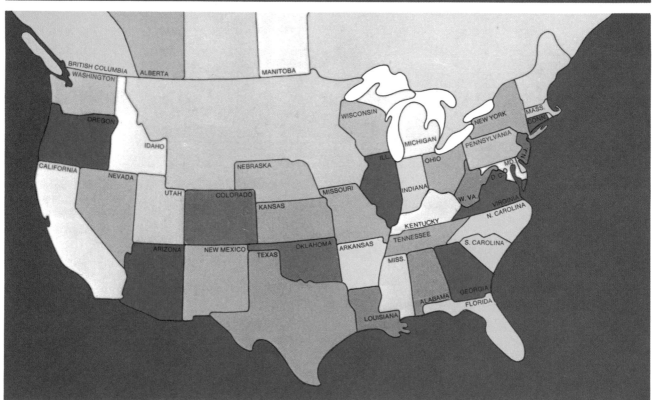

Southland's corporate logo (above) was introduced in 1968.
The maps illustrate a decade of growth—from five states
and the District of Columbia in 1959 to 38 states, the
District of Columbia and three provinces of Canada by 1969.

B etween 1965 and 1969 7-Eleven's growth exploded. In what may have been the most rapid buildup of individual retailing units in American business history, 7-Eleven soared from 1,519 stores on January 1, 1965, to 3,537 stores in operation by December 31, 1969. It was an unprecedented expansion based on the principle that John Thompson had invoked after the company's successful move to the East Coast in 1957. Sears' Herbert Murphy had counseled Thompson then to "take the ball and run with it in all of your good markets. Build all the stores you can, as fast as you can."

Southland's new management team of Thompson and Hartfelder based their expansion-oriented strategy on this advice. In area after area where 7-Eleven already was known and accepted the company moved quickly to build new stores and establish its position in the market.

Southland first concentrated on securing its position as the leading convenience store chain in the company's oldest and best-established regions: Texas, Florida, the East Coast and California. These areas became the scenes of heavy 7-Eleven store construction programs. The "Big Red 7 and Bright Green Eleven" signs erupted by the hundreds in front of the little 60- by 40-foot stores which were now playing host to more than one million customers every day.

The record supports the blazing pace of new 7-Eleven store openings during the 1965–1969 period:

Year	Opened	Closed
1965	398	30
1966	469	42
1967	323	40
1968	508	37
1969	563	94
	2,261	243

7-Eleven's California operation was an example of how this stepped-up growth was accomplished. Division manager Sam Meyer viewed the boom in 7-Eleven construction: "We grew on the West Coast through a combination of a few small acquisitions and the construction of new stores. Mostly, though, it was just the brand new starts that caused the huge increase in our numbers. In fact, 1968 was our most prolific year for building new stores. From scratch we built and opened 198 new 7-Elevens. And I really think if you look back on it from a production standpoint, no one else had ever done that before. It makes you so proud because many of our key people were fairly new in the business. For those young people like Dick Dole, Ray Berry, Don Burnside and on and on, to muster up the energy to build and open that many new stores, it was really something. Also, if you just consider for a minute how many new employees and franchisees that kind of expansion represents, it staggers you. You know the franchisees had to find employees to staff their stores and this was no small effort. I think the real key to success on the West Coast was the foresight of Jere Thompson in insisting that we have nothing but the finest in training. We had a training plan out here that was second to none. It was a centralized school where we brought all of our new people to the same point. Everyone was taught the same way and in the same manner. But all in all it was just a phenomenal thing, this growth. One thing that John Thompson kept repeating was that we simply were not going to abandon the West Coast market. And we didn't. Just as important, never once did we show any red ink while we were expanding and establishing our position. At the time Southland acquired Speedee Mart 126 stores were open. By 1971 we had 700 7-Eleven Stores operating up and down the West Coast."

THE TEXAS STORES' TALENT

The addition of more than 2,200 7-Eleven Stores in the 1965–1969 period must be regarded as a phenomenal accomplishment. Jere Thompson explained some of the positive factors that contributed to this growth: "We were able to grow so rapidly because of the strong nucleus of qualified 7-Eleven people that we had in our Texas stores. True, we had been in Florida, but then we had only been there about 10 years. Since we were expanding there also, we kept our Florida people in their own market rather than sending them to other parts of the country. Our Texas stores had to furnish most of the talent for our expansion. First we took David Burke, then Forrest Stout, Delano Womack, Billy Ruffeno and quite a few other outstanding men and sent them east to operate our stores there. Most of these people, with the exception of Forrest, eventually returned to Texas. When we went to California we sent only one man because they already had a strong management team. However, when we moved into Atlanta we had to send almost an entire management group. Again we called upon the expertise and experience of our people in Texas. There is no question that without this nucleus from the Texas operation we definitely could not have expanded so quickly."

In the Fall 1968 issue of *The Southland Family* Southwestern Division manager Vaughn Heady stated: "As our company has grown and expanded into new markets, it has been a matter of great satisfaction and pride for all of us in the Southwestern Division that we have been able to supply some of the key manpower to help get 7-Eleven Stores off to the right start in new areas. While at times it has been difficult for us to let go of some of our capable and experienced men, I am glad that our company's growth has provided such wonderful opportunity for advancement for so many of the fine men who started their careers with us."

Heady's comments were no understatement. The 7-Eleven managers who began their careers in the old Texas Division proved to be the key operations personnel during this period of expansion: Vaughn Heady in Southwestern; Forrest Stout in Eastern; David Neale in Southeastern (Florida); Sam Meyer in Western; Ben Holland in Mountain; H. R. Brasuell in Southern. All of these division managers were long-time Southland and 7-Eleven veterans, thoroughly knowledgeable in the company's system and operating philosophy. All had started their Southland careers as 7-Eleven store managers with the exception of Holland, who had moved into operations from merchandising. These managers had all been reared in the extremely profit-conscious atmosphere of Southland's chart meetings, which reviewed and analyzed sales, profits and expenses on an item-by-item basis. There was little misinterpretation of company goals and objectives by this experienced group, as they were well-attuned to the Southland system which concentrated strongly on the operations side of the business.

A NEW PHILOSOPHY

Another factor that influenced the 7-Eleven growth was a turnabout in the philosophy of new store site selection. Jere Thompson discussed the policy change: "One of the first decisions we made after Dad died and I moved back to Texas was that we were going to allow the 7-Eleven division managers to select their own sites. In the past Dad used to select them all, or perhaps John, Clifford Wheeler or I might be involved. We realized that if we were really going to expand we had to decentralize that very important part of our business, which we did. True, we made some mistakes, but we also made some very good choices. I think we have continued to improve our site selection process, especially with the help of the computer. However, we still depend on the man in the field, the division manager. In the long run it's his responsibility to operate that store properly. We're not looking for sheer numbers, we're looking for profitable stores. You know Dad used to say that proper site selection was about 80–90 percent of the success of a store. The rest is the people inside the store, as well as having the right merchandise. If you've got an excellent location and run a poor business, there is still a chance you can be profitable. But if you've got an excellent location along with excellent people plus the right merchandise, you can have a super store."

THE *ICEE* PHENOMENON

As 7-Elevens grew in number other unexpected events were occurring in the merchandising area. A spectacular development in a new product aimed primarily at the "kid" trade greatly enhanced the personality, attractiveness and profitability of the little neighborhood 7-Eleven Stores. Ironically, the product introduced by an outside company bore a name which once had been owned and later abandoned by Southland.

The *Convenience Store News,* an industry trade publication, reported about the beginning of the new product: "In 1959 on, appropriately, a cold and icy winter day, two enterprising young inventors, Dean Sperry and Omar Knedlik, approached a prominent Dallas machinery manufacturer, the John E. Mitchell Company, with a truly 'icy' idea. Their new concept was a technique for freezing a carbonated soft drink (cola, lemon-lime, cherry and other flavors) so as to be able to serve it in a sherbet-like form to be sipped through a straw. Thus began a new product development destined to be intertwined with another development—the spread of the nation's convenience stores. Out of this idea, the Mitchell engineering and manufacturing resources created a sophisticated piece of refrigeration equipment to become known as the 'Icee Machine.' With a compact freon refrigeration system, the machine's capability was to mix syrup, carbon dioxide and water in a precisely-controlled fashion under pressure in a freezing chamber. From the chamber a fully-carbonated soft drink could be served through a faucet in a sort of toothpaste-like fashion at a frosty 28 degrees for dispensing to customers. As early Icee advertising proclaimed, Icee was a revolution in the soft drink field. As its manufacturer, Mitchell between 1960 and 1965 sought to sell the machines to drugstores, drive-ins, and other conventional soda-fountain type outlets. Results after the sale of a few hundred units were disappointing because many of the store clerks were not able to keep dispensers working properly as a result of inadequate refrigeration maintenance know-how."

At this point Southland and 7-Eleven entered the Icee story. Dick Turchi, Southland's corporate merchandising manager in 1965, remembered: "One evening I received a call from Bev Hopkins, a 7-Eleven zone manager in Dallas. He was in a competitor's convenience store in Carrollton, a Dallas suburb. He wanted me to see this strange product that he felt had great sales potential for our stores. So I drove out and sampled the product, which was called Icee. I agreed with Bev about the possibilities that it had for 7-Eleven. However, there was just one slight hitch. The machines cost about $3,000 apiece and that represented a pretty good commitment in those days. But we decided to test it. We bought three units in the fall of 1965. They were an immediate sensation. We quickly ordered 100 more units. Then by the spring of 1967 we hit full stride with machines in most every store. Bob Stanford and the agency folks put together some outstanding radio commercials and a super promotional effort which introduced our own Slurpee name for the product to the general public. The Stanford Agency, which then numbered only about eight people, took the program out to the radio disc jockeys around the country. These local personalities got behind the product, had a lot of fun with it and really sold it to their listeners. I personally think it was one of the most successful new product introductions ever."

The Slurpee name dovetailed the switch in many 7-Eleven markets from the original Mitchell unit to the Taylor frozen carbonated beverage dispensing machine. However, the Mitchell machine was still used extensively in some company areas for many years. Overnight the Slurpee name and an inventive promotional campaign helped this new frozen drink sensation—and 7-Eleven—to achieve profitable results. Bob Stanford recalled the introduction of Slurpee to the public: "Yes, we coined the word Slurpee. The first time I heard that sound through a straw it just came out 'slurp.' We added the two e's to make a noun. It was just a fun name and we decided to go with it. When we introduced Slurpee around the country, we wanted to make it a real 'show biz' type of happening. First we tossed away the old idea of calling the Slurpee flavors cola, lemon-lime, cherry or whatever, even though that's what they really were. We started from zero and created a brand-new personality for each flavor. We conjured up a fun name for every flavor and built the radio commercials around spoofing the names. The flavors were given names like 'Fulla Bulla' or 'Firewater' or 'Red Eye' or something outrageous like that. As I remember, we had about seven in all. Then we put together a special meeting that we could take out to the different markets to explain our new Slurpee product. We used the presentation at store managers' meetings, of course, but we especially concentrated our efforts on the local disc jockeys or personalities who worked for the radio stations which would be running our

The frozen sensation that captured a nation's taste buds—first Icee, then Slurpee, almost synonymous with 7-Eleven.

commercials. We felt if we could turn these guys on with the fun of the strange names and the story built around them, then they would give us the extra excitement by communicating this feeling to their listeners. The whole agency hit the road for about two months to personally take this program to the store people and the radio stations involved. Howard Greene, Dan McCurdy, Bob Peck—literally everyone was traveling up one end of the country and down the other telling the Slurpee story. The results were unbelievable. The radio folks came unglued when they heard the spots. They literally tore back down to their stations to tell their listeners about this crazy new product available only at a 7-Eleven Store. The sales were just astronomical in all of the markets and it really put 7-Eleven on the map in the minds of a lot of people, especially many of the radio folks."

Other items also received increased merchandising emphasis in the last half of the '60s. Hot coffee, cold sandwiches and popcorn were popular new items in the stores. Floor polishers, rug shampooers and television sets were available for rent. Motor oil was added and at some locations self-service gasoline was introduced on the parking lots.

Slurpee's appeal has no age limit!

A DECADE OF ACHIEVEMENT

Although specific 7-Eleven accomplishments were impressive between 1960 and 1969, Southland's achievements as a corporation were spectacular:

During the 1960s—

• Southland recorded a compounded annual revenues growth of 23.8 percent

• Southland achieved a compounded average earnings growth of 19.9 percent

• Southland increased net investment in property, plant and equipment from $11.1 million to $125.7 million

• Southland increased shareholders' equity from $10.9 million to $95 million

• Southland paid cash dividends totaling $10.5 million

Total Southland revenues in 1969 were $826,462,000 compared to $88,-955,000 in 1959. Total net earnings had increased to $12,434,000 in 1969 from $2,035,000 in 1959, which also included a special item of $449,000. The number of shareholders advanced from 300 on December 31, 1959, to 8,079 exactly 10 years later.

All things considered, it represented the type of growth rarely seen in retailing. A summary of the specific milestones of the crucial five years from 1965 through 1969 illustrates the magnitude of Southland's development in such a brief span:

1965

• The Southland Corporation was rated as one of the nation's 50 largest merchandising firms by *Fortune* magazine.

• The frozen carbonated beverage Icee was introduced in 7-Eleven Stores.

• Southland acquired Adohr Farms and Spreckels-Russell Dairies.

• Southland won Best 1964–65 Radio Commercial in the Southwest award from the Association of Broadcast Executives of Texas.

• For the first time the company printed an annual report (covering 1964) to be presented to its shareholders.

• Construction began on first 7-Eleven Stores in Chicago.

• Southland established a real estate department with representatives in each division and site selection procedures.

• The new Southland Chemical Division began operation.

• 7-Eleven Stores opened during 1965, 398. 7-Eleven Stores to date, 1,887. All stores, including seven Bradshaw's supermarkets, 1,894.

1966

- Sales of Slurpee and Icee totaled 150 million cups.

- Harbisons Dairies in Philadelphia and Delvale Dairies in Baltimore were purchased. Southland now operated 29 dairy processing plants and 84 distribution outlets in 19 states and the District of Columbia.

- Southland climbed from 49th to 45th in the *Fortune* ranking of top U. S. merchandisers, based on '65 performance.

- The 2,000th 7-Eleven Store opened in Madison Township, New Jersey.

- Southland's dairies began marketing milk in a new plastic gallon jug in addition to the regular paper carton.

- Southland purchased American Service Company in Atlanta, encompassing 86 Handy-Pantry convenience stores in Georgia and Tennessee.

- New stores opened during 1966, 469. 7-Eleven Stores to date, 2,314. All stores, including Bradshaw's, 2,321.

1967

- Southland's '66 results moved the company into 33rd place on the *Fortune* merchandising list.

- For the first time Southland's total revenues passed the half-billion dollar mark.

- Southland's dairies developed uniform product identification for national use. This "New Image" introduced in Memphis, Tennessee, featured an instantly recognizable logotype design while maintaining the long-established firm name of each of Southland's dairies.

- Ice operations, for the first time in nearly 20 years, reported significant increase in profits.

- New stores opened during 1967, 323. Total 7-Eleven Stores to date, 2,597. All stores, 2,605, including eight Bradshaw's supermarkets.

1968

- Southland acquired the 115 stores of Gristede Bros., Inc., the largest and best-known prestige grocery chain in the Greater New York City area.

- Southland entered the New England market with the acquisition of 14 Quik Mart convenience stores in Boston.

- Southland granted the first area franchise for the operation of 7-Eleven Stores to Garb-Ko, Inc., a Saginaw, Michigan, business organization.

- A new training center for stores and dairies management improvement programs opened in Richardson, Texas, a Dallas suburb.

- The entire fleet of 2,500 dairy trucks and trailer-transports was repainted featuring the "New Image" logotype.

- Southland's first public stock offering of 750,000 common shares was well-received by the financial community.

- The first 7-Eleven Stores opened in Detroit.

- The Southland Chemical Division occupied spacious new quarters in Dallas, a two-story, 51,250 square foot office, production, warehouse and laboratory facility.

- Southland's board of directors voted to split the company's stock on a three-for-two basis.

- The 3,000th 7-Eleven Store opened in Deltona, Florida.

- New stores opened during 1968, 508. 7-Eleven Stores to date, 3,068. All stores, including 115 Gristede's and eight Bradshaw's, 3,191.

1969

- The board of directors named John P. Thompson chairman and H. E. Hartfelder president of The Southland Corporation.

- Southland purchased the Barricini Candy Company, headquartered in New York City. The purchase included 145 individual candy shops in 50 major cities.

- A new fully-automated Reddy Ice plant and a new modern facility for the preparation and distribution of Smiley's sandwiches and salads opened in Fort Lauderdale, Florida, to serve 7-Eleven Stores and other retail outlets in the Gold Coast area.

- Southland granted the second and third 7-Eleven area franchises to Handee Mart, Inc. for Western Pennsylvania and Lar-Lin, Inc. for an 11-county area of South Texas.

- Western Division 7-Eleven Stores were divided into two new divisions, with the Southern California and Las Vegas stores comprising the Western Stores Division and the San Francisco, Sacramento, San Jose, Reno, Portland, Seattle and Vancouver, British Columbia, stores comprising the Northwestern Stores Division.

- The Stanford Agency introduced a new advertising theme, "Oh Thank Heaven for 7-Eleven" on radio and television stations from coast to coast.

- Southland purchased Wanzer Dairies in Chicago, giving the company dairy representation in this important market for the first time.

- Southland established a computer systems department responsible for developing and integrating all present and future field computer operations into a central corporate information system.

- The first 7-Eleven Store was opened in Calgary, Canada.

- As a result of extensive research, Southland announced plans to construct its own merchandise distribution centers on a regional basis. This program of computerized control of inventory and distribution was developed by Joseph S. Hardin, a new Southland vice president who during his military career had created the modern distribution system for the United States Army and Air Force PX operations.

- Southland opened an ultramodern milk processing plant at Santa Ana in Orange County, California, with the capacity to produce more than 100,000 gallons of milk per day. Additionally, the original milk plant at Southgate was completely remodeled, giving Adohr two highly-automated processing plants to serve the growing Southern California market.

- During the year Southland purchased Briggs Dairy, which operates in the Buffalo, New York, area.

- The company's dairies were now distributing milk, ice cream and related products through 30 processing plants and 87 principal distribution outlets in 22 states and the District of Columbia.

- New stores opened during 1969, 563. Total 7-Eleven Stores to date, 3,537. All stores, including 121 Gristede's, 145 Barricini and seven Bradshaw's, 3,810.

Here's to Slurpee! Kids immediately latched onto Slurpee and made it their own.

By the end of 1969 Southland was operating in 38 states, the District of Columbia and three provinces of Canada. 7-Eleven Stores were open in 31 states, the District of Columbia and Canada. Of the 3,537 7-Eleven Stores, 1,286, or 36 percent, were now franchised.

It had clearly been a period of incredible progress. In 10 brief years the company had seen 7-Eleven expand nearly seven-fold in number of stores. Southland, the originator of the convenience store concept in 1927, suddenly found that its little 7-Eleven Stores had been embraced by America as the corner grocery store of the '60s—and as a favored place which catered specifically to the new leisure lifestyle based upon convenience. It had to be considered a revolutionary development in modern retailing. As the company prepared for its fifth decade, its positive momentum continued to be evident. The era of the neighborhood store had arrived, and 7-Eleven was the cornerstone of what was becoming the fastest-growing segment of the nation's retail food business—convenience stores.

As the success of 7-Eleven became more visible, other entrepreneurs and retailers began to realize the potential of the convenience store concept. Southland had pioneered virtually alone for decades: creating the original idea, making the inevitable mistakes, learning the customer's likes and dislikes, building an operating system and refining the merchandising techniques.

Now, as the 1960s ended, convenience stores were no longer an oddity. They were beginning to appear almost everywhere in virtually every section of the nation. Their increased presence was attracting widespread attention and respect, both within food industry circles and in the larger outside world of general retailing. A booming new industry had been born—and was blossoming far more rapidly than any other phase of food distribution. What many had still not yet perceived, however, was that 7-Eleven and other convenience markets were actually much more than simply "food stores." Certainly these little stores devoted most of their retail selling space to grocery products. But their sales mix varied considerably from that of the traditional supermarket. The best sellers in the average convenience store were usually single purchase items, such as cigarettes and tobacco products, milk, bread, beer, soft drinks and health and beauty aids. Dry groceries were far behind in terms of popularity with convenience store shoppers. The true lure of the bantams was pure convenience, whether for immediate needs, fill-in items or whatever. The handy location, extended hours, ease and speed of shopping and front door parking simply made a neighborhood convenience store a more practical choice for time-conscious individuals. The working person, perhaps more aware of the demands on his or her time, seemed most attracted to the quick-stop brand of store. Working people appeared to begrudge the extra minutes required by supermarket shopping, especially if only one or two specific items were required. The predominant supermarket customer, the non-working housewife, was the least attracted to convenience stores. Since the full-time homemaker usually shops for a week's supply of groceries at a time, her needs differ completely from the typical convenience store patron. Also, the penny-conscious housewife properly recognizes that convenience stores are slightly more expensive in many, but not all, instances. This small extra cost for some products is the price willingly paid by convenience-minded customers. Their personal time seems far more valuable to them than the few extra pennies involved.

MORE THAN "A FOOD STORE"

The emerging convenience store industry was prospering with its customers by being more than just a "food store." The real difference between the supermarket and the convenience market was that the big store provided a product and the little store provided a service. Even to those doubters who worried over the possible competitive damage that one might cause the other, it was becoming obvious that the two stores actually complemented each other. No realistic convenience store operator could possibly expect a housewife to spend her morning browsing through the little store. No practical supermarket manager could truly fault anyone for wanting to save several minutes on a one-or-two-item shopping trip by choosing the neighborhood convenience store. Although industry watchers admitted there probably always would be some blurring of the roles of supermarket and convenience market, the broadening appeal of the handy little stores showed that, by the end of the '60s, their day with the American consumer had definitely arrived.

Industry figures confirm the phenomenal growth of convenience stores between 1957 and 1970. In '57, there were only about 500 true convenience stores. The store count rose to 2,500 in 1960, 5,000 in 1965 and approximately 13,250 in 1970. Total sales and market shares also reflected this remarkable growth.*

Year	Total Sales	Share of U. S. Grocery Market	
1957	$ 75 Million	Less than	.2%
1960	357 Million	Approximately	.7%
1965	720 Million	Approximately	1.1%
1970	2.415 Billion	Approximately	2.7%

The annual sales volume per convenience store was also rising, spurred by increased customer acceptance and some inflation. The average convenience store saw its total volume move up to approximately $182,000 per year in 1970, about a 21 percent gain over 1957 figures.

As the popularity of the little stores expanded, important changes began to occur as the relatively new industry sought to keep up with customer demands and solidify its own spectacular gains.

THE INTRODUCTION OF EXTENDED HOURS

Since service was the prime appeal of a convenience store, it was natural that new ways to serve the customers would be explored. One of the first experiments built upon the already accepted concept of extended hours. Most convenience stores had followed 7-Eleven's original lead of being open for business from 7 A.M. to 11 P.M. However, as America changed, so did the shopping habits of its population.

The country was becoming younger in terms of the average age of its citizens. Younger people tended to be more restless, more active and more likely to be in need of products and services at all hours, not at just the normal shopping times. The work routine of the nation was being altered, too. More and more jobs required late-night or early-morning schedules. Many U.S. factories were running around the clock with three full shifts. America was beginning to stay out late and its people needed a place to shop in these early hours. Since the neighborhood convenience store was already providing extended-hours service anyway, it was the most obvious candidate to fill this new customer demand. Again 7-Eleven was among the first to sense the potential for the 24-hour convenience store. Not unexpectedly, one of the first areas to try the all-night concept was the 24-hour city of Las Vegas, Nevada.

7-Eleven's Gene Ford was involved: "Opening up our 7-Eleven Stores 24 hours was very easy to do in Las Vegas because everyone is out and around 24 hours of the day. We had one store very close to the Strip, so we decided to open it 24 hours as an experiment. We had very good success with this first one and we soon tried several more in Vegas. That was in the summer

* Based on information published by *Progressive Grocer/Convenience Stores* magazine.

of 1963. To my knowledge, no other convenience chain and few supermarkets had tried 24-hour stores up to that time. The immediate result of going to 24 hours was an increase in sales and profits. We really didn't have a lot of problems. Of course it was a new venture at first and we didn't have any supervision on the midnight shift. We had to supervise the stores ourselves and work with the employees (they were still company-operated at the time) to make sure everything was working out satisfactorily on that shift. We then discovered some other advantages we hadn't counted on—we completely eliminated burglaries. On a positive note, people could depend on our being open and we began to increase our overall business more than the amount we ran on the midnight shift. People just seemed to find their way to us more often after we went to 24 hours. Since we started the round-the-clock operation in Las Vegas, we have always continued on the program. In fact, we now have some 7-Eleven Stores there that have never closed since the day they were first opened. Whose idea was it to open that first Vegas store 24 hours? I guess it was probably the store employees' idea. They were on commission and there was a lot of activity in Vegas, and they felt they could capture a lot of sales."

24-HOUR STORES IN TEXAS

Vaughn Heady, 7-Eleven's Southwestern Division manager, also was being introduced to the 24-hour potential in Texas about the same time that the Las Vegas experiment was taking place. He observed: "I don't remember the exact date, but we really got started with the 24-hour operation by accident. The first store to open 24 hours was in Austin, Texas, at 607 West 19th, which is close to the campus of The University of Texas. It so happened there was a football game in Austin this particular Saturday night and the store was so busy that at 11 o'clock they couldn't get it closed. They just continued to do business and never did get it closed that night. By accident they stayed open the entire night.

"It was in the early 1960s. The store did so well that the next time there was a football game it stayed open 24 hours again. It continued to do well and they kept it open every week-end whether or not they had a football game in Austin. That made us wonder if perhaps it might do well on week nights because it was located close to the University and the students were wandering around all night. They started keeping it open every night and the store did quite well.

"As a result of the store's success in Austin, we opened a 24-hour store in Fort Worth on Berry Street just across the street from Texas Christian University. It did very well, and it appeared then that stores near universities would do well on a 24-hour basis. The third all-night store we opened was on Mockingbird Lane in Dallas near the Southern Methodist University campus. It also did very well. Then we got to wondering if there were other stores in major traffic patterns that might do well on that basis, so we opened such a store on Northwest Highway near Marsh Lane in Dallas. It did quite well and we then thought, if that one does well then there are a lot of others that would do well, too. From that point we started the 24-hour stores."

1

2

3

4

A MULTITUDE OF NEW DEVELOPMENTS

As the trend toward 24-hour operations accelerated other major developments in convenience store operations were occurring. These various changes included a substantial increase in the number of women store managers; a constant introduction of new products and services such as frozen carbonated beverages, fast foods, ice (yes, in a modern form—primarily packaged for home entertainment use) and gasoline; a new emphasis on relatively unpromoted items such as health and beauty aids, books, magazines and candy; and an increase in the number of convenience stores in neighborhood minicenters with one to three other retail stores, as compared to the usual freestanding sites.

Not all of the new developments were positive. As the convenience store business expanded scattered problems began to surface. Employee recruitment, training and retention became serious challenges to most convenience store companies. The percentage of personnel turnover was too high by any standard and was an increasing source of concern as the number of stores continued to grow. In addition, security problems were beginning to merit considerable attention. Internal theft, pilferage and armed robberies were worrisome situations that seemed to defy solution. The convenience and speed of shopping so attractive to customers seemed to offer the identical advantages to thieves—both internal and external.

With the multitude of positive and negative changes swirling around the little neighborhood store one conclusion was undeniable: without a doubt it had become a dynamic growth industry, the fastest growing segment of America's retail food business.

Southland, the industry's founder and leader, as it had done in the past, surveyed the years ahead and began to chart several innovative moves that would help prepare it for the predictable opportunities to come.

1 By the late 1960s the number of 24-hour stores began to increase.

2–4 Magazines, candy, Slurpees and new grocery items were important products of the late '60s.

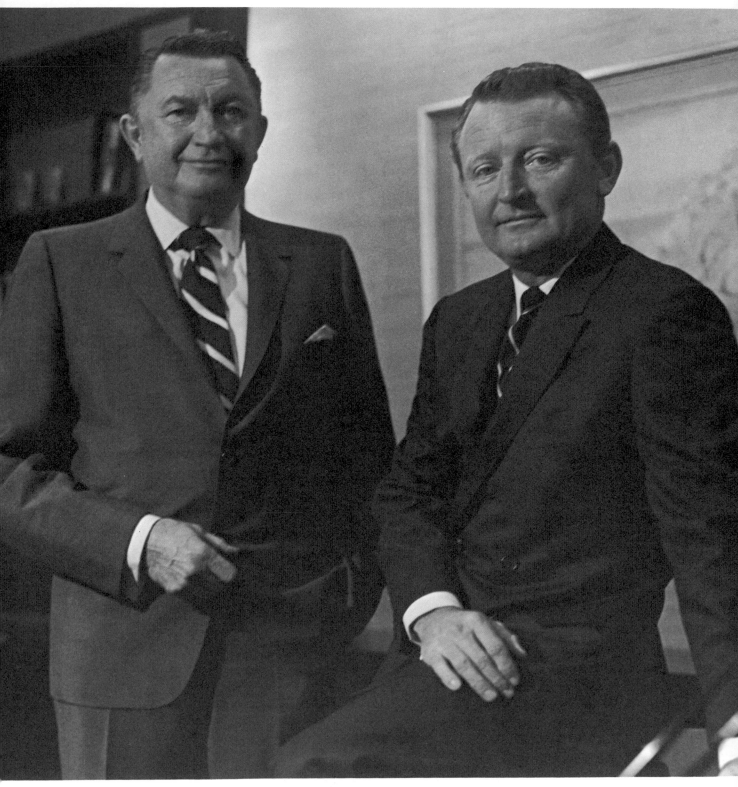

1969—John P. Thompson, right, and H. E. Hartfelder
were named chairman of the board and president of Southland.

In the late 1960s, as Southland looked with anticipation toward a new decade, the company began deliberate preparations to successfully cope with the growth potential being projected —and desired—by its top management.

Several changes were made at the highest levels, including the election in 1969 of John P. Thompson to chairman of the board, a position which had remained unfilled for eight years since the death of his father. H. E. Hartfelder was named president succeeding John Thompson. Other Southland officers at the end of the decade included: Jere W. Thompson, vice president of store operations; M. T. Cochran, Jr., vice president of dairy operations; Clifford Wheeler, vice president of new areas; Walton Grayson III, vice president and general counsel; Joseph S. Hardin, vice president of planning and development; J. Y. Ballard, vice president; J. B. Langford, corporate secretary; W. K. Ruppenkamp, treasurer; R. G. Smith, controller. The board of directors included John and Jere Thompson, Hartfelder, Wheeler, Grayson, Ballard, Webster Atwell and W. W. Overton. The board had remained unchanged since 1965.

HARDIN'S ADDITION SIGNIFICANT

The addition of Joe Hardin to Southland's management team was especially significant to the company's future plans. Before joining Southland Hardin was a U. S. Army brigadier general. At the time of his retirement from active military service in February 1969 he was in charge of the Army and Air Force Exchange Service, a $2 billion worldwide military merchandising business. In sales volume the Exchange Service was the third largest retail merchandising operation in the United States at the end of the '60s, exceeded only by Sears and Penney. During Hardin's tenure with the Exchange, sales to military personnel and their dependents through post exchange and base exchange stores increased from $1 billion to $2.25 billion. Its earnings, funneled to the military services' various welfare programs, were approximately $115 million.

In announcing Hardin's new association with Southland in March 1969 John Thompson said, "General Hardin is ably experienced in all phases of retailing, computerized controls and procedures, buying, merchandising, money management and employee training. We feel fortunate indeed to have him join our company at a time when our operations have grown and expanded throughout the country. His successful direction and management of the Army and Air Force Exchange Service, which supplies and operates 19,000 military retail outlets in all parts of the world, will help bring the most modern and efficient methods and procedures to our business."

Herb Hartfelder recalled how he first met General Hardin and how important the able military executive became to Southland's growth: "Joe Hardin had been successful in moving the PX headquarters from Long Island City, New York, to the Oak Cliff section of Dallas. It was quite a move and meant a lot to our city. The Oak Cliff Chamber of Commerce and the Oak Cliff Bank and Trust, of which I have been a director for many years, were both instrumental in convincing the PX to make the decision to locate in Dallas. At one point when Joe first came down he appeared before the bank's board of directors in his capacity as chief of the PX. That is where I first met him. I subsequently found out that he had a very interesting EDP (electronic

Joseph S. Hardin

data processing) system at the PX. Of course they had thousands of branches and were doing substantially more than $2 billion a year. We had a weak EDP program at Southland. We hadn't been able to get it off the ground. We even bought the wrong computer originally and then could not get it serviced properly. We also had great difficulty in getting qualified personnel to staff the computer part of our business. So again, as we had done at other times in our past, we looked back on what our mistakes had been and tried to avoid making the same ones in the future. We decided the wise thing would be to hire someone who had run a much larger computer operation than our own so that the person would not be appalled at tackling something as huge as ours. We contacted Joe and asked him to join Southland. He made the decision to come with us and this computer problem was like apple pie to him. He had been through the same problems before. Joe brought in Rulon Brough (now head of the company's EDP group) and in turn we staffed the department with some very competent people. We very shortly not only caught up but I believe we are now ahead of most other companies.''

THE NEW DISTRIBUTION CONCEPT

A new distribution concept, with three regional distribution centers and a sophisticated data processing system stream-lined Southland's inventory control and distribution.

1 Southland Distribution Center (SDC), Orlando, Florida.

2 Tyler, Texas SDC

3 Fredericksburg, Virginia SDC

4 A bird's-eye view of store orders being "picked" at Tyler SDC.

5 SDC truck leaves with deliveries for 7-Eleven Stores.

Hardin also was to lead Southland into the new decade with a new distribution concept considerably more advanced in theory and design than that of any other retail food company. In the "Message to Southland Shareholders" in the 1969 annual report, chairman Thompson and president Hartfelder said: "As a result of extensive research and in-depth cost studies, Southland plans to establish its own merchandise distribution centers on a regional basis. We believe that by creating and operating our own warehouses and distribution systems Southland can more effectively meet the day-to-day stock requirements of its stores and minimize the growing complexities of mass distribution to small retail outlets. This program of computerized control of inventory and distribution should prove to be one of the most significant forward steps in Southland's history.''

Herb Hartfelder elaborated: "The distribution centers were a great step forward for Southland. This was another concept that Joe Hardin brought with him from the PX. Joe's system was to break down full cases of products and deliver to the stores on an exact basis the specific number of items needed. Without question this system of distribution put our stores in a better and more realistic stock position. Of course the distribution centers work hand in hand with the computer system. We now have made a substantial investment in our computer technology. Shortly after the first moon landing in 1969 we hired IBM to put a complete computer team together for us. It was at this time that the distribution centers' computerized ordering, order filling and reordering systems were installed and subsequently we went into a revision of our entire accounting procedure.''

HARDIN EXPLAINS THE NEW SYSTEM

Joe Hardin, who was operating at the center of these new directions for Southland, commented: "The basic plan of the Southland distribution system was developed in 1969, at which time it was accepted in principle by corpo-

198

1

2

3

4

5

1

1 Orders from the stores are placed through a central computer to the SDC.

2 Final destination—a 7-Eleven Store receives its order of merchandise from SDC.

2

rate management. The very beginning of the system involved a task force of Southland planners plus a team of IBM specialists who put the plans into workable computer programs. The system is actually made up of many, many concepts—buying from vendors, controlling the warehouse operations, distributing the merchandise and providing the store people with the necessary tools to control the merchandise in the stores. Literally dozens and dozens of people were involved as the whole system was conceived. Those people and numerous others are still involved as the system is being constantly refined. The task force earlier mentioned went to Orlando, Florida, early in 1970 and set up a distribution center in miniature—a small warehouse providing merchandise for 22 7-Eleven Stores with the use of one truck. We proceeded to field test the underlying concepts of the system, which included testing various types of delivery equipment, warehouse conveyer systems, order picking and the impact on the stores. The test ran for 18 months. We actually broke ground for the first Southland Distribution Center (SDC) in Orlando while the test was still in progress and while we were still developing the computer system needed to support the SDC operation. We found that the SDC system affected 7-Eleven store performance in many ways. Most items supplied by the SDCs are price marked before delivery to the stores—this permits the stores to place the merchandise directly on the store shelf. The storing of excess merchandise in the back room of the store is minimized. Another significant feature of the SDC system is that the quantities supplied to the stores represent actual sales requirements. Previously a store would have to accept a complete case of a given product, storing the excess in the back room or placing excess items on the store shelf. The average store was able to reduce its inventory substantially on SDC-supplied items after conversion to the system. This reduced inventory and freed up valuable shelf space, which allowed the stores to add new merchandise programs."

Three regional distribution centers—in Orlando, Florida; Tyler, Texas; and Fredericksburg, Virginia, would be planned, built and operating between August 1971 and October 1973. By the end of 1976 they would serve more than 3,300 7-Eleven Stores.

1 Gristede Bros., Inc., New York City's most prestigious grocery chain, dating back to 1891, merged with Southland in 1968.

2 With the Gristede's acquisition came Charles & Co., gourmet specialty food outlets.

W hile the planning was beginning on the revolutionary distribution system, other interesting developments were occurring. In the mid- and late-1960s several acquisitions and entry into several new businesses took place, thrusting Southland into previously unexplored areas.

SOUTHLAND AND GRISTEDE'S

On October 15, 1968, Southland announced that its board of directors and the directors of Gristede Bros., Inc. of New York City had agreed in principle to a plan of merger into Southland of Gristede's 115 grocery, liquor and gourmet specialty stores in the New York City metropolitan area. Without question Gristede's represented the largest and best-known prestige grocery chain in New York City, an area void of 7-Eleven Stores or any Southland presence. The stores, which specialized in fine groceries, produce and meat, had an annual sales volume of about $60 million.

The original Gristede's store had been opened in 1891 at 42nd Street and Second Avenue in New York City by the brothers Charles and Diedrich Gristede. Of the 115 stores, 58 were in Manhattan proper, with others located in the Bronx, Queens, Nassau, Suffolk and Westchester Counties in New York and in Fairfield County, Connecticut. Gristede's also operated four gourmet specialty food outlets under the name of Charles & Co.

While Gristede's stores were several times larger than the 2,400 square foot 7-Eleven Store, there were some similarities. Gristede's slightly higher prices reflected the New York firm's own special brand of quality and convenience. For its customers Gristede's provided home delivery, took telephone orders and allowed merchandise to be charged. Charge accounts had been a feature in Gristede's service stores since 1891 and were later extended to its supermarkets. By the 1970s, tens of thousands of New Yorkers could boast of a Gristede's charge account. The stores themselves were hailed by their customers as providing an array of first-class produce, the finest in prime beef and an uncompromising quality in all of their products. The stores also had a reputation for the friendliest and most efficient store managers and clerks in the city, no small accomplishment in itself.

The merger was a happy one. John Thompson, in the Winter 1968 edition of *The Southland Family,* said, "I was proud to hear Otto Haass, president of Gristede Bros., tell us that one of the major factors of his company's decision to merge with Southland was the recognition by Gristede's executives that Southland's management people and employees were of the same high calibre as the men and women of Gristede's. There is no doubt of this, I think, and I believe sincerely that together as a team this 'marriage' of fine employees and mutual business interests will lead to great success and achievement."

BARRICINI JOINS SOUTHLAND

In July 1969 another New York-based company joined the Southland ranks. The Barricini Candy Company was purchased from Restaurant Associates, Inc. Barricini, like Gristede's, had an excellent reputation among New Yorkers. The company had been founded in 1928 by two young brothers, Mac and Jack Barricini, and their wives. From their first small family-operated

1

2

3

candy kitchen on Broadway, between 157th and 158th Streets, the company had grown until by 1969 its fine candies were sold in 145 Barricini shops in 22 states and the District of Columbia. Barricini products also were carried in hundreds of drug stores, gift shops and supermarkets. Again Southland had opted for a quality name well-established in its market.

THE CHEMICAL DIVISION IS FORMED

However, the company did not rely on acquisitions alone to enter potentially profitable new businesses. The Southland Chemical Division had been created in March 1965 primarily to service the company's dairy operations. From these modest beginnings the Chemical Division progressed in just a few years to become a solid manufacturer and distributor of a wide assortment of chemical products and food and beverage flavors. These specialty products and flavors were used not only by 7-Eleven Stores and Southland dairies but also by manufacturers and retailers in approximately 40 states. The division's output for dairies included ice cream flavors, stabilizers, fruit drink concentrates, sherbet bases and eggnog base. Specially prepared flavor concentrates for Icee and Slurpee flavors also were produced. Another important category for the Chemical Division was the manufacture and distribution of washing powders, dry and liquid cleaning compounds and conveyer belt lubricants. In June 1966 Southland purchased the Cre-Mel Company in Dallas, one of the Southwest's oldest and best-known manufacturers of flavors and fountain syrups. This acquisition gave the new Chemical Division an additional base of manufacturing strength as well as the benefit derived from an established brand name.

1 By the late 1960s the Southland Chemical Division had become a manufacturer and distributor of chemical products and food and beverage flavors.

2,3 Ice sales grew in the same period, due to increased leisure-time use and new factory packaging of fragmented ice.

ICE TAKES ON A NEW LOOK

An important contribution to Southland's past achievements returned to a place of importance in the mid- and late-'60s. Ice, the company's original business, was making an unexpected comeback. Paul Reed, manager of Southland's Reddy Ice Division, recalled: "I first came to Southland in early 1966 after working in the packaged ice business in Oklahoma City and Houston with other companies. These other firms had been able to keep their sales up, even though tonnage had dropped, by introducing a small package of ice designed primarily for convenience stores. At this time 7-Eleven was still grinding ice in the vault, sacking it in the stores and then selling it to the customers. We felt that this procedure simply had to go. Labor was expensive, the ice was bulky, there was not enough room and the women store employees just could not handle the physical work required. My goal was to get this block ice entirely out of our stores. We wanted to get rid of the melting mess it caused, improve and begin focusing on packaged ice. Besides it was so expensive to deliver bulk that it was just better for us to make packaged ice. The stores were still using block ice to refrigerate soft drinks and beer. We had to wage another campaign to get some modern refrigeration equipment so that we could eliminate block ice entirely. In the 10 years from 1966–1976 we have converted from all block ice to packaged ice. We have gone from a 90 percent wholesale to 97 percent retail market. We have

205

Wanzer's, one of Chicago's leading dairies, joined Southland in 1969.

changed our manufacturing methods from the old ice tanks to fragmentation, where we can make pure ice automatically. Now Reddy Ice sales are greater than Southland Ice sales ever were. Where we used to talk in tonnage, now we only talk in packages and dollars."

SOUTHLAND DAIRIES CONTINUE PROGRESS

Besides the excitement of the new distribution system, the expansion into previously untried but somewhat related businesses and a rebirth of the original phase of the company's operations, there was continued activity in the Southland dairies. On January 2, 1969, the company acquired the 111-year-old Sidney Wanzer & Sons, Inc. dairy in Chicago. Wanzer, following the pattern of other acquisitions, brought an excellent reputation for quality milk and dairy products. Using the advertising phrase "Wanzer's on Milk is Like Sterling on Silver," Wanzer's was considered to be the number one seller of milk in Chicago. The Wanzer acquisition also enabled Southland to enter the populous Chicago area with its dairy products just as 7-Eleven's presence in the market was increasing rapidly.

By 1969 Southland's dairies sales for the year, including intracompany sales, had reached an all-time high of almost $200 million. Southland's nine dairy divisions were: Harbisons in Philadelphia and adjacent areas, Embassy in Washington, D. C., and nearby states, Velda Farms in Florida, Midwest Farms in Tennessee and surrounding states, Oak Farms in Texas and Colorado, Cabell's in Texas and Oklahoma, Spreckels in San Francisco and Northern California, Adohr Farms in Southern California and Wanzer's in Chicago.

The company's dairies were processing and distributing milk, ice cream and related products through 30 plants and 87 principal centers in 22 states and the District of Columbia. And the dairies were quite aggressive in embarking on new projects for the coming new decade. Initial plans were being formulated to manufacture a complete line of yogurt, sour creams, dips and sterile creams. Also the dairies planned to introduce a complete line of low-fat products—milk, cottage cheese, yogurt and ice milk—to be merchandised in new and distinctively designed packages.

PREPARING FOR A NEW MILESTONE

In all corporate areas—7-Eleven, the dairies, new or reborn operations such as the Chemical Division, the Specialty Division (a service arm of the dairies), the Ice Division, other store operations such as Gristede's, Barricini, seven Southland-operated Bradshaw's supermarkets in Southern California—the future appeared promising. From a slender one-product beginning the company had grown and diversified into the unchallenged leader in one business—convenience stores—and an important factor in other businesses, especially dairy operations. From $120 million in sales at the time of Jodie Thompson's death, Southland had grown until it was ready to tackle a now possible goal, its first $1 billion year in total sales.

A new look for the 1970s. The red roof that soon became the identifying mark of the little neighborhood stores answered the need for a standard store design. A remodeled store is pictured, before and after.

CHAPTER
26

How does any corporation reach the billion-dollar sales level? In Southland's case it was a fortunate combination of several powerful—and some lucky—circumstances.

Of course the premier reason for the company's success was the basic soundness of its own convenience store concept. Combined with the changing lifestyle of a nation, it was an idea whose time had come. Added to this positive factor was the entrepreneur's vision of Joe C. Thompson, who had kept alive and built a struggling young company through the highs and lows experienced by almost any new business. A nucleus of loyal and talented people, thoroughly dedicated to profit-minded goals, had provided the intelligence, muscle and perseverance needed for the company's survival and growth. There also existed still one other element that had been critically important to this once tiny company as it neared this achievement—proper timing.

Southland's timing in beginning a major 7-Eleven expansion program in 1962 was extraordinary. No one could possibly foresee the exceptionally favorable results of this decision to rapidly build hundreds upon hundreds of new 7-Eleven Stores. As Southland crossed over into the '70s, it was this single decision to expand—and expand quickly—that had been perhaps the most important key in bringing the company near its first billion dollars in sales.

There was now another consideration for the company's board and officers to ponder: Southland certainly did not plan on halting its growth at a billion dollars. Therefore the question now was being asked: "What does it take to become a $2 billion company?" With the favorable outlook for the convenience store industry as an additional spur, there was little time to squander.

THE SOUTHLAND "IMAGE"

As Southland prepared to mark the first billion in sales, planning and discussion began on the opportunities that awaited beyond this milestone. While many of the company's operational needs remained constant, there were other more subtle changes in style and direction required as the organization shed its smallness. One of the first items on top management's agenda was the necessity for standardizing the "look" of the company. Then-president Herb Hartfelder was among those who considered a company's image important, especially as the organization attained the size which Southland was quickly approaching. He said: "As you know, we had just completed the 'New Image' program for the dairies and it was very successful. At the time of the dairy image project we started looking skeptically at the design of our 7-Eleven Stores. At that time we had a 7-Eleven design that was beginning to have a dated look. It had been a good design for its time but it was not as handsome a store as we felt we needed for the 1970s. Also, and even more important, there was a lack of consistency in our store look. Our signs and stores varied from division to division. They weren't the same shape, sometimes not even the same color. After the dairy program was completed we decided to pursue a new standardized store design. It's kind of funny how it evolved. The idea for 7-Eleven's new mansard roof came from a competitor. We were visiting their stores one day and I noticed it. I recall saying, 'Gosh, that's a good-looking roof.' I could envision a similar design on our stores with some new framing and other modifications. We needed a brighter color, something like the orange being used by another national chain. Our competitor's roof had been done in gray with a sort of metallic shingle. We set out to design our own colorful mansard roof with our architect, Alan Dodds, doing the work. Well, we did this and consequently it has been refined and upgraded over a period of time. That's the origin of the mansard roof and the standardization of the store appearance. From that we got into the redesign of practically everything in the company. We began standardizing items all the way from the letterhead on our stationery to the company's checks. We redesigned Barricini candy boxes, the trucks serving the Chemical Division—just about everything needed standardization. In order to promote our corporate image we tried to bring anything that was part of Southland into this family of related designs. We are still adhering to them. Every time we start to wander off from being consistent, we get right back where we should be."

SOUTHLAND AND PUBLIC RELATIONS

Hartfelder recalled another change in company thinking that took place as Southland marched toward its billion-dollar goal: "When we decided to expand, it involved a number of changes in our thinking. Prior to 1964 Southland really had very little recognition as a company. We just did not have any 'public relations' to speak of. We simply did not grant very many interviews to the media about our business. As we became larger and more diversified John and I decided that we would change our previous posture and begin talking extensively about the company to our various publics. We actively pursued a more 'open' policy with the news media. We also began to place more emphasis on items such as our annual report. We did interviews just about coast to coast, including appearances before security analysts' groups. In 1969 we appeared before the New York Society of Security Analysts for the first time." The commitment to an organized public relations effort was confirmed by the selection in 1965 of *The Southland Family* editor Frank Harting as the company's first public relations manager.

THE PERSONNEL FUNCTION

Other crucial areas receiving special attention were personnel and training. Southland's sudden expansion had triggered a heavy requirement for qualified people. R. L. (Bob) Moore was the company's personnel manager as it completed the transition into a billion-dollar organization. He recalled: "As the company grew we expanded our personnel department to parallel the changes in the corporate structure. In 1966 we also started getting into training more than we ever had before. Palmer Waslien wrote the text and set up a store supervisors training program on how to manage people. We took this program out to our people in the field. We would set up our little training school in a hotel room and the supervisors would come and stay the whole week, Monday through Friday afternoon. We had various people from the corporate office available to explain their different lines of work. For instance, Earl Monk would talk on accounting, W. F. Leonard on safety, Dick Turchi on merchandising, and I would do the personnel part. We practically made a traveling faculty out of the Dallas office. This kept up for at least a year until we had every division participating and most of the supervisors had been through the program. We then set up a formal training school in Richardson, a suburb of Dallas. This is when Palmer Waslien brought in Lew Maddox from Speedee Mart. Lew had been conducting the franchise training program on the West Coast for several years. We started out with just Lew and a secretary. Now there are about 15 people in the training department and they have moved to the corporate office. They write all their own textbooks, have film strip and videotape capability and prepare all of the employee manuals. We have two basic courses for our 7-Eleven operations management: profit manager for the district managers and profit maker for the supervisors. Both programs are constantly updated to incorporate the latest in training techniques. As far as the personnel department is concerned, there were 13 people when I started the department in 1966; we now have 31 people serving 34 separate Southland divisions. It is no secret that we have an especially large turnover of personnel in the stores and I guess this will always be our challenge. I believe we have managed to keep up with the growth and needs of the stores. As we have in the past, we especially must be able to keep our employees with potential because it is these people who help us cope with our future needs.''

THE FIRST BILLION DOLLAR YEAR

While Southland was beginning to polish and update its visual corporate image, pursue its new-found interest in media and financial relations and move ahead on its continuing program of upgrading personnel selection and training, it reached the billion-dollar sales mark in 1971 as revenues totaled $1,085,-107,334. The company had barely missed the $1 billion level in 1970 when revenues were $951,901,487.

In the 1971 Southland Annual Report Thompson and Hartfelder noted that the billion dollars had been a goal attained three years ahead of schedule and had generated the highest profits ($17,299,759) and earnings per share ($1.30) in the company's history.

Thus, the company had finally achieved the status of a billion-dollar corporation. If anyone assumed that the company might now pause to digest the tremendous gains of recent years, they were wrong. The forward momentum generated by Southland's expansion was still gathering strength, pushing the company toward another goal that Jodie Thompson had once predicted would be witnessed within the lifetime of his three sons—the opening of the 5,000th 7-Eleven Store.

The world's first convenience store was rededicated in Dallas on October 16, 1970 with the opening of a new 7-Eleven Store on the site of the original ice dock.

On October 16, 1970, a special event in Dallas attracted considerable attention. The world's first convenience store was officially rededicated when a new 7-Eleven Store was opened on the site of Uncle Johnny Green's original ice dock.

The new 7-Eleven Store #1 at Twelfth and Edgefield in the Oak Cliff section of Dallas was far removed in design and product mix from the first little Southland store. The modern new store featured 2,400 square feet of selling space, was air-conditioned and fully stocked with approximately 3,000 different items available for its customers. The original 1927 hot box had been little more than a tiny office and an ice vault.

The new store was constructed of antique brick with the usual glassed-in front. A red shingled mansard roof overhung the store's front walk and a back-lit 7-Eleven sign illuminated red and green colors against a raised brick pylon. The world's first drive-in food store had progressed quite some distance.

Besides two U. S. congressmen, Dallas civic officials and Southland's own officers and top management, the dedication ceremonies also were attended by several honored guests. One of these was B. C. Glenn, a retired 7-Eleven manager who had operated Store #1 from 1929–1931. He went behind the sales counter long enough to wait on several of the store's original customers, such as Mrs. L. S. Wilson, Mrs. Emma Morrow and Mrs. Lawrence Flusche. Special newspaper sections in the *Dallas Morning News* and the *Dallas Times Herald* noted the event with 12-page inserts detailing the company's founding and growth, with emphasis on Southland's importance to the economy of Texas. By 1970 Southland was ranked as Texas' fifth largest corporation in terms of total revenues. The company employed more than 3,000 Texans in various positions, with a total annual payroll of approximately $23.5 million. 7-Eleven's Southwestern Division now operated about 600 stores in Texas, including nearly 250 in the Dallas-Fort Worth area. The division, which had served as the training laboratory for many of Southland's management, also was approaching a milestone of its own. Construction was nearing completion on a 6,000-square-foot division headquarters building at the corner of Monticello and Cole Avenue in North Dallas.

OPEN PANTRY AND PAK-A-SAK

The rededication of the original store was only one example of 7-Eleven's forward thrust. Despite a national economy which was beginning to experience its first tinge of inflation and tight-money uncertainty, the company continued to add new stores at a solid pace. In 1970 Southland purchased the Northern Illinois Open Pantry Food Marts, Inc., franchisors of 60 convenience food stores in the Chicago area. And in July 1971 a treasured friend returned to the Southland family. G. Allen Penniman, Sr., who had been one of the earliest and most accomplished members of Jodie Thompson's management group, had founded the Pak-A-Sak convenience store chain in Louisiana in 1947. Pak-A-Sak now operated 153 stores in Shreveport, Baton Rouge, Lake Charles, Mobile, Montgomery, Pensacola and other southern markets. Allen Penniman, Sr. had personally been responsible for many of the innovative management policies and techniques introduced by Southland in the 1930s and 1940s. He had then been extremely successful in starting and building his own Pak-A-Sak chain into one of the most highly regarded

213

organizations in the entire convenience store industry. Pak-A-Sak was especially noted for its unusually good employee relations and exceptionally low personnel turnover, which could be traced partly to an outstanding savings and profit sharing fund similar to Southland's. Mr. Penniman, Sr. concluded his active management career with Pak-A-Sak's merger with Southland. The stores, after an orderly transition period during which they were referred to as Pak-A-Sak/7-Eleven, became Southland's new Mid-South Division under the leadership of G. Allen Penniman, Jr. The younger Penniman, a contemporary of John and Jere Thompson, had long been a member of Pak-A-Sak's management group and was a thoroughly knowledgeable and able executive.

The Pak-A-Sak acquisition provided Southland with market penetration in a growing area of the United States. By the end of 1971 7-Eleven was operating or franchising 4,114 stores in 34 states, the District of Columbia and three provinces of Canada. During the year a total of 472 new 7-Eleven Stores had been added through both new construction and acquisitions. Continuing the Southland philosophy of closing unprofitable or outdated locations, the company terminated 92 outlets, giving the Stores Division a net of 380 new stores during the year. Besides the 7-Eleven Stores, there were 207 Barricini/Loft's, 130 Gristede's and nine Bradshaw's supermarkets for a total of 4,460 stores.

In 1971 Pak-A-Sak, with 153 stores, was acquired.

1971 ACHIEVEMENTS

The year 1971 was proving to be another watershed year in Southland's development as the company raced toward its 5,000th 7-Eleven Store. The '71 achievements ranged from those bearing immediate significance to others with longer-term potential. They included:

- On August 2, 1971, Southland's first regional distribution center, located in Orlando, Florida, began delivering merchandise to 29 7-Eleven Stores. By the end of the year this highly automated facility was serving 562 Florida stores.

- The company made its initial entry into the European market through the purchase of a 50 percent interest in 370 specialty shops comprising the retail operations of Cavenham Limited, a large manufacturer, distributor, exporter and wholesaler of grocery, bakery, liquor, tobacco, candy and pharmaceutical products in England and Scotland. Further penetration occurred in 1972 when Southland purchased a 50 percent interest in a corporation formed to acquire a controlling interest in Wright's Biscuits Ltd. and Moores Stores Ltd., which operated 840 retail grocery outlets in England, Scotland and Wales.

- Construction of a new 11-story corporate office tower on Haskell Avenue in Dallas began in early fall. Scheduled for completion in spring 1973, this new building complex of 200,000 square feet was required to provide the necessary space for a growing corporate office staff previously housed in several locations. This centralization of the general office was regarded as an important and necessary move if the anticipated Southland growth was to be properly supported and controlled.

- During the year Southland invested $31.5 million in capital expenditures, a record for any year.

- With the purchase of four Hudgins Truck Rental Companies, Southland entered a new business field. The Hudgins fleet of more than 750 trucks began serving Southland operations as well as other outside companies.

- The company entered new market areas with the Pak-A-Sak acquisition; the purchase of Bancroft Dairy Company of Madison, Wisconsin, a distributor of dairy products in 16 states, including some not previously served by Southland; the purchase of a substantial part of the business of Loft Candy Company (including 69 Loft Candy Shops in New York, New Jersey, Connecticut, Pennsylvania, West Virginia and Maryland); and an entrance into the Dayton, Ohio, market by assuming operation of 17 convenience food stores previously operated by Convenient Industries of America, Inc. Southland, in conjunction with one of Mexico's leading business organizations, opened the first Super-7 Store in Monterrey during April 1971. The new store, located across the highway from one of Mexico's leading universities, featured merchandise and service similar to that of its 7-Eleven counterpart in the United States.

- The number of 7-Eleven Stores in Canada reached 49 with operations in Calgary, Winnipeg, Edmonton and Vancouver.

- The use of microwave ovens to prepare such fast food items as chicken, french fries, pastries and sandwiches was beginning to herald new merchandising possibilities. Plans for expansion of fast food service in 7-Eleven Stores included a variety of recipes for such favorites as barbecue, fish and chips, onion rings and pancakes, as well as the other staple items.

- The three Southland Food Centers produced and distributed a variety of salads and approximately six million Smiley's sandwiches during 1971.

- Southland's new private label products, including 11 flavors of 7-Eleven soft drinks distributed in both bottles and cans, were introduced in 7-Eleven Stores. In the company's newly-formed corporate design studio, headed by Hans Streich, displays and packages were being designed to promote the company's private label products ranging from the soft drinks to a new line of hosiery, Sheerly Beloved.

- 7-Eleven began a substantial move toward 24-hour store operations in many locations, a significant step that was expected to affect dramatically company total revenues and net earnings.

- Management began to formulate specific plans for reaching the $2 billion mark in sales, with concentrated attention devoted to establishing long-range corporate goals in the areas of financing, personnel requirements, organizational structure and operational expansion.

- 7-Eleven continued to enlarge its testing of self-service gasoline. This relatively new merchandising program received a strong boost from the Pak-A-Sak acquisition since most of these stores had long provided this additional customer service.

Southland's corporate headquarters were considerably expanded with the completion of an 11-story tower in 1973.

Developments of the early 1970s:
1,2   New private label products were introduced with the logos and packaging designed
by Southland's corporate design studio.

3   Self-service gasoline was introduced.

4   Southland entered the United Kingdom with
CTN (candy-tobacco-news) stores.

5   Mexico's first Super-7 Store.

6   7-Eleven expanded in Canada.

7   Hudgins Truck Rental was purchased.

HEADY AND STOUT NAMED REGIONAL MANAGERS

To properly manage the expanding 7-Eleven operations two regional manager positions were created in late 1971. The executives named to the new regional manager jobs, effective January 1, 1972, were two 7-Eleven veterans who had clerked together in the old Bluebonnet Circle store in Fort Worth 24 years before. Vaughn Heady was named to direct the operations of the new Central Region's 1,200 stores and Forrest Stout was selected to head the 1,000-plus Eastern Region stores. Four new 7-Eleven divisions also were created and managers designated for them. The Eastern Region included the Northeastern Division managed by Ken Bishop, the Washington-Baltimore Division under Frank Kitchen and the South Virginia Division with Sterling DeLoach in charge. The Central Region consisted of the new South Central Division under Delano Womack; the already established Southwestern Division, managed by Don Barfield and the Mountain Division, which remained under the leadership of Ben Holland.

"OH THANK HEAVEN FOR 7-ELEVEN"

7-Eleven's advertising and merchandising also continued to share special importance. Southland's Stanford Agency originated a popular advertising slogan in 1969: "Oh Thank Heaven for 7-Eleven." This theme was first used exclusively by the Southwestern Division stores in Texas and New Mexico as its dominant promotional theme for the entire year. "Oh Thank Heaven" proved so successful in this one particular store division that all 7-Eleven areas chose to utilize the theme in 1970. In 1971 the slogan was modified to include the convenience store's most telling sales advantage: "Oh Thank Heaven for 7-Eleven—It's About Time." Members of the in-house advertising agency continued to produce scores of radio and television commercials, storefront banners and point-of-sale posters. The humorous and light approach that had helped define 7-Eleven's unique personality continued to draw a multitude of customers to the friendly little store.

One unusual facet of 7-Eleven's advertising and merchandising structure was the autonomy granted to individual divisions in planning their respective programs. While an eastern area division might choose to devote the majority of its advertising dollars in January to selling coffee and hot chocolate, the Florida stores might at exactly the same time be strongly advertising sunglasses and suntan lotion. This local decision-making responsibility for advertising and promotion gave 7-Eleven a marketing flexibility unlike most other large retail chains.

SOUTHLAND MERCHANDISING CHANGES

7-Eleven's merchandising techniques underwent an alteration in the late '60s and '70s, resulting in a modernization compatible with both the changing times and the company's billion-dollar size. Dick Turchi, Southland's corporate merchandising manager during that period, was involved in many of the changes in style and substance: "When I joined Southland in 1963 as assistant merchandise manager of the Texas Stores Division, I spent the first few days on the job literally closeted in a 7-Eleven dairy vault. I was getting firsthand knowledge of how the company merchandised crushed ice. For several hours each day I would attack 300-pound blocks of solid ice with an old-fashioned icepick. We reduced each of these huge blocks to 12½-pound sections for feeding into the store's ice crusher. It was a laborious operation but it was just the way we did things. Now we have our own Reddy Ice trucks which are efficiently loaded with quality-controlled merchandise for quick distribution. Believe me, we've come a long way from the icepick stage. There is no doubt that we have become far more effective in our merchandising techniques. But to compete and survive we have had to change. We must constantly be anticipating and providing the type merchandise wanted by our particular kind of customer. We pay special attention to regional preferences. One of our strengths over the years has been the adaptability of Southland in keeping up with the changing needs of our customers. This is quite a challenge, especially in the merchandising function. There are about 10,000 new products introduced every year. Only a few hundred will survive for any length of time. The life cycle of a product was five years back in the 1950s. Now the cycle is down to 18 months on many products. Our overall merchandising concepts have greatly improved. Not too many years ago we were sitting down in our 7-Eleven store divisions in June to plan what we would merchandise and promote in July. Now every division has its merchandising and advertising plans drawn up a year in advance. We can still change or adapt to new situations if necessary, but basically we know where we are going when each new year starts.''

SOUTHLAND GOES ON ''THE BIG BOARD''

As the 1970s began to unfold, evidence that Southland was maturing as a national company was considerable. One of the most noteworthy happenings from an investment standpoint occurred on August 21, 1972. On that day the company saw its common shares listed on the New York Stock Exchange for the first time. Trading in Southland common, using the symbol SLC, began on the Big Board with the traditional first transaction of the day occurring at Post 22, Section D on the floor of the exchange. Chairman John P. Thompson, acting as a trustee of the Employees' Profit Sharing Plan, placed a purchase order for 100 shares at a price of $32⅞ a share which was immediately executed by Fowler and Rosenau, the specialist firm operating Post 22. The electronic and paper tape had been ''up'' for a moment bearing the following message: ''ADMITTED TO THE LIST AND TO DEALINGS . . . THE SOUTHLAND CORPORATION COMMON STOCK . . . $0.01 PAR VALUE . . . TICKER SYMBOL SLC . . . POST 22 SEC. D . . . NEW YORK STOCK EXCHANGE INC . . .'' Now the data on daily trading in Southland common would be carried in newspapers and financial journals around the world.

The value of Southland stock and number of shareholders had greatly increased over the years. Long-time shareholders benefited from three-for-two stock splits in 1968 and 1971 and a usual year-end stock dividend of three percent. As recently as 1958 the company listed only 284 shareholders. This number advanced slowly at first: 317 in 1960, 1,228 in 1965, 2,816 in 1967, jumping to 7,457 in 1968 and beginning to level off at 9,418 in 1972.

August 21, 1972. Southland common stock was traded on the New York Stock Exchange for the first time, opening at $32⅞ per share. Left to right: Jere W. Thompson, M. T. Cochran, Jr., J. Y. Ballard, John P. Thompson, NYSE vice president Merle S. Wick, H. E. Hartfelder, Walton Grayson III and W. W. Overton, Jr., are pictured on the floor of the NYSE.

Other corporate activities continued to build in the early '70s, with an eye toward the second billion. The company strengthened its managerial foundation in 1972 by establishing three executive vice president positions. Jere W. Thompson was named executive vice president in charge of stores and dairies operations, Walton Grayson III became executive vice president for administration and services and Joseph S. Hardin was selected as executive vice president for planning and special operations. Three new 7-Eleven store divisions were created: Great Lakes, which encompassed the Chicago/Detroit area and the remainder of the Midwest, managed by George Davis; the Northwestern Division, with Ray Berry as the manager; and the Canadian Division, led by John Neely. 7-Eleven operations now consisted of two regions, 14 divisions, 48 zones and 151 districts compared to seven divisions, 24 zones and 80 districts just five years before. There were 4,455 7-Eleven Stores open for business at the end of 1972 compared to 2,597 in 1967. The number of franchised stores in 1972 had grown to 1,875 or 42 percent of the total stores.

As the company expanded it was legitimate to question whether a saturation point could possibly be reached as far as the number of convenience stores servicing certain individual markets. But on a close evaluation it appeared that market penetration in 1972, based on one 7-Eleven Store per 12,500 population, was still lacking in many key areas. The New York, Chicago, Los Angeles, Boston, Philadelphia, Detroit, San Francisco-Oakland, Pittsburgh, Cleveland, Minneapolis-St. Paul, Milwaukee, Cincinnati, Indianapolis and New Orleans markets were all large metropolitan areas with a relatively small percentage of 7-Eleven Store penetration. Washington, D. C., the Dallas-Fort Worth Metroplex, San Diego, Miami, Tampa-St. Petersburg, Denver and San Jose were the areas with the heaviest saturation of convenience stores.

Besides the availability of more room for expansion in the United States, Southland began seriously considering the international potential for convenience stores.

By the end of 1973 the company's international operations consisted of its 50 percent interest in two United Kingdom retail food operations with 1,096 outlets, 75 7-Eleven Stores in three provinces of Canada and four Super-7 Stores in Mexico. And in December 1973 a historic agreement was concluded. The shareholders letter in that year's annual report stated, ''We are extremely pleased that Southland will be participating in the modernization of Japan's retail food distribution system. Agreements were finalized in December for the introduction of the 7-Eleven concept into Japan through an area license granted to Ito-Yokado Co., Ltd., one of that nation's largest and most successful retailers. We are extremely optimistic about the future of this venture.''

7-ELEVEN IN JAPAN

Palmer Waslien, Southland's area license manager, Vaughn Heady, veteran 7-Eleven operations executive, and Dick Turchi, who would later become manager of Southland's International Division, were heavily involved in the formation of the Japanese venture. Heady commented: ''Dick Dole, Dick Turchi and I went to Tokyo in April 1973. We spent about 10 days in Japan analyzing the markets and visiting with the Ito-Yokado organization. We came back with the recommendation that we grant an area license to them. Ito-Yokado operates very successfully in Japan. They operate general merchandise stores in multi-level buildings with a supermarket on the ground floor. They are like a J. C. Penney except with a supermarket thrown in. They are, I believe, the third largest retailer in Japan. We did grant an area license to them in late 1973 and they started building stores. Since then I have made two other trips to Japan, once to assist on selecting store locations, and this year I went to help in advising them on store operations as well as real estate. They are already far ahead of their projections on opening new stores. They opened about 25 7-Eleven Stores in their first year of operation. Frankly, when you get down to it, the stores over there are basically the same as here except that some of the products are different. For instance, they sell a large amount of fresh and dried fish and a lot of fresh produce and fresh meats. The overall potential for convenience stores in Japan is wonderful. The Tokyo metro area has a population of 24 million people. Japan as a whole has over 100 million people in an area of 146,000 square miles. About 85 percent of that area is mountains, so the amount of livable space is limited. There may be as many as 30,000 to 40,000 people living within a half-mile radius of a store. The stores themselves are on busy streets and the 7-Eleven franchise owner usually lives above the store. It makes for a very good arrangement. As far as Ito-Yokado and York-Seven, its subsidiary which operates the 7-Eleven company in Japan, are concerned, we have built up some very fine friendships with them. We trained them over here in all the various aspects of our business. A lot of Southland people have gone to Japan to help train them right in their own country. I think they are very pleased with the relationship. Because of the success of convenience stores in Japan, I think our company is looking for opportunities all over the world.''

1 In 1974 7-Eleven was introduced to Japan. By late 1976, 188 7-Eleven Stores were open for business in Japan.

2,3 A shop owned by a Japanese family, with living quarters on the second floor, was remodeled when the owner became a 7-Eleven franchisee.

4,5 Newly-built 7-Eleven Stores in Japan are similar to their American counterparts.

Dick Turchi added: ''The Japanese program seems to be moving along with great success. Ito-Yokado, our area licensee in Japan, is well-managed and aggressive from the standpoint of development. In June 1976 they opened their 100th store, which is far ahead of schedule. Our posture is to continue counseling and training their people in our 7-Eleven system. We have their top management personnel coming over here on a regular basis and we send our people over there. In Japan the store is a duplicate of the convenience store as we know it in the U. S., including the 7-Eleven sign. We have some free-standing buildings and we have some very small stores that have been remodeled. To give you a little background, one of the most important things in Japan is the land. A piece of land may have been in the same family for generations. Land is very expensive since it is so limited. What this program does is to appeal to the individual who owns some land. Many landowners in Japan have a small retail shop already in operation. When they get together with our licensing company, York-Seven, they are able to secure financing to go in and completely remodel or, in some cases, build a brand-new store. Many times, in fact in most cases, these stores will have living quarters built above them so that the franchise owner can have his home and business at the same location. It seems to make for a very happy franchisee.

''Our program is well received in Japan because it really offers something to the country's small businessman. He is able to learn the newest management skills from a large company yet still remain an individual businessman. So the concept has received many favorable comments, especially from banking institutions. They seem happy to help in developing the system. This is one of the factors that has allowed the rapid growth of our stores in Japan, and now we literally have people lined up to get into the program. This is the reason that we can be optimistic about the 7-Eleven growth rate in Japan.''

2

3

4

5

7-ELEVEN'S AREA LICENSE PROGRAM

The Japanese venture's licensing concept was a refinement of Southland's area license agreement, first introduced in the United States. In 1968 the company granted its initial area license to Garb-Ko, Inc., a Saginaw, Michigan, company. Garb-Ko was given the license to build and operate 7-Eleven Stores in certain northern and central Michigan markets. It opened its first 7-Eleven Store in Saginaw, Michigan, on July 11, 1969, the 42nd anniversary of Southland's birth. In the news release announcing the opening Guy Garber, Jr., president of Garb-Ko, said, "This is the first of more than 50 7-Eleven Stores we plan to open in central and northern Michigan areas during the next five years. We have two stores just about ready for opening in Flint and by the end of the year we will open four additional stores there. We plan seven more stores in Saginaw and we will open other stores in Grand Rapids, Muskegon, Port Huron, Bay City and Midland and other areas." Garber added that "Southland originated the convenience food store concept and has always been the leader in this field of business. They have the finest and most experienced men in the business in all departments of operations. The name 7-Eleven is well-known from coast to coast and we feel especially fortunate to be the first business firm to be granted an area franchise by Southland."

Palmer Waslien, formerly Southland's training manager, was now directing Southland's expansion into this form of franchising. He explained the reasons for the company's interest in area franchising and licensing: "About 1967 I was put in charge of franchising and had to give up some of the other things that I was doing in the training area. Most of my time was spent helping our 7-Eleven field people explain the franchise program. One day I attended a managers' meeting where Mr. Hartfelder spoke about the importance of increasing our net return on sales. He thought that even though our profits were good, especially for a food chain, we should work toward a larger percentage of net on the bottom line. I had an idea at the time, and I went back to my office and started working on a plan that would generate income for the company without the profits having to come from sales. If we could add to our net profit in a way that wouldn't be a function of sales, then we would achieve a larger bottom line figure and we would have a bigger percentage of net against recordable sales. So, in that framework I designed what we now call our area license program. I don't know that Mr. Hartfelder knows it, but that's how it came about. It just so happened that the very day after I presented the program to John Thompson, Jere Thompson and Herb Hartfelder, I got a telephone call from Saginaw, Michigan. These people said that they had just visited some 7-Eleven Stores in Florida and wondered if there was any help that we might give them in starting up a business in northern Michigan. I said, 'By the way, I have something in my briefcase, and I will be up tomorrow.' After a short period of negotiation we ended up with our first area franchisee in Saginaw, and we expanded from that. The whole idea of the program is to bring in royalties in exchange for our help, system and name so as to generate more profit for the company without the function of sales. Of course another very, very important benefit is that it allows us to expand the 7-Eleven

 At the end of 1976, area licensees operated or franchised
7-Eleven Stores in parts of 16
states and overseas in Japan
and Australia.

The first 7-Eleven area license
agreement was signed in
1968 with Garb-Ko, Inc. Left to
right are Devere Kostoff,
Guy Garber, Jr., and Richard
Kostoff, representing Garb-
Ko, and Jere W. Thompson and
Palmer Waslien of South-
land.

name in areas where we might not be planning to develop ourselves for some time."

By the end of 1976 Southland area licensees encompassed the following areas: Garb-Ko, Inc., northern Michigan; Lar-Lin, Inc., the Rio Grande Valley of South Texas; SBR, Inc., West Virginia and areas of Kentucky and Ohio; Contemporary Industries, part of Nebraska and western Iowa; Wymodak, Inc., Wyoming, Montana, North Dakota, South Dakota and part of Nebraska; Mako, Inc., eastern Oklahoma, southern Kansas, southwestern Missouri and northwestern Arkansas; Handee Marts, Inc., southwestern Pennsylvania; and Steveco, Inc., various counties in Kentucky and Indiana. Total area licensed 7-Eleven Stores, including Japan, numbered more than 350.

1973: ANOTHER SUCCESSFUL YEAR

Meanwhile, in 1973 the company neared the 5,000th 7-Eleven Store by concluding "the most successful and exciting year in your company's 46-year history," according to the annual shareholders letter. The letter, which for some years had borne the signatures of John P. Thompson and H. E. Hartfelder, gained a new signee in '73. On December 31, 1973, Southland's board of directors elected its first vice chairman and a new president. Hartfelder moved up to the post of vice chairman of the board and Jere W. Thompson became the fifth president in Southland's history, following Claude Dawley, Jodie Thompson, John Thompson and Herb Hartfelder. Two other vice presidents were assigned separate operational responsibilities for company-operated and franchised convenience stores. Vaughn Heady was named to head the company-operated stores and Dick Dole, a veteran of the original Speedee Mart operation, was chosen to oversee 7-Eleven's franchised stores.

The year also was remarkable in several other areas. For one, Southland and the entire country were both still struggling with various economic uncertainties, including unprecedented inflation, rapidly changing government stablization programs—including limits on retail prices and profit margins—and higher costs, including government-imposed increases. Despite these handicaps, revenues and earnings increases again reached all-time highs. From the preceding year revenues increased 13.7 percent to $1.396 billion and net earnings soared to $23.3 million, a 14.5 percent gain.

Gasoline, although comprising less than two percent of Southland's corporate revenues, was the most publicized national shortage of 1973. Nevertheless, sales and profits of 7-Eleven's self-service gas installations were up substantially during the year and another gain was anticipated in 1974.

Accentuating its basic confidence in the future, Southland's capital expenditures during 1973 were $78.6 million, the largest single-year investment ever. Of that total $66 million was invested in 7-Eleven store expansion and the new convenience store distribution system, while $12.6 million was devoted to dairy plant modernization and automation programs and the expansion and improvement of various other operations. The innovative distribution center

On December 31, 1973 Jere W. Thompson was named the fifth president of The Southland Corporation.

concept was further strengthened in 1973 with the addition of the second and third SDC in Tyler, Texas, and Fredericksburg, Virginia, respectively. The three distribution centers, located in Orlando, Tyler, and Fredericksburg, were providing 52 percent of the 7-Eleven Stores with about half of their merchandise by the end of the year. In other capital improvements, the building program to enlarge and modernize the Dallas corporate office was completed and the company soon began realizing the efficiencies of centralizing the corporate staff in one location.

In 1973 Southland opened 426 new convenience stores while closing 80. This boosted the operating total to 4,801 at year-end. As of December 31, 1973, Southland retail stores numbered 5,041 with 240 units under construction.

THREE MILLION CUSTOMERS A DAY

Customers were now shopping 7-Eleven Stores at the rate of 600 per store per day. The customer count for the little stores was reaching just about three million on a daily average. These shoppers were spending an average of three and one-half minutes in the store and their typical purchase was slightly over $1. More than two-thirds of 7-Eleven customers were male, indicating a decided preference for convenience by the male shopper. In 1973 more than 40 percent of the customers were between the ages of 21 and 35 while 35 percent were children or teenagers. An additional 18 percent were between 36 and 50 years of age and the remaining seven percent were past 50. Although the general merchandise classification of groceries was still the most popular single category, with 18.2 percent of total sales, other specific product groups more truly reflected the 7-Eleven convenience appeal. Tobacco products, at 15.8 percent, beer/wine at 13.6 percent, non-food items at 11.4 percent, dairy products at 11.3 percent and soft drinks at 10.8 percent were the most popular merchandise in 7-Eleven Stores. These figures, compiled for Southland by its own in-house research staff, gave the company an excellent insight into the most important public—the customer.

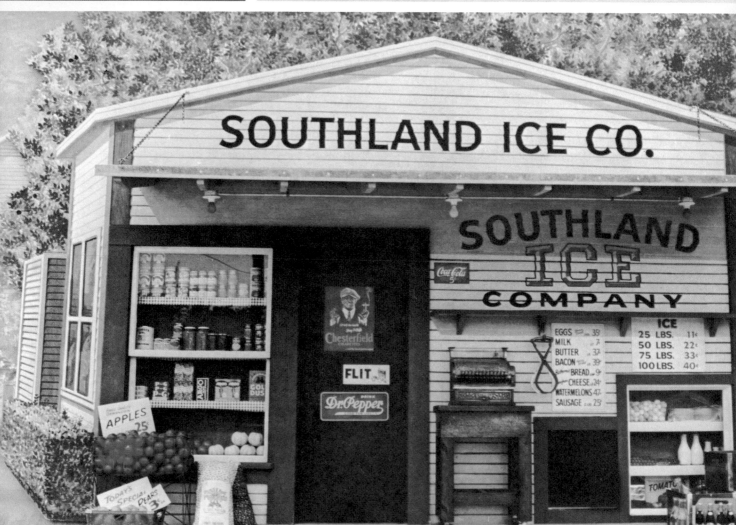

*August 1974—The 5,000th 7-Eleven Store and a replica of
the first Southland Ice store, built especially for the occasion.*

CHAPTER

29

On Friday, August 9, 1974, a large contingent of Southland corporate officials and guests gathered at 8440 Park Lane in Dallas to celebrate the opening of the company's 5,000th 7-Eleven Store. Jodie Thompson's prediction, made 16 years earlier, had been proven correct far sooner than expected. Because the opening of the first Southland retail outlet had also taken place in Dallas in 1927, the company chose to celebrate the 5,000th store event in a nostalgic and spectacular way. Visitors and guests arrived to find the new storefront entirely concealed by a full-sized replica of the company's Store #1. A Dallas design company had built the carefully researched set especially for the occasion.

As chairman John Thompson completed his welcoming remarks, Dallas mayor Wes Wise arrived in a 1923 Cadillac convertible touring car. After Wise's brief speech, during which he commended Southland as being a "good corporate citizen," he accepted the first of a limited series of commemorative 5,000th store medallions "on behalf of the City Council and the citizens of Dallas." Then the replica of old Store #1 was rolled aside, revealing the new 5,000th store. An elaborate set had been prepared from a black-and-white photograph of the original store and was rendered in color. It exhibited great authenticity—from the picturesque white frame homes in the background to the painstakingly acquired or specially constructed props displayed in the windows and in front of the store. The prices of items featured at the first Southland Ice store were researched from 1927 newspaper files. Among the bargains available in that boom year were non-homogenized milk at seven cents a quart, Longhorn cheese (wrapped in cheesecloth) at 24 cents a pound, two pounds of sausage for a quarter and bread at 9 cents a loaf. Ice was offered at 11 cents per 25 pounds (or a saving of a penny per 25 pounds for a 100-pound block).

The opening of the 5,000th store was attended by all three of Jodie Thompson's sons, all now active in the company's management. Besides John and Jere Thompson, Joe C. Thompson, Jr. (who was christened Joe C. Thompson III, but after his father's death changed his name) was now serving as manager of 7-Eleven's Central Region, comprised of several store divisions located in the southern, southwestern and Rocky Mountain areas of the country. But, although the 5,000th store ceremonies had attracted widespread interest among company officials and employees and local Dallas civic leaders, as well as within the convenience store industry, there was a noticeable lack of outside news media interest in the historic event. For at 11 A.M. central daylight time on August 9, 1974, as the replica of old Store #1 was being rolled aside to reveal the 5,000th 7-Eleven Store, another important ceremony was occurring in Washington, D. C. Gerald R. Ford was being sworn in as the 38th President of the United States.

MANAGING A 7-ELEVEN STORE

As the physical appearance of the stores had changed drastically from old #1 to the 5,000th, so also had the duties and outlook of the individual 7-Eleven store manager altered over the years. A long-time store manager, Lewis Tucker of Dallas, reflected on these differences: "I have been with 7-Eleven now just over 25 years, starting in 1951. I've been a store manager for 24 years, including 18 years at my store at Hillcrest and Northwest Highway. It was one of our best stores then and is still a very good store. I must say that it is a lot easier being a store manager today than it was 10 or 20 years ago. Back in the old days we had to grind our own ice for our customers and for the produce and cold drink boxes. We also gave curb service, so we did a lot more walking and running. We had stalks of bananas hanging outside the store that we had to carry out in the early morning and back in at night when we closed. We definitely have less bookkeeping today than we used to have. Then it would take at least two hours every day just to do your bookkeeping. Also, back then it was not unusual to work seven days a week, with no day off and no vacation. I get four weeks vacation now and really enjoy it. We have better help now, too. My assistant manager, Will Parker, and I have worked together for 20 years. It is a real advantage to have someone like that who can take over when you are not here. I have a real good overall crew, too, and consider myself very fortunate in that respect. The merchandise we carry hasn't really changed much over the years except for the variety in the selection. When I first came with the company we had only one selection for cold drinks, the six-ounce bottle. Now we have a dozen different sizes. I have been real lucky as far as customers are concerned. Mine have always been pretty easy to get along with. In fact, I have 'raised' most of the kids out here. Now if they live out of town they will bring their kids by to see me when they come back for a visit. It sure makes me feel good. Of course July 4 and Labor Day are still our biggest single days and we also still close on Christmas Day, the only day of the year that we are not open. One year I came down on Christmas morning just to check my motors, to see that everything was okay. Two young boys followed me in the store and wanted two Icees. I just couldn't refuse to serve them, even though we were closed, so I gave them the Icees. In the old days when we didn't have air-conditioning it could get as hot as 120 degrees inside the store on some summer days. The customers wouldn't tarry long then. I think the air-conditioning definitely helps sales because the customer will stay longer and look around the store more. Back several years ago it took you a long time just to open up. You had to lift all the overhead doors, put all of the merchandise outside and so forth. Now that we're open 24 hours the store stays a lot cleaner. I have had customers ask me how we can keep it so clean, and I tell them that being open 24 hours we have to stay on it.''

With the opening of the 5,000th store successfully completed, Southland began to concentrate on the next major milestone—$2 billion in total revenues. During 1974 and 1975 progress toward this goal continued without interruption. Revenues climbed to $1.613 billion in '74 and $1.789 billion in '75. Net earnings in these years were $29.7 million and $34.3 million, respectively.

The number of 7-Eleven Stores continued to mount with a net increase of 778 stores during this two-year period. On December 31, 1975, there were 5,579 7-Eleven Stores in operation, including 3,391 company-operated and 2,188 franchised, in 39 states, the District of Columbia and Canada.

7-Eleven now could—and did—boast of serving more than one billion customers each year. In the company's 1974 annual report (judged best in the retail food industry by *Financial World* magazine) Southland graphically illustrated just who its customers were, how old they were, when they shopped and what they purchased:

PERCENT CONVENIENCE STORE SALES (BY PRINCIPAL PRODUCT CATEGORY)

	1970	1971	1972	1973	**1974**
Groceries	18.7%	17.9%	18.2%	18.2%	**17.1%**
Tobacco Products	13.7	14.0	15.6	15.8	**15.7**
Beer/Wine	11.9	12.6	13.5	13.6	**14.1**
Non-Foods	11.7	11.3	10.7	11.4	**12.0**
Soft Drinks	11.2	11.2	11.2	10.8	**11.6**
Dairy Products	13.2	13.4	11.8	11.3	**10.5**
Baked Goods	5.8	6.1	6.0	5.9	**5.9**
Candy	5.0	4.9	4.9	4.8	**5.3**
Health/Beauty Aids	6.9	6.5	5.6	4.9	**4.0**
Other Food Items	1.9	2.1	2.5	3.3	**3.8**
TOTAL	100.0%	100.0%	100.0%	100.0%	**100.0%**

The report also profiled the typical 7-Eleven customer:

WHO?

685,000,000 male customers
315,000,000 female customers

HOW OLD?

8.8% under 12
16.4% 12–17
32.0% 18–24
21.0% 25–34
14.8% 35–49
7.0% 50 and over

WHEN?

71.4% on weekdays
28.6% on weekends

19.1%— 7:00 AM to 11:00 AM
21.6%—11:00 AM to 3:00 PM
24.9%— 3:00 PM to 7:00 PM
26.1%— 7:00 PM to 11:00 PM
5.7%—11:00 PM to 3:00 AM
2.6%— 3:00 AM to 7:00 AM

The typical 7-Eleven customer.

Male
Under 35 years
Married
Two Children
Lives less than 1 mile
from 7-ELEVEN
Earns more than $10,000
a year
Shops in 7-ELEVEN 6.1
times per month
Spends $6.16 per month
at 7-ELEVEN
Is in store 3½ minutes
per trip

7-ELEVEN'S MERCHANDISING PHILOSOPHY

The ability to know its customers and their needs continued to be a major factor in the company's success. Much of the responsibility for following Jodie Thompson's philosophy to ''give the customer what he wants, where he wants it and when he wants it'' lies with Southland's corporate merchandising department. Bob Gallana, the firm's merchandising manager, explained the current Southland marketing philosophy: ''First of all, our merchandising concept is exactly today like it was when Mr. Thompson designed the store theory years ago. Of course some important things have occurred recently that have helped our merchandising program. The first improvement would have to be in our product movement analysis. Now we know the movement by major category on every item in our stores. In our Southland Distribution Centers we have the movement analysis by item by store, which is an even further breakdown of category. When I speak of category, I mean milk, bread, Slurpee, candy, fast foods, etc. Our Canada Division went on the system April 1, 1976, so that now every 7-Eleven Store we operate, with the exception of a few stores in Mexico, is on it. We can also compare results by 7-Eleven divisions, and this has been a tremendous help to us. To my knowledge, no other convenience store company has this system. Another plus factor for us has been our store design. We are now building and merchandising our stores nationwide in almost exactly the same way. The locations of the vaults and sales counters are now consistent throughout the country. Overall our 7-Eleven Stores have taken on a more standardized appearance. Prior to this recent development each division had the option to build whatever design it wanted, and this was happening quite often. There was no similarity between stores, so we had no way to research whether we were merchandising properly or even building our stores correctly. We are now remerchandising about 10 percent of our stores per year to conform. Our basic merchandising plan is to continue selling all the things we have always sold (and improve on those) while integrating a Hot-to-Go fast foods department, which is becoming a fast growing area for us. Fast foods are both fairly new—and fairly old—in our stores. We started selling carry-out hot coffee on the East Coast about 13 years ago. Only recently has it expanded to every division in Southland. We have really just begun to work very hard on our sandwich and Hot-to-Go business. Hot-to-Go is a great name for our products. It was created by Bob Peck, a writer for the Stanford Agency. This emphasis on fast foods is causing us to build a somewhat more expensive store because the various health departments require additional stainless steel sinks, counters, better floors, walls, etc. Even though our buildings are more expensive, the return on the investment is good. We do not include soft drink sales in our fast food movement, but we do know that half of our volume is in single units. Increases in that category obviously could be attributed to our sandwich and Hot-to-Go items. If someone comes in the store and buys a sandwich, he usually buys something to drink with it. Overall, I think the merchandising possibilities for 7-Eleven are unlimited. We are beginning to strengthen our merchandising out in the various 7-Eleven divisions, and we have all strong people there. Many of our ideas are triggered from the divisions, either when they ask us for help on a problem or when they suggest products that they want us to develop for them. One of the most important things that will be a major product this year and in the future is 7-Eleven self-service gasoline. We now have over 1,250 gasoline installations in operation with more planned for the future. We plan to push gasoline hard because this is really a new service at our stores. By the way, one of the best things that the product movement analysis has brought to us is an accurate customer count. For example, the daily customer count on one particular day in June 1976 was 4,403,258. That's nearly four and a half million customers who came through the doors of our 7-Eleven Stores on that day. I guess we must be living up to what Mr. Thompson had in mind about 'serving the customers what they want and when they want it.' But I must say that we are still looking for new product possibilities and better ways to serve every day."

A CHANGING PRODUCT MIX

Without question 7-Eleven's merchandising mix had evolved considerably throughout the history of the little store. Products came and went, succeeded and failed. Some, such as ice, came, went and then returned again in a modernistic form. In the late 1950s TV tube testing machines could be found in almost every store. In the 1970s they were nowhere to be seen. The original Slurpee paper cups introduced in the mid-1960s gave way less than 10 years later to slick promotional plastic Slurpee cups featuring sports stars, comic characters and rock and roll performers. Ice-cold watermelon, once one of the Texas stores' favorite summer items, is another product which has virtually disappeared. Shotgun shells, another popular item of the '50s, were practically discontinued in the '70s. And of course private label products, Hot-to-Go fast foods, hand-dipped ice cream, fountain soft drinks and other new merchandising performers had been literally unimagined in decades past. The standard old performers such as the dairy products and soft drinks remained basically unchanged, just undergoing minor refinements, occasional product improvement and usually several major packaging changes over a period of years.

hot to go

Hot-to-Go, 7-Eleven's fast food program, serves customers with little time to spare.

W hile merchandising continued its winning formula with the typical 7-Eleven customer, another operational situation was demanding attention. It was a simple consideration but absolutely critical to the success of any organization with a substantial number of retail outlets. In 7-Eleven's case it was simply: "How do you effectively control more than 5,000 individual stores?"

KEEPING AN EYE ON THE STORE

An article in the *SLC News,* a special company publication prepared for Southland's April 29, 1976, appearance before the New York Society of Security Analysts, attempted to answer that basic question. Headlined "Keeping an Eye on the Store," it explained:

"When Joe C. Thompson, Southland's founder, opened the first convenience store, he learned that to stay abreast of the business he had to know what was happening in each store every day. He continued to visit the stores on a regular basis until his death in 1961.

"Keeping an eye on the store is still the number one priority of Southland's management team and the company's financial reporting system. Developed to keep pace with the rapid growth that started in the 1960s, this management structure is capable of staffing, merchandising, servicing and controlling 5,600 7-Eleven Stores with the flexibility to handle future expansion.

" 'We've never forgotten that we are in a nickel and dime business,' said Eugene Pender, Southland's corporate controller. 'Because we know how important it is to really know what's going on in each store, we've developed a relatively simple financial reporting concept that, with the help of sophisticated technology, gives us the ability to know daily what any given store is doing.'

"The system starts with the district, the basic unit of 7-Eleven's organizational structure. A district's geographical area can vary in size, depending on the concentration of stores, with an average of 32 stores per district (in April 1976, 7-Eleven operations are divided into four regions, 17 divisions, 54 zones and 198 districts).

"In 1969, Southland initiated a program to develop a computerized financial reporting system designed specifically for a convenience store operation. 'It is based on the manual accounting system which we have developed through the years,' said Pender, 'and continually refined to its present high level of sophistication, providing a much broader spectrum of information both daily and monthly.' A sending and receiving terminal, linked to the data processing center in Dallas, is located in each district office. Every morning, the district manager has a complete up-to-date record of sales, cost of sales, gross margins, retail inventory and other information for each store in the district.

"After the end of the month, within five or less working days (compared to 20 days when produced manually) monthly reports are available to the district, zone, division and regional offices. Included in the reports provided are a profit and loss statement for each store, as well as an operating exception report, and trend and comparison reports analyzing the most important aspects of the operation. 'One of the beauties of the system is that a person can be trained to use the computer terminals in a very short period of time,' Pender said.

"The key link in the flow of information from stores to district office is the supervisor (or field representative in franchise areas), the first level of management in 7-Eleven. There are generally four supervisors to a district, and each has the day-to-day responsibility for about eight stores. Among a supervisor's duties (in addition to counseling store operators, assisting in training employees and general trouble-shooting) is collecting daily reports which summarize the day's happenings—sales, purchases, etc. to take to the district office."

THE 7-ELEVEN SUPERVISOR AND FIELD REP

The recognition of the supervisor as the key link in 7-Eleven management had begun many years before. At the second annual convention of The Southland Corporation in 1959 Jodie Thompson had surprised everyone in attendance by including a sealed pamphlet in the convention brochure. He asked that no one open it until he gave the word to do so. Later, in the middle of his speech he paused and asked everyone in the audience to open the seals. The pamphlet, when opened and unfolded, displayed two organizational charts of Southland management. The first chart featured president Joe C. Thompson at the top and 7-Eleven supervisors listed at the bottom. Thompson told the audience, "This is supposedly where the top men are." He then called their attention to the second chart, where the supervisors were now shown at the top and the executives at the bottom, and said emphatically, "This is where the real top men are."

By the mid-1970s 7-Eleven supervisors (company-operated stores) and field representatives (company franchised stores) numbered more than 700 and included many top men—and women. A survey of Southland executives showed that most of the top management had served at one time or another in the supervisor/field representative position. And their comments indicated their appreciation of the importance of the job:

Vaughn Heady, vice president, company-operated stores: "Southland built its business on convenience—but it has made its profits through good supervision and tight control. Supervisory work is the first place where the job must be done correctly. Everything starts there."

Forrest Stout, vice president, Southern Stores Region: "Getting to be a supervisor was the best thing that ever happened to me at the time. It was my first job in management. Today I'm doing some of the same things I did when I was a supervisor. In that job I picked up the basic ingredients of management knowledge."

S. R. (Dick) Dole, vice president, company franchised stores: "The field representative is the *second* most important member of our team. The most important person, of course, is the person who makes the 'bells ring,' the

7-Eleven supervisors (company-owned stores) and field representatives (franchised stores) are key management links in the organization.

franchisee or store manager who actually operates the store and takes care of our customers. The field representative is our eyes and ears in the field, the most important link between our owners and local management. His ability to select qualified franchise owners is our profit key to the present and well-trained, aggressive field representatives are our profit keys to the future. Virtually all management, from the district managers to the chairman of the board of Southland, have been field representatives or supervisors at one time in their career. This experience is invaluable to future personal growth and promotion. Our field representatives and supervisors are truly the key element in the future growth of our company."

Ray Berry, 7-Eleven Western Region manager: "The field representative has a more complicated job today, even though many of the duties are the same as they were years ago. The field rep was more involved with physical labor in the past. Now the job is more mentally demanding and more sophisticated. Due to our broad base, Southland is expanding quickly and the opportunities for advancement become greater every day. Some of the men who may be division managers five years from now may not have been hired yet."

How do the supervisors/field representatives themselves view their role in the company's management structure? Ken Peters, Larry Jasinski and John Banker are field representatives in the company franchised Las Vegas Zone. They said: *Larry Jasinski:* "There is no real routine to our job. Every day is different. I feel that I have a lot more responsibility now at my age than I would have with any other company. I don't particularly like the late night phone calls that I get sometimes, but that is part of the job. It is challenging." *Ken Peters:* "The franchise owners in one district will sometimes be entirely different from those in another district. Being a field representative is the best place to get a lot of good experience working with all types of business situations. You are operating where the action is, where the money is made. We represent the company to the owners and the owners to the company. If we didn't feel that we have the opportunity to advance, we wouldn't be here. The company is always getting into new fields. For instance, now we even have a gasoline division." *John Banker:* "I like working with the franchise store owners. I feel they are hard workers since they have their own businesses. It is difficult to say what makes one franchise owner better than another. When you interview a prospective owner, it sometimes is hard to tell what he will really be like when he gets out to the store. We are always trying to isolate what makes a good owner. I know that one thing that helps any owner to succeed is a good field representative."

7-Eleven Stores from east to west, from north to south.

Save A Living Thing

The successful 7-Eleven campaign which involved employees, franchisees and customers and resulted in a refuge for the American Bald Eagle.

A s Southland's growth continued, a few problem areas existed. Certainly no business organization can operate indefinitely without encountering some troublesome situations.

Probably the most nagging problem facing Southland was the heavy personnel turnover in the 7-Eleven Stores. Some industry watchers have advanced the idea that high employee turnover is a natural phenomenon experienced by this particular type of retail store. Others have stated that many convenience store workers are younger people who regard the job as a stopgap while attending school or waiting for another position to open up. Whatever the reason, the turnover of store clerks in the 7-Eleven Stores continued to create concern among Southland management. To help slow the rate of this turnover the company began reinforcing its commitment to proper hiring policies which, hopefully, would reduce the number of unqualified employees who might slip through the screening process. Another area receiving a renewed emphasis was training, which always has been a source of major concern and concentrated effort. But, although every method was being explored to decrease the number of workers who pass through the company's employment rolls each year, employee turnover remained a worrisome area.

Another more recently emerging problem was the rising incidence of robbery and violence occurring in all retail establishments, including convenience stores. During the late 1960s the number of armed robberies in small retail outlets, such as liquor stores, dry cleaners, gasoline stations and convenience stores, began to increase dramatically. The general upswing in criminality manifested itself in a startling gain in "stranger-to-stranger" crimes such as armed robbery.

SOUTHLAND FORMS CRIME COMMITTEE

Faced with a substantial increase in the number of armed robberies in 1975, Southland took action. In early 1976 under the chairmanship of company franchised stores vice president Dick Dole, the company organized a crime prevention committee. The members included Dole; Vaughn Heady, company-operated stores vice president; Joe C. Thompson, Jr., Central Region manager; Seth Burgess, corporate security manager; Mark Rigg, operations manager for the personnel department; Clark Matthews II, vice president and general counsel; W. K. Ruppenkamp, vice president, financial relations; Bob Gallana, corporate merchandising manager; Lew Maddox, training manager; and Allen Liles, public relations manager. The simple purpose of the anti-crime committee was to find a way to reduce the amount of robberies and violent crime which were adversely affecting the company's 7-Eleven operations. One of the first projects launched by the committee was to join with a social science research team from the Western Behavioral Sciences Institute (WBSI) of LaJolla, California, in conducting a robbery deterrent experiment in Houston, Texas. A similar anti-robbery test completed during the prior year in Southern California had resulted in a 30 percent reduction in robberies in 60 test stores. The follow-up experiment in Houston was seen by the crime committee as a prelude, if successful, to introduction of the concept to all 7-Eleven store divisions. The basic thrust of the special program centered around preventive techniques that could be utilized by store personnel to prevent a robbery from ever occurring. The new techniques also involved surveying the physical layout of each store, including its overall accessibility to potential robbers and the visibility of the store interior. The project, introduced in Houston in April 1976, was judged a moderate success after a few months of observation. In late fall of that year the strongest elements of the Houston program were introduced in 7-Eleven store divisions across the United States and Canada. Meanwhile Southland's anti-crime group continued its efforts to reduce the potential dangers to customers and employees by considering and testing other various approaches to the problem. In mid-1976 the robbery trend seemed to have begun a noticeable decline from its previous high rate. Still, store robberies remain worrisome and of concern to Southland officials.

Another relatively negative development which in part could be traced to the robbery problem was the attitude in some isolated communities toward convenience-type operations. A few zoning commissions and other civic bodies occasionally encountered strong organized opposition to the construction of 7-Eleven Stores. These objections usually involved complaints about noise and the fear that the stores' presence might encourage criminal activities. Although the number of situations such as these remained small, Southland reacted with a commitment reaffirming its dedication to each community in which it operates.

SOUTHLAND AND COMMUNITY RELATIONS

To that end the company had begun placing heavy emphasis on a structured community relations program. With small stores located in approximately 6,000 individual neighborhoods, 7-Eleven naturally found itself in the midst of many community activities. Therefore Southland decided to accept the responsibility of being "the neighborhood store" in a manner that would be meaningful to the company and its communities. In 1974 Southland joined with the prestigious National Wildlife Federation to raise funds for the purchase and development of raw land which would be designated as the nation's first refuge for the American bald eagle. Through donations from the sale of 20 million special "Endangered Species" plastic Slurpee cups, the company was able to raise $200,000 to buy more than 1,200 acres of eagle nesting ground in South Dakota. An additional $38,000 was collected for the wildlife organization through special canisters placed in all 7-Eleven Stores. This extra money was designated by the National Wildlife Federation for a continuing research program aimed at saving the eagle, America's national symbol.

In other programs during 1975 many of the 7-Eleven divisions served as collection points for the United States Marine Corps' annual "Toys For Tots" effort. Over one million toys were deposited at 7-Eleven Stores for distribution to needy children. Also in 1975 7-Eleven agreed to lend its support to "Operation Peace of Mind," a program of assistance to runaway children and their parents. Texas Governor Dolph Briscoe had established a Houston-based runaway center which could be reached by telephone from anywhere in the United States. Runaways could telephone the center and leave messages for their parents or be referred to locations where they could find shelter, food and first aid. 7-Eleven Stores offered to assist the program by posting on their front windows colorful decals which encouraged the runaways to use a special toll-free number prominently displayed on the decal. In addition the company distributed news and public service announcements about the runaway hotline to news media throughout the country.

1 Many 7-Eleven Stores served as collection points for the U. S. Marine Corps' "Toys for Tots" program. In 1975 over one million toys were deposited at the stores for distribution to needy children. The U.S.M.C. band, pictured, kicked off the 1975 program in Chicago.

2 7-Eleven Stores across the country display a toll-free telephone number for runaways in cooperation with the "Operation Peace of Mind" program.

3 In 1974 Southland presented $200,000 to the National Wildlife Federation to purchase land for a refuge for the American bald eagle. The funds were raised through sales of special Slurpees in "Endangered Species" plastic cups.

1

2

3

1

THE JERRY LEWIS TELETHON

In 1976 Southland made its most important community service commitment yet in terms of actual dollars. The company announced that it would support the 1976 Jerry Lewis Labor Day Telethon with a special campaign designed to raise in excess of $1 million for the Muscular Dystrophy Association. 7-Eleven generated funds for the telethon from several sources, including a donation of 10 cents for each special 24-ounce Jerry Lewis Slurpee sold during the month of August, another dime from the sale of every Hot-to-Go sandwich purchased from August 1 through midnight on Labor Day, September 6, and a 10 cent donation for every large cup of hot coffee sold during the eight-hour period from 11 P.M. September 5 until 7 A.M. on Labor Day. The stores encouraged their millions of daily customers to support the telethon through a campaign to "Let Jerry Lewis Keep The Change For His Kids" by placing the change received from their purchases in a special canister located on the store counter. 7-Eleven also urged its customers to participate in the

244

1 The Stanford Agency's highly successful fund-raising campaign for the Muscular Dystrophy Association featured Jerry Lewis singing 7-Eleven's theme song, "Keep the Change."

2 1976 Jerry Lewis Labor Day Telethon—Southland employees, franchisees, customers, and suppliers raised $3,092,755 for MDA. John Thompson and Jere Thompson appeared on the Telethon to announce the latest contribution totals.

2

fund-raising activities by providing more than one million collection canisters nationally which could be used by individuals to seek contributions from their respective neighborhoods. Many local 7-Eleven areas also staged numerous events to raise additional funds for the telethon. The result: The Southland Corporation raised $3,092,755 for Jerry Lewis and "his kids" in one of the single most successful fund-raising campaigns in memory. A special song, "Keep The Change," with music composed by Larry Muhoberac, noted composer, arranger and long-time associate of Bob Stanford, was sung by Lewis on the telethon. The words, written by Lewis himself and Stanford copywriter Mark James, said, "Can I have your love/ May I hope you hope/ And share my prayer/ And could you arrange/ To let me keep the change for my kids?/ Oh thank heaven is the song I sing/ I shout it to the sky above/ Oh thank heaven for 7-Eleven/ And our Labor Day of love/ And could you arrange/ To let me keep the change for my kids?"

The new Embassy Dairies milk plant in Waldorf, Maryland—opened in August 1975 as the world's most modern dairy facility.

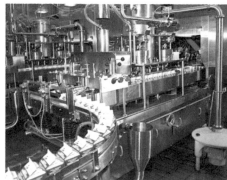

W ith the first $2 billion sales year forecast for 1976, Southland kept its forward thrust in the mid-'70s. Capital expenditures continued strong with $64.5 million committed in 1974 and $71.8 million invested in 1975. This vote of confidence in the convenience store business was especially reflected in the latter year when 566 new 7-Eleven Stores were opened for business, the largest number added in any single year.

SOUTHLAND ADDS DAIRY FACILITIES

Most of Southland's other interests besides 7-Eleven also were growing and prospering. The dairy operations continued to develop, highlighted by the construction of the new Embassy Dairies milk plant in Waldorf, Maryland. This dairy facility, acknowledged to be the most modern in the world, serves Southland's dairy customers throughout the Maryland, Virginia and Washington, D. C., areas. Opened in August 1975, the new Embassy plant features the capacity to process 100,000 gallons of milk in a scheduled work day or 50,000 gallons in an eight-hour shift. The Embassy plant also boasts four separate systems, unique to the industry, which control the entire operation electronically from receipt of raw milk through processing, order-filling and truck load-out. Dairy industry sources hailed the new Embassy plant as the dairy of the future.

Other new Southland dairy properties were added to the growing roster in the '70s when Horten's in the Cleveland market and Bluffview Farms in Dallas joined the Dairies Group through acquisition. In 1975 the Southland Dairies Group's sales and profits reached all-time highs. Sales to outside customers increased 13.3 percent from the preceding year to $208.1 million and accounted for 12 percent of corporate revenues. Total sales rose 10.3 percent to $297.7 million, including intracompany sales of $89.6 million which were not included in company revenues. In 1975 Southland dairies served 3,972 of its convenience stores and supplied 68 percent of the dairy products sold in all 7-Eleven Stores.

Another important part of the Dairies Group was the Specialty Foods Division, managed by C. W. Cochran, a veteran Southland dairy executive. The Specialty Foods Division processed products such as private label fruit juices, dips, eggnog, toppings, yogurt and ultra-pasteurized creams. The division also produced sandwich ingredients for the 7-Eleven Hot-to-Go fast foods program and a variety of Farm Field meat, vegetable and fruit salads. The Packaging Division, now structured as a part of Specialty Foods, manufactured gallon and half-gallon plastic milk containers for three Southland dairies and other customers throughout the Southwest. Expansion, automation and modernization of the company's dairy facilities were scheduled to continue throughout 1976, including a major enlargement of Velda Farms in Miami. In addition Bancroft Dairies in Madison, Wisconsin, was enlarged and its production capacity increased for processing ultra-pasteurized creams and other specialized products.

SPECIAL OPERATIONS GROWS

Southland's Special Operations Group was another interesting area of the company demonstrating solid growth. In 1975 sales of Southland's diversified operations increased 15.6 percent to $26.8 million and represented one percent of Southland's revenues. The Special Operations

Group included Chemical Division, managed by Ronald Goodnight; the Food Centers, directed by Al Boter; Hudgins Truck Rental, led by Don Hudgins; and Reddy Ice, with Paul Reed as its division manager. The Barricini manufacturing and retail operations were sold in 1976, thus ending what was a limited involvement in this type of business.

In 1975 the three Southland Distribution Centers provided 3,184 7-Eleven Stores with about 50 percent of their merchandise from a selection of approximately 2,300 items. Sales of the three distribution centers, which were not included in Southland's revenues, exceeded $225 million in '75, a gain of 14.3 percent over the prior year. The centers attained an average order fill rate of 99 percent with an average inventory turnover of 29 times.

THE PRODUCTIVE SEVENTIES

All in all the first six years of the '70s, from 1970 through 1975, had been extremely productive in terms of continued growth and development. The company had experienced an especially rewarding year in 1975 which was hindered by an unsettled business environment plagued with widespread unemployment, uncontrolled inflation and the most severe recession in a generation. The ability of Southland to withstand the negative pressure of these external forces was extraordinary. The company results, won under the worst of economic conditions, were credited to a strong financial position, geographic spread and diversity of operations, a strong marketing orientation and flexible management. For example, when it became apparent in 1974 that potentially dangerous economic conditions were developing, strong measures were adopted to improve product mix, tighten cost controls and expand profit margins. This "hardnosed" stance by management, unusual in a growth-oriented company, allowed Southland to endure the 1974–1975 recession with no reversal of its record of continuing highs in total revenues and net earnings. The company was tested in the recession and the results were heartening.

Another cheering note was the number of communities being entered by 7-Eleven for the first time. In 1975 7-Eleven was introduced in 153 cities and townships in the United States and Canada. The list included both those established areas bypassed during past expansions and other new, promising communities just now developing. Entered were such diverse markets as San Antonio, Texas; New Orleans, Louisiana; Saskatoon, Saskatchewan; Pismo Beach, California; South Bend, Indiana; and Cape Cod, Massachusetts. This exceptional volume of new market penetration indicated that 7-Eleven was far from reaching its saturation limit.

Probably the most significant change occurring in the '70 to '75 period was a dramatic commitment to the concept of 24-hour stores. As late as 1972 there were only 817 all-night 7-Eleven Stores in operation. By the end of '75 there were 3,703 stores open 24 hours. Almost 12 percent of the total day's shoppers were visiting the stores between 11 P.M. and 7 A.M. 7-Eleven had truly become "The Little Store That Never Sleeps." With the almost complete swing to 24-hour operations in two-thirds of its outlets, 7-Eleven was offering its customers the ultimate convenience, a store which was *always* open when needed.

The various logos of The Southland Corporation, December 1976.

248

**THE
SOUTHLAND
CORPORATION**

SOUTHLAND INTERNATIONAL		PENDING
STORES	**SPECIAL OPERATIONS**	**DAIRIES**
7 ELEVEN ®	CHEMICAL DIVISION THE SOUTHLAND CORPORATION	®
GRISTEDE'S ® PENDING	SOUTHLAND FOOD CENTERS	Cabell's ®
Charles & Co. PURVEYORS OF FINE FOODS	Hudgins TRUCK RENTAL {S} DIVISION OF THE SOUTHLAND CORPORATION	Specialty Foods
R S McColl Limited	Reddy Ice ®	
	southland distribution center	

CHAPTER
34

As Southland neared its 50th year an improving national economy in 1976 provided an additional stimulus to the company's expansion. By the fall of the year many interesting developments had occurred. A sampling included:

1976 SOUTHLAND DEVELOPMENTS

• The company purchased 183 retail gasoline locations from The Oil Shale Corporation which were part of the more than 700 Phillips Petroleum Company gasoline outlets Phillips was required to divest under a court order. The properties, located mostly in California, were scheduled for development as 7-Eleven Stores, although some were slated for conversion into large, modern self-service gasoline stations.

• By February sites for 290 new 7-Eleven Stores in the company-operated areas had been selected, approved and scheduled for opening in 1976.

• Southland restructured its United Kingdom investment with Cavenham Limited by selling its 50 percent interest in approximately 600 Moores & Wrights' grocery stores but acquiring a controlling interest in the 365 CTN—confection, tobacco, news—convenience-type stores. Southland now owned 69 percent of the CTN operation, with an option from Cavenham to buy the remaining 31 percent in two years.

• Continuing a Southland tradition of experimentation with potentially profitable new operations, four new Thomas & Hart mini-department stores were opened on a test basis in Dallas during the spring and summer of 1976. These neighborhood department stores featured a limited selection of sportswear, photographic and electronic equipment.

• On June 4, 1976, just two years after the 7-Eleven concept was introduced in Japan, two new 7-Eleven Stores were completed at the same time and opened simultaneously with the designation of the 100th store. One was located in Koriyama, 250 kilometers north of Tokyo, and the other was in Chiba, a Tokyo suburb.

• The Washington/Baltimore Division opened its 400th 7-Eleven Store in Ocean City, Maryland, on July 1.

• For the third consecutive year Southland's Annual Report (1975) was named the Bronze Trophy Winner in the grocery chain category by *Financial World* magazine.

• The three Southland Food Centers projected that they would prepare approximately 40 million sandwiches during 1976, including 10–12 million which would be sold to outside customers.

• In July the Reddy Ice Division completed construction of a new ice facility in Houston. Called the most modern ice manufacturing plant in the nation, it has the capacity to produce 160 tons of ice per day.

• The company's 1975 results moved it up to 18th place on *Fortune* magazine's list of the top 50 merchandising firms in the U. S.

• Southland's cash dividend was raised to 50 cents per share per year, a 25 percent increase from the previous rate.

Australia—the next new area for 7-Eleven. John P. Thompson, foreground, Southland's chairman of the board, and R. G. Withers, managing director of Pacific-Seven of Melbourne, signed an area license agreement in late 1976.

• For the 10th consecutive year, a three percent stock dividend was declared.

• In the second quarter total company revenues were $538,904,000, the first half-billion-dollar quarter in the company's history.

• Southland signed an area license agreement with Pacific-Seven, Pty., Ltd. of Melbourne, Australia. The first 7-Eleven Stores in Australia are expected to open in the Melbourne metropolitan area sometime in 1977.

JERE THOMPSON VIEWS THE FUTURE

So the company pressed forward. But what about the future? It certainly appeared positive based on current trends. Jere W. Thompson discussed 7-Eleven's future in his presentation to the New York Society of Security Analysts on April 29, 1976: "Now, what do I see for the future of 7-Eleven? When you, the investment community, look at our growth you may wonder if Southland can keep it up. Frankly, I believe we can. In 1971, our 45th year, the company reached a goal of $1 billion in revenues, and in 1974 our 5,000th store opened. We are now approaching $2 billion and look ahead to a milestone of 10,000 stores. As I pointed out earlier, 7-Eleven now commands slightly over a one-cent share of the American food dollar and certainly one of our goals is to double the share. Having more than 5,600 stores naturally creates some problems by sheer numbers, but there are tremendous advantages. It is the same as having 1,000 test markets. It's a great proving ground, one that's delivered profitable products for us in the past, and there's no reason to believe it won't do the same in the future. Slurpee, our semi-frozen carbonated drink, is a perfect example. At first it was sold in only one store, then in a few stores and then in a division. We tracked its sales, experimented with advertising and in effect worked out our own product development system. By the time we completed countrywide expansion we'd sold over a billion cups. Our Hot-to-Go fast foods line is proving to be a winner in much the same way. No doubt there must be a dollar limit on sales volume for one 7-Eleven Store, but so far we haven't been able to discover what that limit is. Twenty years ago if a store had an annual volume of $140,000 it was an outstanding performer. Today an average performing store would almost double that and the top 7-Eleven Store in 1975 had sales in excess of $800,000. That gives you an idea of the possibilities we see in convenience stores and the potential for increasing a store's volume. For that reason when we think of growth we look first at the stores currently in operation and constantly search for new products and services to increase sales and improve profitability. A second way we plan to facilitate growth is through opening new stores in markets where 7-Eleven is well-known. As the population continues to shift from central cities to surrounding suburban areas, each new neighborhood becomes a potential market for 7-Eleven expansion. Of the approximately 500 or more stores to be opened this year, many will be in areas already familiar with 7-Eleven. A third area of expected growth is in many rural and smaller communities bordering major population centers in every part of the country. Recently we opened a store in a small Texas town and sales in its first year of operation were $480,000. We believe there is potential for duplicating that situation in many other markets. In addition, the first 7-Eleven Stores in New Orleans opened recently and there are still other areas of high population density where we do not operate. Independent research studies estimate that the convenience store segment of the retail food industry will have sales in excess of $15 billion by 1982 and will represent almost seven percent of industry sales. We are confident that 7-Eleven will attain its share of that market.''

JOHN THOMPSON LOOKS AHEAD

In a separate interview Southland's chairman, John Thompson, talked about the company, its future and his father: ''We are very bullish for our company and the whole industry. We will always try to do a better job in our stores—provide better service and offer new products. It will change as we go along. We always have to stay alert and get in and out of products with the times. But that flexibility has always been one of our strengths. You know, I think Dad would be amazed by the growth of the company. I don't think he really felt it could be as geographically successful as it turned out to be. He was just beginning to think about expansion when he died. Don't think for a moment that he didn't want to expand, but I think he probably would have been more cautious about it. You have to remember that he started working in the '20s. He went through the Depression and saw the company go into bankruptcy. This would naturally make you very cautious. Yes, Dad wanted to expand, but he was just more cautious about it than we have been. One point that I would especially like to make about him is that he had such a wonderful way with people. He attracted some very competent and talented people to our company and I hope I learned something from him in that regard. He always loved doing things for people inside and outside the company.''

Southland's Employees Savings and Profit Sharing Plan, originally conceived by the elder Thompson in the late 1940s, remained the best example of this concern for employee welfare. By the end of 1975 the participants' equity in the fund had grown to $83,088,477. Substantially all of the assets of the plan were represented by investments in 7-Eleven store properties, purchased from and leased to Southland, and in shares of Southland common stock. The assets of the plan had increased by six-fold just in the 10-year period from 1966 to 1975.

One participant in Southland's profit sharing is Elmer Eiland, a sales representative for Oak Farms Dairies in Dallas. Eiland said: ''I celebrated my 30th anniversary with the company on July 28, 1976. I had been with Southland three years when the profit sharing plan first started. They told us how good the plan was going to be but we had no idea it would be anything like it turned out. When it first began we had meetings and the company presented charts showing us what they thought our plan would do over the years. It sounded great at the time, that's for sure. During the 27 years from 1949 through 1975 I contributed $9,579.75 to the plan. My account as of December 31, 1975, stood at $137,601. You just couldn't imagine that it would grow like that. In talking to other people who work for other companies that have their own

plans, ours seems so much better. It just makes you feel proud to be with Southland and Oak Farms. One thing I'll say, getting up early and working hard over the years has really paid off. I plan to retire at the end of 1976. We have 10 acres of land southeast of Dallas and my wife and I hope to start building a house on it soon. None of this would have been possible without profit sharing. There is no way that the average working person could possibly save the kind of money that I have in the fund today. And since I'll only be 60 my next birthday, my wife and I will have some time to enjoy it."

In addition to profit sharing, other special employee programs were still being carried forward. A four-year college scholarship plan for the children of Southland employees was begun in 1955. By 1976, 311 scholarships had been granted. An employee credit union begun in November 1956 had accumulated more than $4 million in savings by the end of 1976. More than 10,000 Southland employees held "share accounts" in the credit union.

A COMMITMENT TO SERVICE

John Thompson had, himself, carried on one important family tradition. His father had strongly believed in contributing his time, money and efforts to a variety of worthwhile activities outside the company. As Southland's chairman and chief executive officer, John Thompson continues this commitment. He currently serves as a director of the National Wildlife Federation, the Cotton Bowl Athletic Association, the State Fair of Texas, the Dr Pepper Company and First International Bancshares. He also is a trustee of the Presbyterian Hospital in Dallas, a member of the advisory board of the Salvation Army, chairman of the Texas Turnpike Authority, a member of the development board of The University of Texas and a member of the board of directors of the Dallas Citizens Council.

THE JOE C. THOMPSON CONFERENCE CENTER

The University of Texas at Austin had always been a Thompson family love. The highlight of this involvement came on October 30, 1970, when Texas business, civic and educational leaders gathered in Austin for the formal dedication of the Joe C. Thompson Conference Center. Among those present were Mrs. Joe C. Thompson, the three Thompson sons and their families. The modernistic new center features a 300-seat auditorium, 17 conference rooms of varying sizes, a special VIP conference room, a large dining room with catering kitchen, a library and snack bar area. Among other uses, the conference center was slated to provide facilities for short-term continuing education and public service programs conducted for off-campus adult groups by teaching or administrative units of the University.

The speaker at the center's dedication was former Texas governor Allan Shivers. He described the conference center as "a place where people can meet face to face with mutual respect and a mutual goal of broadening understanding and constructive planning in an era that so urgently needs both."

Gifts amounting to $300,000 from Southland, the Thompson family, devoted friends and long-time employees of Southland who had been with Jodie Thompson during his lifetime aided in the establishment of the center.

The building itself was located on an oak-shaded hill on the University's campus just north of the Lyndon B. Johnson Library. It was an additional honor to the memory of the former student manager for the various Longhorn athletic teams, 1922 senior class president, member of the Board of Regents of the University and holder of Life Membership Number One in the University's Ex-Students' Association that the dedication ceremonies were attended by the man whose library neighbored the conference center, former President Lyndon Baines Johnson.

The Joe C. Thompson Conference Center at The University of Texas at Austin, dedicated October 30, 1970.

255

CHAPTER 35

As Southland approached its 50th anniversary in 1977 it was bolstered by a favorable outlook for the continuation of its growth and progress. The company did reach its goal of $2 billion in sales in 1976. Net profits were again at record highs, reaching $40 million.

THE "RIGHT IDEA"

In reviewing the company's first 50 years, it appeared that Southland's development into a major corporation simply illustrated the correctness of the American business system. First and most important, the right idea had been present with the innovative concept of convenience-oriented food stores. Then the right man, in the presence of entrepreneur Joe C. Thompson, was able to hold off economic catastrophe long enough to mold an organization capable of making the idea profitable. The right timing was certainly favorable in that a nation was moving into the unprecedented mobility of the automobile age, thus creating a population shift to outlying suburban areas. Timing had again proved its importance when the new generation of Southland management perceived the promise of opportunities of the early 1960s and vigorously expanded to capitalize on them.

PEOPLE: THE KEY INGREDIENT

Despite these powerful forces that dominated the company's fortunes, there was one factor impossible to ignore. It was simply Southland's ability, or good fortune, to attract and hold uncommonly talented people. As the company surveyed its past 50 years, the "people factor" loomed as one of the most crucial elements affecting the achievements of the past. H. R. Brasuell, a long-time Southland employee and former 7-Eleven division manager, illustrated this feeling by saying: "Southland isn't mortar, bricks, steel or glass. Southland is people. The people will still be standing when the buildings have all fallen down. I think Southland will always be the leader in the convenience store field because of our people. So many of the ideas don't originate at the top—they come from the bottom up. This is where Southland's strength comes from—the people. I can sit back and compare 25 years ago to today and I am amazed at the new products we now sell. Where did these new ideas all come from? Many of them came from our people in the stores and our top management who wanted and encouraged these ideas. This is why I say The Southland Corporation isn't mortar, bricks, steel or glass. It's the people who have made our company what it is today."

John Thompson summed up Southland's past half century: "Dad once described Southland's success as being a happy accident. Whatever the reason, there is no question but that we have been blessed with a unique history of growth and progress. Certainly the Southland people—from the store personnel to the officers and board members—have all contributed greatly to our past 50 years. But I really must point to the customer as being the final judge as to whether or not we have succeeded. It is the millions of people who shop every day in a 7-Eleven Store and the additional families or individuals purchasing our dairy and other products who are our most important critics. They are the ones who keep us constantly working to serve them better. They tell us every day if we are measuring up to their standards of service. As long as we pay attention to our customers I think you will be able to look back 50 years from today and see a hundred years of serving the public with what they want and when they want it."

ABOUT THE AUTHOR

Allen Liles was a staff writer for several Texas newspapers following his graduation from Baylor University in 1959. He joined Southland in 1967 and was named public relations manager for the company in 1974.